PRAISE FOR QABALAH FOR WICCANS

"A fascinating mix of Witchcraft and Ç ˙ ˙ ˙ ˙ ˙ ˙ ˙ ˙ ˙ ˙ the many sim-
ilarities between both magical system  nould
enjoy it and learn a great deal from ea ded."
—Migene González-Wippler, au ˙ Angels,
Kabbalah for ˙ ˙adows

"Don't let your knowledge of the system sway you from reading this work,
because there is so much to be gained. Chanek takes what can be a complex
system and makes it approachable, friendly even, to the beginner and skilled
alike."

—Mortellus, author of *Do I Have to Wear Black?*

"This is the book we've all been waiting for. Magical practitioners of all vari-
eties will find it provides a clear and accessible entry point and road map to
the wisdom of the Qabalah. Jack Chanek not only sheds a brilliant light on
the interdependent nature of the ten Sephiroth of the Tree of Life, but he
also brings greater clarity to the energetic dynamics of our everyday magical
work. And he does it all in a friendly, inclusive, reassuring way. I'm certain I
will be recommending this book for decades to come."

—Tess Whitehurst, cohost of *Magic Monday Podcast* and author of
You Are Magical

"Chanek's book draws you in and holds you close with this helpful and practical tool for modern magick practitioners. You feel as though you're taking
a gentle, but deep, walk through the Tree of Life with a kind friend holding
your hand. *Qabalah for Wiccans* is an invaluable resource for deepening one's
spiritual journey and will appeal to Pagans wishing to add complexity to both
their ritual and personal practice."

—Courtney Weber, author of *The Morrigan: Celtic Goddess of Magick
and Might*

"Now and then a new teacher emerges who will change the face of magical practices for generations to come. Jack Chanek is one such teacher. When books-a-plenty promote nebulous, ungrounded, and unfounded paths toward spiritual learning, along comes Chanek's smart, insightful, and clearheaded approach to the Qabalah meant for all practitioners of Pagan witchcraft. *Qabalah for Wiccans* provides a systematic, rational, yet engaging application of a complex magical system to well-known Craft practices."

—Timothy Roderick, author of *Wicca A Year and A Day*

"From page one I was learning not only interesting things about the Qabalah, but historical information about modern Occultism … Chanek's approach to working the Tree of Life is both esoterically smart and deeply profound…. This book will take you on an exploratory dance with the Qabalah using language any modern Wiccan can connect with."

—Phoenix LeFae, author of *What Is Remembered Lives*

"A refreshing and practical text on how the Qabalah can enhance one's spiritual practice. Written especially with Wiccans in mind, author Jack Chanek's text will prove extremely useful to any magical student, regardless of their spiritual path … *Qabalah for Wiccans* is an insightful text which practitioners will want to keep within easy reach of their sacred space."

—Chic Cicero and Sandra Tabatha Cicero, Chief Adepts of the Hermetic Order of the Golden Dawn and authors of *Golden Dawn Magic*

"If you are new to the Qabalah, Chanek's introduction will help you to understand the sephiroth in a way that is imminently relatable and immediately useful. Even experienced Qabalists will find that Chanek's fresh approach highlights different relationships and teases out subtle meanings hiding in the Tree."

—Amy Hale, PhD, author of *Ithell Colquhoun: Genius of the Fern Loved Gulley*

QABALAH
FOR
WICCANS

About the Author

Jack Chanek is a Third-Degree Gardnerian Priest, a Slavic polytheist, and a Tarot reader. Outside of Paganism and the occult, he is an academic philosopher working on a PhD in the history of philosophy, specializing in Immanuel Kant's philosophy of science.

JACK CHANEK

QABALAH
FOR
WICCANS

CEREMONIAL MAGIC
ON THE PAGAN PATH

LLEWELLYN PUBLICATIONS
WOODBURY, MINNESOTA

FIRST EDITION
First Printing, 2021

Cover design by Shannon McKuhen
Editing by Holly Vanderhaar
Interior art by Llewellyn Art Department
Interior yoga figure by Mary Ann Zapalac
Tarot card illustrations are based on those contained in *The Pictorial Key to the Tarot* by Arthur Edward Waite, published by William Rider & Sons, Ltd. London 1911

Llewellyn Publications is a registered trademark of Llewellyn Worldwide Ltd.

Library of Congress Cataloging-in-Publication Data (Pending)
ISBN: 978-0-7387-6866-3

Llewellyn Worldwide Ltd. does not participate in, endorse, or have any authority or responsibility concerning private business transactions between our authors and the public.
    All mail addressed to the author is forwarded but the publisher cannot, unless specifically instructed by the author, give out an address or phone number.
    Any internet references contained in this work are current at publication time, but the publisher cannot guarantee that a specific location will continue to be maintained. Please refer to the publisher's website for links to authors' websites and other sources.

Llewellyn Publications
A Division of Llewellyn Worldwide Ltd.
2143 Wooddale Drive
Woodbury, MN 55125-2989
www.llewellyn.com

Printed in the United States of America

DEDICATION

For Alex, who read an early draft of this book
and told me it was "not a total snooze fest." You inspire me.

CONTENTS

Meditations, Exercises, and Rituals

Chapter 13

Foreword

When I first met Jack Chanek, he was nineteen years old, and I stood him up.

Jack was applying for membership in my Wiccan training group, and we had scheduled our first face-to-face meeting. The night before, there was a massive, record-breaking blizzard: more than two feet of snow fell in a matter of hours. When I got up in the morning, my thoughts were entirely focused on the weather, and the fact that I had a meeting scheduled went right out of my head. Jack waited at the designated restaurant, and sent a polite email that I eventually noticed. I ran down the block (between corridors of snow piled six feet high) to find him. This may have set the tone for our relationship—Jack ever patient with my foibles, and flawlessly polite whether I deserve it or not.

The young man I met was charming, bright, genuinely interesting, and definitely full of rough edges that needed knocking off. From an occult point of view, he was all fire and air, with little earth or water in sight. He also knew exactly how bright he was. I happen to find arrogance charming, so I was not at all put off by that. We hit it off right away.

My philosophy, as a Wiccan priestess, is that it is my job to help those who come to my group find their own paths. Sometimes those paths take them away from me. I don't try to twist anyone into being my sort of Wiccan. So I am incredibly lucky that Jack's path turned out to guide him directly into my group, where he remains today.

He's really impossible. He's sweet, helpful, generous, and crazy smart—Ivy League smart, to be precise. At a Wiccan gathering, I attended a class he was teaching, and dammit, he's a good teacher too. A very good teacher. After he taught an introductory class on Qabalah a few times, attendees said he should write a book. And dammit, he's a good writer too.

Jack's entry into the occult was through the tarot. He became obsessed with it as a child, and studied occult subjects related to it, beginning with the Qabalah. At the time we met, my knowledge of the subject was minimal. I'd read a couple of books and a few articles. I knew that the subject informed occultism, and I've been an occultist for nearly forty years, but I'd only ever scratched Qabalah's surface.

Like many people who become Wiccan as adults, my relationship with the religion of my upbringing—Judaism in my case—was complicated. If it was perfect for me, I wouldn't have sought elsewhere. Yet I fundamentally understand myself to be Jewish. It is common for Jews to know ourselves to be ethnically, culturally, or tribally Jewish, and feel that connection deeply. But while that was true for me, it was also unsatisfying in some way. I tried, in my early twenties, to incorporate Jewish elements into Wicca. Some people do that successfully, but it didn't work for me. I abandoned the idea of spiritual Judaism sometime in the 1980s.

At the same time, in Wicca and Paganism, I frequently encountered people who said things along the lines of, "You're Jewish? You should study Qabalah!" This always made me uncomfortable. In hindsight, I'd call it a microaggression—pointing at my ethnicity or background and telling me what I "should" be good at. It's not a lot different from assuming an African-American is good at basketball. Because I was definitely not drawn to Qabalah anyway, and because of the unwelcome remarks of many (probably well-meaning) people, I mostly avoided Qabalah, and even managed to write a well-received book on the tarot—*Tarot Interactions: Become More Intuitive, Psychic & Skilled at Reading Cards*—without any Qabalistic content whatsoever.

Then a funny thing happened. According to my daughter (a professional astrologer), the funny thing was my second Saturn return. Perhaps you're more familiar with the first Saturn return—you know, the thing where sometime before turning thirty your life enters a state of upheaval as you confront the restrictions and limitations of your life? That thing where you suddenly feel old, or feel inadequate because you don't feel old, or everything somehow changes? That's what happens when Saturn, the planet of restriction, returns to the position it was in when you were born, completing its orbit of approximately twenty-seven years. The second Saturn return, which is more like the classic "midlife crisis," happens about twenty-seven years after the first one.

Saturn is one of the best-aspected planets in my chart. Saturn and I flow together. At my first Saturn return, I had a baby. At my second Saturn return, I returned to Judaism.

Following the anti-Semitic massacre of eleven people at the Tree of Life synagogue in Pittsburgh in 2018, I felt a need to be among my people, and attended services at a local synagogue. To my surprise, I was drawn to it, and began attending every week.

I am deeply devoted to Wicca; I have been Wiccan since I was twenty-one years old. I didn't wish to feel like I was living a double life; I wanted my Jewish life and my Wiccan life to be a single life. To bridge the distance between Wicca and Judaism in a way that would allow me to feel integrated and whole, I began to study the Kabbalah. In fact, I study both Qabalah and Kabbalah (as Jack defines them)—both the Hermetic and Jewish versions.

After two years, I'm still very much a beginner, but a passionate one. My many years of occult work have helped my studies move swiftly. And of course, I have Jack in my life, airing ideas with me, and spurring my studies along.

There has never been a book like *Qabalah for Wiccans*. There's no translating of the Qabalah into a familiar Wiccan context; instead, it's right there. Here, the rituals, structures, deities, and language of Wicca are treated as the norm; here, you are not working to figure out how to fit the Qabalah into your spiritual life—it already fits. There has never been a book that allows Qabalah and Wicca to simply flow.

—Deborah Lipp

Acknowledgments

Deciding to write a book is, on some level, an inescapably egotistical project. You have to believe not only that you have something worth saying, but also that no one else has said it before. Nonetheless, actually writing a book is deeply humbling, and *Qabalah for Wiccans* was only made possible by a wide network of people supporting and encouraging me.

First and foremost, I owe incredible thanks to everyone on the Llewellyn team who worked to make this book a reality: Alisha Bjorklund, Donna Burch-Brown, Heather Greene, Markus Ironwood, Terry Lohmann, Sami Sherratt, and Holly Vanderhaar, as well as anyone with whom I didn't have the privilege to speak directly. This book would never have happened without all of your work, and I am immensely grateful.

Thanks to Deborah Lipp, who taught me everything I know about the Craft, plays a mean game of cribbage, and has put up with incessant early-morning discussions about the placement of the magical circle on the Tree of Life, the role of polarity magic in post-Victorian society, and much more besides. "We can talk about this after I've had coffee" has been a constant, and welcome, refrain of our friendship. No other priestess would have known what to do with me, and I am so grateful to have found my way to you.

I am indebted to the dear friends who read early drafts of this work and encouraged me to keep going. I owe particular thanks to Shane Mason, my first and greatest cheerleader, who spent many late nights drowsily listening to me reading chapters aloud over the phone, and who never once complained. Thanks also to Tom McArthur, the loveliest witch east of the Atlantic, whose constant support and enthusiasm has meant more to me than I know how to say.

I owe thanks to all the authors who took the time to read this book and say a kind word, for promotional purposes or otherwise: Lyam Thomas Christopher, Tabatha and Chic Cicero, Lon Milo DuQuette, Migene González-Wippler, Christina Oakley Harrington, Phoenix LeFae, Thorn Mooney, Mortellus, Timothy Roderick, Courtney Weber, and Tess Whitehurst. Thanks especially to Amy Hale, whose sharp observations about the left-hand path and Victorian sexual politics made the book better than it was.

And finally, thanks to all the members of my coven, past and present. You are the greatest magical family I could have hoped to have, and it is my honor to walk this path beside you.

WHAT IS QABALAH?

I'm going to say the Q-word. Don't freak out.

Anyone who spends enough time in the occult or Pagan communities will eventually run into the Qabalah. The word is spoken in hushed tones, with a sense of awe, as if the mere mention of it will awaken some sleeping demiurge. Reading through classic books on the occult—titles from the likes of Franz Bardon, Dion Fortune, and Francis King—it's easy to get the impression that occultism just *is* the Qabalah. These authors treat Qabalah as if it is the beginning and end of all magic, as if one cannot be an occultist without also being a Qabalist. The contemporary occult community is full of people talking about Qabalah, whether they're praising it or condemning it. On one hand, there are Thelemites and Golden Dawn magicians who work an explicitly Qabalistic system of magic. On the other, there are hedge witches complaining that Qabalah is too complicated and intellectual, as well as grimoire magicians who write the whole thing off as an unnecessary modern invention. Somewhere in the middle of that mess, there's a group of wayward Wiccans who aren't entirely sure what Qabalah is or whether it's relevant to what they do. This book is for that last group.

Before we proceed any further, though, it is important to answer two basic questions, which motivate the rest of this book. First, what is Qabalah? And second, why is it worth our time to study?

As it turns out, the answer to the first question is rather complicated. This book is about the magical practice of Hermetic Qabalah, but in order to understand that practice, we have to trace its origins. Hermetic Qabalah is an appropriation of a form of Jewish mysticism that first emerged in medieval Iberia, blending Jewish theology with astrology, Hermeticism, and Neoplatonic philosophy. The word *Qabalah* comes from the Hebrew קבלה; in Hebrew, קבלה literally translates as "that which is received." Jewish Kabbalah, then, is received wisdom: It is a body of esoteric lore connecting the Jewish people to their God.

This book is emphatically not about Jewish Kabbalah. That is a living, thriving mystical tradition belonging to a closed culture, of which I am not a member and about which I have no authority to speak. As we approach the subject of occult Qabalah, we should be attentive to this fact; to that end, I employ a spelling convention that distinguishes Hermetic Qabalah (Qabalah-with-a-Q) from the Kabbalah in Judaism (Kabbalah-with-a-K). Both are transliterations of the Hebrew word קבלה, but the spelling difference helps to clarify that the two practices are not the same thing.

This is a sensitive subject, and it merits close evaluation. From the early days of Kabbalah, Christian missionaries in Europe had started to incorporate Kabbalistic concepts from Judaism into their own mysticism, forming a Christianized version of the Cabala (Cabala-with-a-C). Given the rampant anti-Semitism of Renaissance Europe, we should understand that this Christianization of Kabbalah was not done in the spirit of open and mutually beneficial sharing between cultures. It was, rather, part of a concerted effort to eradicate Jewish culture by diluting it and dissolving it in Christianity. The reason for this culture war was the doctrine of supersessionism, which taught that Judaism was a mere prefigurement of Christianity and that the teachings of Christ invalidated and replaced the Jewish covenant with the God of Abraham.[1]

By the sixteenth century, Christian Cabala was being incorporated into Christian magic, featuring prominently in Cornelius Agrippa's *Three Books of Occult Philosophy*.[2] From there, it worked its way into much of Western occultism, most notably and most influentially in the magical system of the

---

1. Yaacob Dweck, *The Scandal of Kabbalah*, 149–170.

2. Henry Cornelius Agrippa, *Three Books of Occult Philosophy*, 468.

Hermetic Order of the Golden Dawn. The Golden Dawn was a secret society founded in England in 1887 by S. L. MacGregor Mathers and William Wynn Westcott. Modeled on initiatory lodge systems like Freemasonry, the Golden Dawn had a system of degrees and initiations based on the Qabalistic Tree of Life.

Although the Golden Dawn only lasted sixteen years, collapsing in 1903, it was a remarkable society. To this day, it remains quite possibly the single most influential occult organization in Western history. The Golden Dawn attempted to synthesize all of Western magic, creating a single unified system that brought together disparate subjects such as tarot, astrology, Enochian magic, Goetia, the Key of Solomon, and geomancy. And the keystone in this grand unification theory of magic, the thing holding it all together, was occult Qabalah. The Golden Dawn loaded their magical system up with correspondences of all kinds, connecting magical tools, colors, tarot cards, Pagan deities, flowers, gems, incenses, and more. Though its ritual structure was vaguely Christian on the surface level, the Hermetic Order of the Golden Dawn was more preoccupied with magic than with religion; it is with this order that non-Christian magical Qabalah takes the form most familiar to us today.

Moreover, the landscape of Western occultism was forever changed after the Golden Dawn. Occult societies such as Aleister Crowley's Ordo Templi Orientis (O.T.O.), Paul Foster Case's Builders of the Adytum, and Dion Fortune's Society of the Inner Light were all explicitly Qabalistic. They worked an initiatory degree system structured around the Tree of Life, and the magic they taught was a ceremonial, systematic Qabalah. Likewise, the overwhelming majority of tarot decks published in the twentieth and twenty-first centuries draw on Qabalistic correspondences established by the Golden Dawn. Some of this Qabalistic symbolism is explicit, as with esoteric decks like the Thoth tarot. Some is more hidden, but is still there for those who know how to look; an astute observer will see that the coins on the Rider-Waite-Smith Ten of Pentacles are arranged in the shape of the Tree of Life.

The Ten of Pentacles

Even non-ceremonial forms of modern occultism have been affected by Qabalah. The use of four elemental tools in magic—a staple of Wicca—derives from the four elemental weapons of the Golden Dawn. The practice of casting a circle and invoking the elements at the four cardinal points is, likewise, an echo of the Lesser Ritual of the Pentagram, an Enochian and Qabalistic rite of the Golden Dawn's outer order.

Does this mean that all Wiccans have to be expert Qabalists? Of course not. I firmly believe that knowing the Qabalah is in no way necessary to the practice of witchcraft. Some of the best witches I know have never cracked a book on ceremonial magic in their lives, don't give a damn about the difference between Malkuth and McDonald's, and are still skilled magicians and devoted worshippers of the Gods. However, I maintain that while Qabalah is not necessary for Wiccans, it is nonetheless edifying. It can help us to enrich our understanding of the things we do in Wiccan ritual, of why we do them, and of our magic more broadly. It can give us access to a model of the universe, and of the human soul, that can help with practical magic, with acts of worship, and with self-improvement.

Where does that leave us with regard to Qabalah? There is a serious question about how appropriate it is for us, as Pagans, to use a body of occult teaching that has its roots in Jewish mysticism. Judaism is a closed religious and ethnic culture. It's not our place, as outsiders, to pick up something belonging to that culture and claim it for our own. But at the same time, we would be rewriting occult history if we ignored the way Kabbalah was appropriated by Christian magicians, or if we denied its prevalence in Western magic. We would be doing a disservice to history if we denied that Qabalah had anything to do with, or any influence on, modern Wicca.

Just as current-day residents of the United States must grapple with the history of colonialism and indigenous genocide on the land we inhabit, modern practitioners of Western magic—including, but not limited to, Wiccans—have a duty to consider the troubling history of Qabalah, how it entered our occult canon, and how we choose to relate to that history. Do we reject it altogether, strip our Paganism of anything Qabalistic, and start over from the beginning? Or do we take what we have inherited, oppressive history and all, and try to find the most respectful way to carry it forward while acknowledging the harms that have been done?

Either approach is legitimate, and there are many Wiccans (and non-Wiccan witches) who choose the former route. For myself, though, I find that the kind of Wicca I practice is a synthesis of "low" folk magic and "high" ceremonial magic (with a healthy dose of initiatory mystery cult thrown into the mix). If I were to scrub away everything Qabalistic from my practice and keep only the low European folk magic, my witchcraft would be all but unrecognizable. It would not be worse, or lesser, but it would no longer be the Wicca that I know and love.

The second difficulty with trying to remove Qabalah from Wicca is that once you start studying Qabalah, you'll quickly find that *everything* can be understood in Qabalistic terms. Qabalah contains many disparate elements that were part of Western occultism before Kabbalah came onto the scene, but those elements have since been synthesized in a way that makes them nearly impossible to disentangle from each other. Because of the sprawling, all-encompassing nature of Hermetic Qabalah, just about every color, number, plant, animal, incense, and stone can be viewed through a Qabalistic lens.

Qabalah shifts the way we perceive our surroundings, so that everything is laden with symbolism and esoteric meaning. Someone accustomed to seeing the world in that way cannot simply decide not to see it anymore, just as someone who has had corrective eye surgery cannot simply decide to go back to wearing their old prescription glasses. For those Wiccans who choose never to learn anything about the Qabalah, this poses no issue, but for those of us who have studied Qabalah, there's no way to put that genie back in the bottle.

How, then, do we approach Qabalah respectfully? Different people will answer this question differently. I can only tell you what my approach is, and encourage you to think about the issue for yourself.

First, remember that Qabalah is not Kabbalah. While Hermetic Qabalah has its roots in Jewish Kabbalah, the latter is still a living mystical practice to which outsiders have no access and no right. The Hermetic magical practice has not replaced Kabbalah, nor are the two identical. Some things are done in magical Qabalah that aren't done in Kabbalah, such as pathworking the tarot. Likewise, many things are done in Kabbalah that are intimately tied up with Judaism and cannot meaningfully be done outside of a Jewish context; one such example is the Lekha Dodi, the greeting of the Sabbath Bride performed in some synagogues. Keep these differences in mind, and remember that even though Qabalah is part of our occult legacy, some doors remain closed to non-Jews.

Second, talk to Jewish friends. You know who the authority is on whether something is respectful to Judaism? Jewish people. Communicate with your Jewish friends and see how they feel about the matter. Remember that Judaism, like any other religion, is not a monolith, and different people will have different opinions, ranging from "This is totally fine" to "Any engagement with Qabalah is disrespectful and appropriative." Moreover, no one owes you their time, and if the people you know don't want to talk about Qabalah, that's entirely their right. The most important thing you can do is to listen in good faith, and then proceed (or not) based on the boundaries that people have set around their religion and their culture.

Qabalah is not the only magical system in the world, nor is it the only good one. But it is *a* good one, and I think, one that maps particularly well to Wicca. It is my hope that in reading this book, you will find a useful supplement to your extant magical and religious practice. Even if you don't end up becoming a hardcore Qabalist, this book will give you enough information that you can comfortably have a conversation about the Qabalah. By the time you're done reading, you will be able to:

- understand the structure of the Tree of Life and the significance of the individual Sephiroth
- apply Qabalistic concepts for magic and spellwork
- use the Tree of Life for pathworking and meditation
- enrich the worship of Pagan deities using a Qabalistic ritual framework
- draw Qabalistic connections to Wiccan theology and practice

This book is not comprehensive, nor is it intended to be. Rather, it is a Pagan-oriented introduction to the basics of Qabalah, in theory and in practice. The hardest part about Qabalah is getting started, because there is *so much* information and no easy point of access for a beginner. Someone coming to Qabalah for the first time sees tables upon tables of correspondences, but little explanation of what those correspondences mean, why they matter, or how they might be relevant to that person's practice. My goal is for you to finish this book and feel that you've learned the basic, essential information you need in order to look at the Tree of Life without panicking. There will still be more to learn after you finish this book, because there is always more to learn, but this will get you started and give you that much-needed point of entry.

Because we are using Wicca as our starting point for learning Qabalah, this book does presuppose that you, the reader, have some basic familiarity with Wiccan ideas and practices. You don't have to be a seasoned practitioner by any means, but you'll get the most out of reading this if you know which end of an athame to hold. Throughout the book, I explain Qabalistic concepts by reference to Wiccan ones—such as casting a circle, using a magical name, or consecrating cakes and wine—and it will be helpful if you already have a frame of reference for the latter. As we're getting started, it's important to note that "Wicca" is an umbrella term for a diverse array of religious beliefs and practices, ranging from lineaged and coven-based to solitary and eclectic. Different Wiccans believe, and do, different things, and that's as it should be. In discussing Wicca, I speak primarily from the perspective of British Traditional Wicca, simply because that is what I practice and what I know best. Nonetheless, this book is written for Wiccans of all kinds.

Before reading further, you should get yourself a journal or notebook in which to take notes and document your reflections and experiences. It doesn't have to be anything fancy; a regular old spiral-bound notebook is fine. This is the place for you to build your personal understanding of the Qabalah. As you work your way up the Tree of Life, you may find connections, or make observations about your own magical and religious practices, that aren't mentioned in the book. Your journal is the place to note these down, as well as to keep a record of your Qabalistic studies for later reference. The end of each chapter includes a selection of journal prompts to help you get started.

By the time you're done with this book, you will have a sense of what Qabalah is, how it works, why it matters, and how it might be relevant to your practice. From there, you will be equipped to pursue further study if you choose, or—so to speak—to take the money and run. Either way, my hope is that you'll learn a lot, and you'll find Qabalah much less intimidating than you might have previously feared. It will be fun. I promise.

Let's dive in.

Journal Prompts

- What have you previously heard about Qabalah? What are the preconceptions you bring to this book? Write them down so that you can keep track of how your impressions change as you learn.

- Why are you reading this book? What are you hoping to learn from it? Is there a particular Qabalistic concept that you've heard about and want to understand better? Do you hope to become a serious Qabalist? Are you just looking for a broad overview? Take a moment to specify what you want to achieve.

- How do you feel about the tumultuous history of Qabalah and its roots in Kabbalah? Do you feel that there's a respectful way to practice Qabalah while acknowledging the anti-Semitic erasure of Jewish culture that accompanied Qabalah's development? If so, how? It's okay if you don't have all the answers, but this is an important question to at least start to think about.

CHAPTER 1

WHY THIS BOOK?

The information in this book is presented differently from what you will find in any other book on Qabalah. For one thing, it's targeted at a Pagan audience; it is as much a book about Wicca as it is a book about Qabalah. To this end, I keep the lists of angels, archangels, God-names, and the like to a minimum. Qabalistic texts tend to be front-loaded with these, but they're generally not relevant to the interests of a Pagan readership, and part of why so many Wiccans are turned off of Qabalah is the wearisome task of filtering out all that theurgy.

Our purpose in this book is to show that Wicca and Qabalah are already compatible with each other, and that all the magical energies of the Qabalah are already present in Wicca and can be explored without fundamentally altering Wiccan religious and magical practice. You will find sample rituals, meditations, and exercises throughout this book. These will look like other Pagan rituals you may have encountered, and may not appear superficially Qabalistic at all. The goal is for them to feel familiar, Pagan, and workable. Rather than unlearning Wicca and learning Qabalah as a wholly new way of viewing the magical world, we are going to use the Qabalah as a lens through which to view the things we already do as Wiccans, exploring the ways that Qabalistic energy manifests in Wiccan ritual structure even when it's not made explicit.

As you read this book, what you know about Wicca will provide a point of entry to help you understand the Qabalistic concepts we introduce. Conversely, what you learn about Qabalah will help to enrich your knowledge of Wicca. As we introduce Qabalistic ideas, we will tie them back to Wiccan theology or rit-ual, showing how Qabalah and Wicca weave together. This book will show you how to connect Qabalah with concepts like the coven, the Goddess and God, and the ceremony of cakes and wine. These concepts don't feature in other Qabalah books, because they are unique to Wicca, but they are essential to our project here. They provide a way for us as Wiccans to understand Qabalah, relate to it on a personal level, and find it in our own magical work. They show us why Qabalah might matter to a Wiccan, as well as how Qabalah is already implicitly present at the heart of Wiccan ritual, magic, and worship.

THE TREE OF LIFE

The heart of our study of the Qabalah will be a symbol known as the Tree of Life. The tree is the central glyph of Qabalah, a symbol that at once serves as a map of the universe and of the human soul. The fundamental cosmology of Qabalah is one of emanations: There is one ultimate source of divinity, from which all things flow and in which all things take part. The material universe is understood not as separate from the Divine, but as a different facet of it.

The Tree of Life picks out ten such facets, each of which is called a "Sephirah," from the Hebrew ספירה; the plural is "Sephiroth," from ספירות. Although the standard transliteration of ספירות in English is "Sephiroth," the more accurate way to pronounce it is *sfee-ROAT*. Likewise, if we're trying to pronounce Hebrew words as correctly as possible, the pronunciation of "Sephirah" would be *seh-FEE-rah*. Throughout this book, I will stick to stan-dard transliterations for the sake of consistency with other texts, but I will also provide a pronunciation guide for any Hebrew words, and all pronuncia-tions are listed in Appendix I.

Each Sephirah is, depending on your interpretation, a plane of existence, an aspect of the psyche, a stage in the mythical creation of the universe, or a face of God or the Gods. In fact, the Sephiroth are all of the above, complex expressions of divine energy pouring forth into the world. In an emanationist worldview, everything participates in the Divine; the energy of the Gods flows through everything, ranging from abstract metaphysical principles to the physi-cal bodies we inhabit. The ten Sephiroth on the Tree of Life are ten emanations of that divine energy, ten specific manifestations of the Gods' presence at all levels of reality. The tree itself maps those emanations and puts them in relation to each other, connecting them with twenty-two "paths" that show the flow of energy between the Sephiroth. The names of the Sephiroth, in order from the top of the Tree of Life down to the bottom, are:

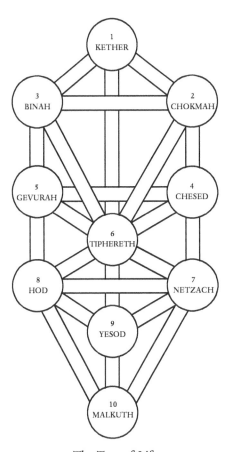

The Tree of Life

1. Kether (כתר, pronounced *KAY-tehr*)
2. Chokmah (חכמה, pronounced *KHOAKH-mah*, where the KH sound is like the Scottish "loch")
3. Binah (בינה, pronounced *BEE-nah*)
4. Chesed (חסד, pronounced *KHEH-sed*)

5. Gevurah (גבורה, pronounced *guh-VOO-rah*)

6. Tiphereth (תפארת, pronounced *teef-AIR-et*)

7. Netzach (נצח, pronounced *NET-zakh*)

8. Hod (הוד, pronounced *HOAD*)

9. Yesod (יסוד, pronounced *yih-SOAD*)

10. Malkuth (מלכות, pronounced *mal-KHOOT*)

One common way to talk about the Sephiroth is as planes of existence—Malkuth is the material plane, Yesod is the astral plane, and so on. This is a useful way to think about them, but we should be careful not to be too rigid in our thinking. All of the Sephiroth express different aspects of divine energy, but that energy is present in all of them. There is an important sense in which they are as much the same as they are different. The Tree of Life shows the nature of reality as simultaneously variegated and homogeneous, much like light refracted through a prism. There are many colors in the rainbow, but all of them share in the nature of light, and all of them come from the same source. The prism simply breaks them apart so that we can see, name, and appreciate each of them individually.

Likewise, all ten Sephiroth are always present in the world. As we start to discuss the Tree of Life in the following chapters, we will see that some Sephiroth are associated with concrete, graspable concepts (things like justice and love), while others express abstract metaphysical principles. There's a sort of creation myth accompanying the Tree of Life, wherein the creation of the universe proceeded in a series of emanations from Kether (the most abstract) to Malkuth (the most concrete). However, we would still do well to keep in mind that the world we inhabit does not only consist of the lowest Sephirah—it's replete with all ten. Just as a beam of white light contains the entirety of the visible spectrum, the universe itself contains all ten Sephiroth. It is laden with divine energy in all its forms, not just with one Sephirah, and Kether is just as present in the world as Malkuth is.

When we talk of the Sephiroth, then, we should think of them dynamically. They are copresent with each other, interacting and affecting each other. We should not think of one Sephirah as "here" and the rest as "there"; *all* the

Sephiroth are here, now, in the world we live in. We just need to learn how to look for them. The Tree of Life is the prism that lets us do so. It allows us to convert the all-pervading presence of the Gods in the world to something more suited to our finite understanding—breaking pure white light down into its component colors, so that we can see the rainbow.

Meditation on Divine Presence

It's easy to feel overwhelmed by wordy descriptions of emanations, Sephiroth, and the flow of divine energy. If you're drowning in jargon and worried that this is all too much, try meditating on it instead. If you like, you can record yourself reading this meditation aloud, and listen to the recording as you meditate; otherwise, just read through the instructions beforehand.

You Will Need

- a quiet room with no distractions, where you can meditate undisturbed.

Instructions

Sit in a comfortable position with your feet planted on the ground, in a quiet room with no distractions. Close your eyes and focus on your breathing. Breathe deeply and evenly, letting stray thoughts slip away, until you feel you've found your center. When your mind is clear and you are calm and grounded, mentally open yourself up and try to feel the presence of the Gods. Feel divine power flowing through you, coming in from the crown of your head, down through your body, and out the soles of your feet.

Say out loud, "I am one with the Gods and the Gods are one with me." Repeat that mantra as you meditate, all the while drawing that power through yourself. Then, when you feel ready, reverse the flow of energy. Feel energy rising up from the earth, through your body, and out the top of your head into the heavens. All the while, keep repeating your mantra, "I am one with the Gods and the Gods are one with me."

Last, open yourself up even further, and let the energy move in both directions. You have two currents within you, one pulling energy down from the sky and the other drawing it up out of the earth. You are the place where heaven and earth meet. You are at the center of the cosmos. The Gods are within you and all around you. You are a conduit for the current of divine energy that connects all things.

Let yourself fall silent. Be still for as long as you like, feeling the energy circulating through you. Then, when you are ready, you may slowly open your eyes and stand up.

DIVISION AND RECOMBINATION

Introductory books on the Qabalah tend to teach the Tree of Life in one of two ways: They either start at the top of the tree and work their way down, devoting one chapter to each individual Sephirah, or they start at the bottom of the tree and work their way up. The rationale behind the former approach is that it follows the order of emanations, starting with the ultimate source of divine energy and following its flow until we get to material reality. The rationale behind the latter approach is that it follows the order in which we, as practitioners, get to know the Sephiroth. We are already intimately familiar with the physical world, and out of all the Sephiroth, Malkuth is the easiest for us to understand. The work of a Qabalistic magician involves elevating one's consciousness by rising up through the Tree of Life and exploring the higher Sephiroth.

However, I am not particularly satisfied with either approach. Both attitudes toward teaching the tree make the same grievous error. They treat each Sephirah as an isolated unit, something to be understood independently of whatever is going on with the rest of the tree. That's simply not how the Tree of Life works. As we've discussed, the Sephiroth flow in and through each other. No Sephirah can be understood in isolation, because the relationship between the Sephiroth is an essential part of what they are. With that in mind, this book will introduce you not just to the energy and symbolism associated with each Sephirah individually, but also to the larger structural principles holding the Tree of Life together. In particular, there is one grand principle sitting at the heart of Hermetic Qabalah: the law of polarity.

Polarity as an occult dogma will be familiar to many Wiccan readers. The basic idea is that sameness is sterile. The original source of divine power may ultimately be One, but oneness is impotent and static. It has no motion, no energy, no differentiation. Without the interplay between *this* and *that*, between *self* and *other*, there is no creation. If everything is the same, then there can be nothing new. Creation is born of the synthesis that comes from division and recombination. Thus, the One becomes Two, and then the poles of that Two reunite to form something new and different, greater than the sum of its parts.

When we divide the poles of a spectrum, a tension emerges between them, and that tension is the source of all potential change. Protons and electrons attract each other due to electromagnetic force, and the electromagnetic fields between them allow for the formation of atoms. Meiosis (sexual reproduction) results in gametes that, when fertilized, create new life. The principle of polarity states that creative power, and power more broadly, comes not from nothing, nor even from one thing, but rather from the union of two. We could list all kinds of polarities, ranging from the scientific to the literary to the mystical: lover and beloved, light and dark, matter and energy, transcendence and immanence, earth and sky. The list goes on forever.

In traditional Wicca, we see polarity most clearly in the relationship between the Great Mother Goddess and her consort, the Horned God. They are the primordial mother and father whose love gives birth to the world. Covens in some traditions expand on polarity-based symbolism with the partnership of a high priestess and high priest as coven leaders. Polarity drives the Wheel of the Year, as the tension between the solstices continually turns the seasons. At Midsummer, when we are at the peak of the light half of the year, the opposite pole draws us toward the darkness and cold of winter. At Yule, when we are in the nadir of the dark half of the year, the polarity is reversed and we find the seasons shifting toward the light and heat of summer. Wherever we stand on the Wheel of the Year, the opposite side of the wheel calls to us, and so the seasons keep turning interminably.

Exercise: Feeling Polarity

Feeling the push and pull of magnetic attraction and repulsion is a great way to experience polarity. Try this exercise to give yourself a practical, embodied understanding of what we mean when we talk about polarity in amagical context.

You Will Need

- two magnets. Stronger magnets are preferable, but refrigerator magnets will do if you don't have anything else on hand
- a partner (optional)

Instructions

Bring the two magnets together so that they are touching; gently tug on them and feel how they resist being pulled apart. Pull them farther and farther away from each other, all the while feeling the attractive force between them. Then, release them and let them snap back into place. Do you feel the sense of relief, of resolution, as they are finally able to come together?

Now, flip one magnet around so that its poles are reversed. Push the two magnets together and feel the repulsive force between them. They will twist around in your hands, driven apart from each other. Focus on feeling the energy that comes from the tension between the two matching poles. Then, once again, release them and let them reorient toward each other. Note again the energetic release that comes from that moment where they conjoin.

Lastly, try it without the magnets. Alone or with a partner, rub your hands together to get your blood flowing. Bring the palms of your hands very close to each other, so that they're almost touching, and feel the tingle of energy between them. Pull them apart, then bring them together. Take note of what you're feeling. How does it compare to what you felt holding the magnets? If you're working with a partner, you can experiment with reversing the poles. Sit facing each other and start by putting your left hand against your partner's right, and your right hand against your partner's left. Then, switch so you're left-to-left and right-to-right. How does the energy change?

THE TWO PILLARS

How, then, does polarity connect to the Tree of Life? Take a moment to look at the tree. The first thing I want you to notice is that the ten Sephiroth are arranged in three vertical columns. On the left, we have Binah, Gevurah, and Hod. On the right, we have Chokmah, Chesed, and Netzach. In the center, we have Kether, Tiphereth, Yesod, and Malkuth. These three columns are known as the "pillars" of the Tree of Life, and they are our first point of access to the essential principle of polarity as it manifests in the Qabalah. The left-hand pillar is known as the "Pillar of Severity," or sometimes the "Pillar of Form." The right-hand pillar is the "Pillar of Mercy" or the "Pillar of Force," depending on what we call the left. (Personally, and for reasons that we will explore further in the coming chapters, I prefer to call them the Pillars of Force and Form, but the names Mercy and Severity are more widely used.) And, of course, the central pillar is the "Pillar of Equilibrium," also known as the "Hermetic Pillar," which mediates between the two poles.

If our goal as Qabalists is to ascend the tree from Malkuth to Kether, in order to raise divine consciousness, a quick glance at the Tree of Life reveals three obvious ways to do so. We can ascend the right-hand pillar (following the Path of Mercy), the left-hand pillar (following the Path of Severity), or the central pillar (following the Path of Equilibrium). No path is better than any other, but each offers different lessons and challenges.

People who talk about working the "left-hand path" in magic are working with the energies of the Pillar of Severity, the left-hand pillar on the tree. This work is not evil or particularly dark, but it is a magical path that tends to prioritize self-actualization and the enforcement of boundaries between one's own needs and the needs of others. The Sephiroth on the Pillar of Severity are contractive, rational, and self-oriented. Archetypally, the magician of the left-hand path uses their magic to elevate themselves, rather than in the service of deities or a broader community and its social mores. By contrast, people working the "right-hand path" are working with the energies of the Pillar of Mercy. This path emphasizes compassion, service, and putting others before oneself. The Sephiroth on the Pillar of Mercy tend to be expansive, emotional, and other-oriented, and the archetypal magician of the right-hand path is a love-and-light healer who veers toward hippiedom.

Different people need to learn different lessons, and both paths are necessary. Often the Sephirah we least understand is the one we most need to delve into. Once again, remember that all ten Sephiroth are present throughout the universe and within ourselves. Part of what we're doing in exploring the Tree of Life is exploring ourselves and doing the hard work of bringing our own psyches into balance. A person who is a pushover, easily cowed and unable to stand up for themselves, needs to cultivate the strident energy of Gevurah. Someone who is insensitive to the feelings of others, ignorant of the way their actions affect the people around them, needs to develop the loving energy of Netzach. The Tree of Life does not just map divine energy in the universe, but also in the human soul, and one of the most important tasks we undertake in studying the Qabalah is the great work of becoming fully ourselves. Each of us, individually, is a microcosm of the universe. We want to bring ourselves into balance just as the Sephiroth are balanced on the Tree of Life, and different people will accomplish that balance differently.

In discussing the left-hand and right-hand paths, I have left off the Pillar of Equilibrium, which stands between the Pillars of Mercy and Severity, and which mediates between the two poles. The Sephiroth on this pillar express the mystery that comes from the union of Sephiroth on the other two. Consequently, they can only be properly understood once we have grasped the polarity expressed by the left and right pillars. Our ultimate goal is to achieve balance, and to walk the Path of Equilibrium, but first we must understand what it is that we're balancing. We have to experience the division before we can experience the union.

Take a look at the High Priestess card from the Rider-Waite-Smith tarot. You'll notice that she sits between two pillars. On the left is a black pillar marked with the letter B, and on the right is a white pillar marked with the letter J. These are the Pillars of Severity and Mercy. If you look very carefully, you can see that the pomegranates on the tapestry behind the High Priestess are arranged in the shape of the Tree of Life. We have two poles, one dark and one light, and we must pass between them in order to access the tree—to attain the mysteries that the High Priestess guards. The letters B and J stand for "Boaz" and "Jachin," the names of the two bronze pillars that flanked the entrance to the temple of King Solomon. Thus, the choice to walk between the two pillars is an initiation of sorts, the first step that takes us from the mundane world into something mysterious and sacred.

The High Priestess

As we delve further into the Qabalah, let us always be conscious of that initial step. So often in occultism, the first mystery we learn is the deepest and most profound. We can quickly gain a superficial understanding of it, and think that we have understood it all, but there is always more depth to be found. Each new mystery sheds light on the first one, and we find that the first mystery contains all the others. With each subsequent revelation, we have a feeling that it is at once obvious and impenetrable: we would never have understood it had it been revealed to us before we were ready, but at the same time its essence is contained in that very first mystery. It is new and familiar, surprising and self-evident, transformative and yet the same.

Keep the Pillars of Mercy and Severity, and the polarity between them, at the forefront of your mind while reading this book. They express the mystical heart of the Tree of Life and of Hermetic Qabalah more broadly. I have laid it all before you, the great secret of the Qabalah: Mercy and Severity, Force and Form. With everything you read, I hope that you will come back to this first mystery. It really is the heart of everything.

THE THREE TRIADS

The dynamic relationship of the pillars is replicated on a smaller scale within the Tree of Life. Look at the tree again, and this time notice that the ten Sephiroth are arranged in three sets of three (with the last one, Malkuth, set apart). At the base of the pillars of Mercy and Severity, there is a triad containing Netzach and Hod, with Yesod balancing between them. This is known as the Astral Triad. Then, one step up, there is another triad consisting of Chesed, Gevurah, and Tiphereth. This one is called the Moral Triad. And finally, at the top of the Tree, we see the Supernal Triad made up of Chokmah, Binah, and Kether.

Each triad expresses a microcosm of the polarity between the two pillars. The Astral Triad does so at the most concrete, relatable level, showing how the energies of the pillars manifest in the individual psyche. The Moral Triad takes those energies and expands them, showing how they manifest at the interpersonal and social level. Lastly, the Supernal Triad expands yet further, taking these same energies and applying them to the nature of ultimate reality. (Heady stuff!)

The three triads provide the structure for our approach to the Tree of Life in this book. We'll start at the bottom of the tree with Malkuth, then address each triad in turn. Because we cannot properly understand a synthesis until we first grasp what it's a synthesis *of*, we'll look at the opposing forces in each triad—the Sephiroth on the left-hand and right-hand pillars—first, in tandem, exploring not just what they mean on their own but also how they relate to each other. Only then will we look at the Sephirah on the middle pillar, to see how it resolves the tension implicit in the interplay of the other two.

That is to say, after Malkuth, we will skip over Yesod in our progress up the tree. We'll look at Netzach and Hod together, and then once we have a handle on them, we'll come back down to Yesod in order to complete the triad. This is an unconventional approach to teaching Qabalah, but it captures the dynamism of the tree and the essential interconnection of the Sephiroth. My goal is to teach you not just what each Sephirah is in its own right, but also how it fits into the bigger picture.

THE SERPENT AND THE FLASH

Before we proceed to our in-depth study of the Tree of Life, I'd like to draw our attention to one last way that polarity manifests on the tree. We have talked about the left and right sides of the tree as magical poles, but the same can be said for the relationship between the top of the tree (Kether) and the bottom (Malkuth). These two Sephiroth represent the starting point and the end point of all creation, the unmanifest and the manifest. The relationship between them is the quintessential marriage of spirit to flesh, heaven to earth, transcendence to immanence. The word כתר in Hebrew means "crown," and the word מלכות means "kingdom." Thus, Kether is the crown of divinity that the Gods wear, the source of divine power that gives them dominion over the earth, while Malkuth is the kingdom that they rule.

The kingdom needs the crown, and the crown needs the kingdom. Without the wellspring of divine energy in Kether, the world would be a barren, disenchanted place devoid of grace and wonder. Without the kingdom of Malkuth, the Divine would have no expression, and the Gods would have no one to love or be loved by. In Wicca, we often encounter the theological notion that the Gods need us as much as we need them. Our worship is good for the Gods, just as the love of the Gods is good for us. The connection between worshipper and deity is reciprocal, a mutually beneficial give-and-take instead of a one-directional relationship where the Gods give to us and answer our prayers without us ever giving anything back in return. Likewise, in Qabalah, the flow of energy on the Tree of Life goes in both directions. It flows from Kether down to Malkuth, but it also flows back up the tree from Malkuth to Kether.

The flow from Kether to Malkuth is the order of creation, by which divine presence is made manifest in the physical world. It is direct, spontaneous, and energetic, and as such, it is visually represented as a flash of lightning starting in Kether and descending sequentially through the Sephiroth. Alternatively, it is sometimes represented as a flaming sword extending from Kether to Malkuth. The image is active and forceful, the power of the Divine penetrating into the material world. In contrast, the flow from Malkuth to Kether is slow and sinuous. This is the order of ascension, the path by which we attain enlightenment and knowledge of the Gods. As any mountaintop ascetic can tell you, the road to enlightenment is long and winding. Divine power may permeate the world all at once, but the process by which we elevate our consciousness requires years of arduous work. It is slower, and less direct, than the path of emanation. Consequently, the visual representation associated with upward motion on the tree is a serpent winding its way through the Sephiroth from Malkuth to Kether.

Energy moves simultaneously in both directions, drawing the Gods down to us and raising us up to the Gods. Together, the Serpent and the Flash form a closed circuit that keeps power constantly moving between the two poles. The Flash is manifestation; the Serpent is liberation. Combined, they maintain the reciprocal connection between Kether and Malkuth that makes the Tree of Life dynamic and alive. In our work with the Tree of Life, we need both liberation and manifestation. We put in the work to experience the higher Sephiroth and gain greater insights and wisdom, but then we also have to come back down the tree, return to the mundane world, and live our lives. No one can spend all of their time rapt in spiritual visions of Kether. Eventually, most of us have to come back down off the mountaintop and go back to our jobs.

With that discussion out of the way, it is time for us to begin a more detailed examination of the Tree of Life. We start at the bottom of the tree, with the Sephirah of immanence and manifestation. Let us now turn our attention to Malkuth.

Journal Prompts

- What does polarity mean to you? How do you use polarity in your magic? Does it factor into your understanding of the Gods? Think about the connection between polarity and Wicca as you understand them.

- In your notebook, copy out the Tree of Life. Mark all the different layers of polarity we've discussed. Draw a black pillar to the left of the tree and a white pillar to the right. Draw a box around each of the triads and label them. Draw the Serpent and the Flash, or use arrows to mark the directions that energy flows on the tree.

- Look over the Tree of Life. We have noted three ways that polarity manifests on the tree: the pillars, the triads, and the Serpent and the Flash. From your first impressions of the visual structure of the tree, what are some other ways we might find polarity on it?

CHAPTER 2

MALKUTH

G o outside on a sunny day. Find a quiet, secluded spot, and if the weather is warm enough, lie down or take off your shoes so that you can stand barefoot upon the earth. Don't close your eyes. Instead, focus on opening up all your senses, and taking in everything around you. Look up at the sky and appreciate just how vibrant and blue it is. Listen for the sound of birds and animals nearby. Take a deep breath, and notice the smells on the air. Feel your toes wriggling in the earth.

Still your thoughts. Let your senses envelop you. Just *be*.

The feeling you get from an exercise like this, the sense of peace and presence in the world, is the experience of Malkuth. For all the words and big ideas you'll read in this chapter, nothing can explain Malkuth better than the simple, wordless ritual of going out in the world and feeling the earth. Malkuth is the easiest of the Sephiroth to understand, because in many ways it is the world we already know. It is the fullness of the material world, everything that is physical, everything that is *here*. It is the endpoint of manifestation, the thing into which the Gods are made manifest. Everything we can see, taste, and touch is Malkuth.

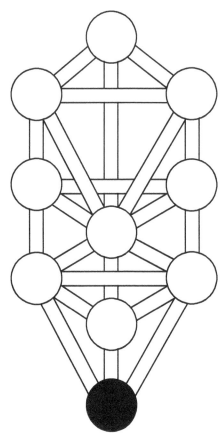

Malkuth

ISIS VEILED

There is a distinction sometimes made in Paganism between two faces of the Goddess, which can help us to understand Malkuth better: Isis Veiled and Isis Unveiled. The language originates with the Greek historian Plutarch, who documented the syncretic cult of Isis. He describes a cult statue of the Goddess at Sais, a city in Egypt. The Goddess wore a veil, and the statue bore the inscription: "I am all that has been, and is, and shall be, and my robe no mortal has yet uncovered."[3] This description gave rise to two different ideas of the Goddess: Isis Veiled is the Goddess as we can see and know her, and Isis Unveiled is

....

3. Plutarch, *Moralia: Volume V*, 25.

the Goddess of mysteries whose true face is hidden from us. This distinction was later picked up by Helena Blavatsky, a nineteenth-century mystic and the founder of the Theosophical Society, in her book *Isis Unveiled*.[4]

What is the veil of Isis, exactly? It is none other than the material world. What we can know of the Goddess is what we can see of her in nature. Think about all the imagery associated with Mother Earth. Isis Veiled is every-thing about nature that Wiccans (tree-hugging hippies that we tend to be) revere. When you are mindful of the changing seasons, the cycles of nature, the beauty of the earth, and the sheer Romantic awe of wild places, you see the face of the Goddess as Isis Veiled. The essence that lies behind all that, the Goddess as she exists when we strip the manifest universe away, is mysterious and unknowable. We simply do not know what Isis looks like when she is not dressed in the veil of the earth and heaven.

Isis Veiled, the Goddess incarnate in the world, is the essence of Mal-kuth. One of the great hallmarks of Wicca as a religion is that it holds this world sacred. The Gods are immanent in everything in nature, every part of the material world. We see the Goddess in the phases of the moon, not just because the moon is a symbol of the Goddess, but because in some sense the moon *is* the Goddess. We worship her as Mother Earth, because she *is* the earth. Yes, she has another face, the face of Isis Unveiled, separate from her manifestation in all these things, but that face is elusive, mysterious, and intangible. The Goddess we know, the Goddess we worship every day, is the Goddess who is here in the world with us. We can literally reach out and touch her, because she pervades everything around us, and makes everything sacred. To see the Goddess face-to-face, all you need to do is go outside on a clear night and spend some time looking at the moon.

Our Gods are alive and embodied. When we honor them with lunar rites or with the seasonal rituals of the Wheel of the Year, we are affirming that this world, this planet we live on, is what we hold sacred. The Gods aren't hidden away in some far-away place, or confined to remote events in ancient history; they are here, now, with us. The whole of the living world is burst-

---

4. H. P. Blavatsky, *Isis Unveiled*.

ing with their presence. Wiccan ritual is ecstatic and embodied, and it makes us feel more aware of the physical world and more a part of it. As a general rule, Wiccans aren't trying to remove ourselves from the world. We're not ascetics; we don't seek liberation from desire, from our bodies, or from incarnation on the physical plane. Rather, we celebrate all of those things. We honor nature as divine, and because our bodies are part of nature, our bodies are divine as well. That ecstatic experience—the physicality of the Divine—is what we seek in Malkuth.

Connecting to Malkuth

In today's industrialized society, most of us are somewhat cut off from the earth as our source of life. We don't see crops being grown and harvested, or livestock being bred, raised, and slaughtered for food. With air conditioning and indoor heating, it is easy to be insulated from nature, to feel like we live in a world of steel and glass. However, Malkuth is present in all of the manifest world. It may be easiest to feel if we go wandering in some lonesome glade, but everything physical, everything in this material world we inhabit, partakes of Malkuth. The world of steel and glass is just as divine—just as natural—as the world of crops and livestock. The Gods are present throughout; it is simply our task to seek them.

Even if you live in a high-rise apartment with no outdoor space and spend your days working in an office cubicle, you can find a connection to Malkuth, because Malkuth is everything. It is the earth, and the trees, and the birds and the bees, but it is also the subway car on your commute to work, and your cramped office chair, and the weird coppery-tasting water that comes out of the drinking fountain in the bus station. There is nothing in this world that is not of the Gods, and Malkuth is the divine connection that ties all things together. The whole world is the body of the Gods, even if we don't typically have overwhelming mystical experiences on the subway.

Importantly, though, just because Malkuth is present throughout the material world does not mean that we're always aware of it. Part of the reason most of us don't have mystical experiences on the subway is that we're bogged down with other thoughts and worries. We're not taking the time to be mindful of the Divine, and to look for the Gods in the world around us. When you're stressed at work, or in the middle of a busy commute, or worrying about whether the water from that bus-station fountain is safe to drink, you're not orienting your consciousness toward the Gods. In order to experience Malkuth properly, you need to stop, still your thoughts, and be wholly present and mindful in the world.

Meditation on Malkuth

This is a simple meditation to help you connect to the awareness of Malkuth and the divinity of the manifest world. It can also be used as a grounding meditation before any ritual or magical work. The first few times you perform this meditation, record yourself reading it aloud, and listen to the recording as you meditate.

You Will Need
* a quiet room with no distractions, where you can meditate undisturbed.

Instructions
Stand with your feet planted shoulder-width apart and your hands at your sides. Close your eyes and breathe deeply. As you inhale, tense all the muscles in your face: your brow, your cheeks, your mouth and jaw. Then, as you exhale, release all that tension and allow your muscles to relax completely. Repeat the process a few times, until your face is totally relaxed. Do the same with the muscles in your neck and shoulders. Then your arms, wrists, and fingers. Down through your chest, belly, and lower back; then your glutes, thighs, and calves. Finally, clench the muscles in your ankles and feet, before letting them relax. You should feel loose and comfortable.

Feel the earth beneath you. Feel its vast expanse, solid, unmoving, eternal. Notice how it holds you and supports you. You are rooted where you stand. You are solid. Powerful. Strong. Feel the energy rising up through the earth, into the soles of your feet, up through your knees and hips. Feel it spread across your groin and up into your belly, expanding and contracting with each breath. Let the power rise up into your heart, spilling over your shoulders and down your arms. Finally, let it flow up your throat and into your head, filling you all the way up to your crown. You are one with the earth, brimming with its power. Feel it moving in you and through you.

Gradually, begin to open up your senses and take note of the world around you. Identify the sounds around you, the smells, the feeling of your fingertips resting against your thighs. Open your eyes and let the vibrant colors of the world wash over you. Everything you see, feel, and hear is sacred. You are in the world. You are of the world. You are at one with the manifest Divine.

MALKUTH AND THE ELEMENTS

We also see Malkuth in the four elements: air, fire, water, and earth. When we talk about Malkuth as divine power brought into the physical world, we would be remiss to pass over the elements in silence, as they are the building blocks that make up the physical world. The concept of four elements goes back to pre-Socratic philosophy, where philosophers debated over which of the elements was most fundamental. This four-element model was later picked up by Aristotle, who added a fifth element, quintessence,[5] which Wiccans commonly call spirit.

Through commentary on Aristotle's works by medieval Christian theologians, the four elements became an important part of late medieval and early Renaissance philosophy. From there, they worked their way into alchemy, and thence into the wider occult canon. By the time Wicca came onto the scene in the mid-twentieth century, the four elements were a cornerstone of Western occultism. In contemporary magic, they are an invaluable way of understanding different kinds of magical energy in the world. The elements are not only physical (although, of course, they are also that; nothing is more fiery than a literal flame). They are also a taxonomy of four different kinds of magical energy. Entire books have been written about the elements alone, so our brief survey of them here will necessarily be inexhaustive, but as a refresher:

- air rules the intellect, thought, speech, and communication
- fire rules the will, desire, spirituality, and transformation

----

5. Aristotle, *On the Heavens*, 8.

- water rules the heart, emotions, intuition, and feeling
- earth rules the body, practicality, action, and being

All four elements can be found throughout the Tree of Life, and we will have the opportunity to explore them at greater length in Chapter 9. For now, though, let us focus on Malkuth, which has a special relationship to the elements. Malkuth is the world, and the elements are the stuff from which the world is made. Without the four elements, there could be no Malkuth. This is true not just in the sense that things like the sky and the ocean are made out of air and water, but also in the sense that Malkuth is where we find the full range of human experience. Our connection to Malkuth, to this world, depends on everything we think, desire, feel, and do. Our lives could not happen without an expression of the four elements. Without the elements, Malkuth would be empty.

One of the primary symbols of Malkuth is an equal-armed cross surrounded by a circle. This is an alchemical and astrological symbol of the earth, but it also shows that Malkuth is the place where the four elements meet. Each arm of the cross, each element, is essential to Malkuth but is only part of the whole. Elemental air on its own is not enough for the world to exist; nor is fire, water, or earth. It is only when they all come together, when the four of them meet in the center of the circle, that Malkuth comes into being.

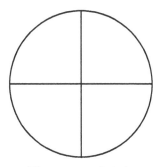

The quartered circle

THE ELEMENTS IN THE QUARTERS

This union of the four elements in the center of the circle will be especially familiar to Wiccans. It is mirrored by the Wiccan practice of calling the quarters in ritual. In a Wiccan rite, after the circle has been cast, it is common for someone to go to the four cardinal points and invoke the four elements. This brings the elements into the ritual, and when they meet in the center, the circle is impregnated with the energy of Malkuth: the union of the four elements. Once the quarters have been called, Wiccan sacred space is transformed into the quartered circle, the symbol of Malkuth. I have said already that Wicca holds this world as sacred, and Wiccans revere nature and everything within it as divine. The structure of Wiccan ritual implements that theology by turning our place of worship into a microcosm of Malkuth.

There is a tremendous amount of variation regarding which elements are assigned to which quarters, but the most common arrangement is air in the east, fire in the south, water in the west, and earth in the north. This arrangement is itself Qabalistic, originating with the Enochian rites of the Golden Dawn. Enochian magic is an angel-based form of ceremonial evocation that was originally introduced by John Dee, the personal magician of Queen Elizabeth I. Dee worked with a medium named John Kelly to develop a system of scrying and communication with angelic spirits; this system was later co-opted and expanded by the Hermetic Order of the Golden Dawn. One addition that the Golden Dawn made to Dee's system of Enochian magic was a set of element/direction correspondences based on the vision of Ezekiel in the Bible. In this vision, Ezekiel describes four living creatures holding up the throne of God: "Their faces looked like this: Each of the four had the face of a human being, and on the right side each had the face of a lion, and on the left the face of an ox; each also had the face of an eagle."[6]

---

6. *The Bible*, New International Version, Ezekiel 1:10.

The World

The four faces of each creature correspond to the four fixed signs of the zodiac, and thereby to the four elements. The human is Aquarius, the lion is Leo, the ox is Taurus, and the eagle is an alternate symbol for Scorpio. If you look at the World card in the Rider-Waite-Smith tarot deck, you will see that the central figure is surrounded by these four creatures, representing the elemental correspondences of the four quarters. Following Ezekiel's description of how the four faces were arranged, the Golden Dawn system put Aquarius (air) in the front of the temple, Leo (fire) on the right-hand side, Taurus (earth) on the left-hand side, and Scorpio (water) in the back. Because the

Golden Dawn designed their temples facing the east, toward the rising sun, the arrangement of the elements came to be aligned with the cardinal directions.

Although there is variation in elemental correspondences for the directions, in Wicca and even in the rites of the Golden Dawn, these are the most widespread and the best known. Within the Golden Dawn system, they are, perhaps, most famous for their use in the Lesser Ritual of the Pentagram, which is the ancestor of the Wiccan quarter calling. In that ritual, the practitioner goes to the four quarters, starting in the east; at each point, they draw a pentagram and intone a name of God. Then, they stand in the center of the ritual space and call the names of the four archangels associated with the quarters and the elements: Raphael for air, Michael for fire, Gabriel for water, and Uriel for earth.

The Lesser Ritual of the Pentagram has a sibling, the Greater Ritual of the Pentagram, which is broadly similar but involves more elaborate ritual gestures and words of power, including the names of Enochian spirits. What both rituals share in common is the basic formula: go to a quarter, draw a pentagram, and invoke or banish an elemental power. This is the formula that has been adopted in much of Wicca.

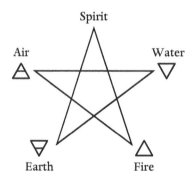

Pentagram with elemental points

THE ELEMENTAL PENTAGRAMS

One of the Golden Dawn's great magical innovations was the introduction of a set of elemental pentagrams that could be used to invoke and banish specific energies. The Golden Dawn associated each point of an upright pentagram with one of the elements: the uppermost point was spirit, the top right was water, the bottom right was fire, the bottom left was earth, and the top left was air. Using these correspondences, the Golden Dawn developed a set of twelve pentagrams for ritual use: invoking and banishing pentagrams for each of the four elements, plus for "active" and "passive" spirit.

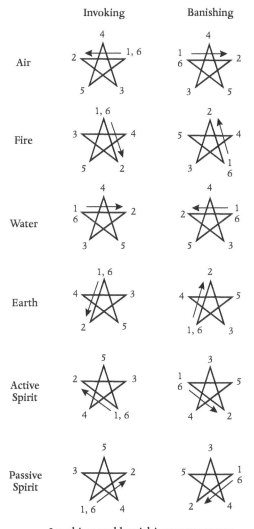

Invoking and banishing pentagrams

Each of the elemental invoking pentagrams begins with a stroke toward the point of the pentagram associated with the element in question. So, for example, the invoking pentagram of earth begins with a stroke from the point of spirit to the point of earth; the first line we draw is from the topmost point to the bottom left, and then we finish drawing the pentagram in a continuous line from there. Likewise, the invoking pentagram of fire begins with a stroke from the point of spirit to the point of fire. The notion here is that we are drawing spirit into earth or fire, respectively, calling that power down to manifest in the element of our choosing.

As there is no direct connection between the points of water or air and the point of spirit, the pentagrams of these elements are drawn somewhat differently. The invoking pentagram of water begins with a horizontal stroke from the point of air to the point of water. The invoking pentagram of air begins with a horizontal stroke on the same line, but in the opposite direction, from the point of water to the point of air. Once again, the core idea here is that we are drawing power from elsewhere toward the point of the element we invoke.

Finally, the invoking pentagrams of active and passive spirit are a bit counterintuitive, in that their first stroke doesn't involve the point of spirit. Instead, the first stroke of a spirit pentagram connects the two active elements or the two passive elements, respectively. The invoking pentagram of active spirit begins at the point of fire and draws a line to the point of air, and the invoking pentagram of passive spirit begins with a stroke from the point of earth to the point of water. By connecting the two active or passive elements, we manifest the power of active or passive spirit.

All of the banishing pentagrams begin with the same stroke as the invoking pentagrams, and simply reverse its direction. Thus, the banishing pentagram of earth begins with a stroke from the point of earth to the point of spirit—effectively pushing earth away, rather than drawing it in. The banishing pentagram of fire starts with a line from the point of fire to the point of spirit, and so on.

All of these pentagrams can feel confusing, complicated, and overwhelming. Let me say right now, you do not have to know and use them all. However, if you choose to use them, they can be incredibly helpful for magic, and the more you work with them, the easier they are to remember. When I'm stuck in a bout of writer's block, I will focus my energy and make an invoking pentagram of air over myself, to help get my thoughts flowing. When I'm in ritual and I can't get the incense charcoal to light, an invoking pentagram of fire works every time. An elemental pentagram is a quick and efficient way to bring the energy of one of the elements to the fore, or to get rid of an excess. And, of course, the pentagrams are used to great effect when we call the quarters in Wiccan ritual.

Some Wiccans call the quarters by using the respective pentagram of each element. Others choose to simplify things, using only the invoking and banishing pentagrams of earth. Either way is fine. In fact, in Golden Dawn magic, the Lesser Ritual of the Pentagram only uses the pentagrams of earth; only the Greater Ritual of the Pentagram uses the pentagrams of all four elements and spirit. Do whatever feels more comfortable and powerful to you.

Ritualizing Malkuth: Call the Quarters

Bring the Qabalistic energy of Malkuth into your rituals by summoning elemental powers at the four cardinal points of your sacred space. This ritual is written with a different elemental pentagram to be used in each direction, but if you prefer, you can always use the pentagram of earth in all four directions.

You Will Need

- a wand or athame
- a ritual space you can move around freely.

Instructions

After you have cast your circle (see Chapter 4), take your wand or athame and walk to the east. Draw an invoking pentagram of air (or earth, if you prefer) in the air in front of you. As you draw it, send power out through your wand or athame; visualize the pentagram shining with a brilliant white light, a beacon that is summoning the elemental power of air to your circle. Say:

"Mighty element of air! I conjure you now in the names of the Lady and the Lord, and I beseech your attendance at this rite. Blessed be!"

When you have finished drawing the pentagram, seal it in place by thrusting your wand or athame through its center. Visualize yourself skewering the pentagram in place, so that it will stay there until you release it.

Then, proceed to the south. Conjure the element of fire in the same manner, using an invoking pentagram of fire. Then conjure water in the west and earth in the north. Return briefly to the east, completing your circuit, and then move to the center of the circle. Before you proceed any further with your ritual, take a moment to feel the energies of the four elements meeting in the center of the circle. Feel how they make your ritual space alive. Feel the energy of Malkuth that you have brought to your rite.

When your ritual is over, before you uncast the circle, dismiss the quarters. Taking your wand or athame, proceed to the east. Draw a banishing pentagram of air (or earth). As you draw it, send power through your wand or athame and visualize it erasing the pentagram you drew there before. Say:

"Mighty element of air! I thank you for attending this rite, and in the names of the Lady and the Lord I give you leave to depart. Farewell!"

Once again, seal your banishing pentagram by thrusting your wand or athame through its center. Then go to the south to dismiss fire, the west to dismiss water, and the north to dismiss earth. Conclude by closing your circuit and returning to the east.

Preparing to Ascend the Tree

Malkuth is the sacrality of the living world. It is the all-pervading presence of the Gods in everything we experience, and seeking Malkuth requires nothing more than a shift of consciousness to perceive divinity in the world we inhabit in our daily lives. The elements, as the building blocks of that world, are an essential part of Malkuth, and working with the elements is a point of access that helps us to understand the tenth Sephirah and to ritualize our worship of the manifest Divine. Calling the quarters, bringing Malkuth into our rituals, is an act of celebration and an affirmation of a theology that venerates nature.

Now, having grounded ourselves fully in Malkuth, let us begin to ascend the Tree of Life, and to explore some remoter, more abstract emanations of divine power.

Journal Prompts

- Write a list of things that feel sacred to you. What are the ways you feel the presence of the Gods in the physical world?
- Meditate on each of the four elements individually, and write down your experiences. How does each element feel on its own? How is that different from when they are brought together in the world?
- Write down ways you bring Malkuth into your ritual practice, besides calling the quarters. What are some techniques you use to ritually honor the Gods as part of nature?

CHAPTER 3

THE ASTRAL TRIAD: NETZACH AND HOD

We begin our ascent of the tree with the Astral Triad, which consists of the seventh, eighth, and ninth Sephiroth: Netzach, Hod, and Yesod. Netzach and Hod represent a polarity that is synthesized by Yesod, so we will start by looking at the nature of that polarity. This means that even though Yesod is the next Sephirah up from Malkuth on the Tree of Life, we are going to skip over it for now, examine the other two Sephiroth in the Astral Triad, and then return to Yesod in the following chapter; we must understand the division of Netzach and Hod before we look at their recombination in Yesod.

The Astral Triad expresses the polar principles of the tree at the smallest scale, within an individual psyche; as such, Netzach and Hod represent two fundamental impulses in the human soul. Their Hebrew names are commonly translated as "Victory" and "Splendor," respectively, but that translation is broadly unhelpful in gaining insight into what these Sephiroth mean in Hermetic Qabalah. Rather, I like to talk about them as the polarity of other and self. Netzach, at the base of the Pillar of Mercy, is the love we feel for others. Hod, at the base of the Pillar of Severity, is the love we feel for ourselves. This pair of Sephiroth captures the delicate balance between self and other, between one and many. Hod looks inward in contemplation of the internal world; Netzach looks outward in concern for the external world.

Netzach encompasses romantic love, but it is also much more than that. Everything that is social, communitarian, and oriented around fostering a connection with other people is in the purview of Netzach. Familial love, friendship, sexuality, mentorship—even our relations with our coworkers. Every part of our lives that is other-regarding belongs to Netzach. In contrast, Hod is the self. It is the ego, not in a pejorative sense of inflated self-image, but in the sense that it is the part of ourselves concerned with who and what we are, independently of how we relate to other people. Hod is an affirmation of individual identity. It's who we are when there's no one else around to see.

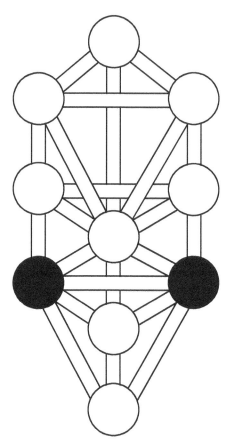

Netzach and Hod

The two Sephiroth balance and complement each other. We need both in our lives. Some people are naturally more social, and others are more inclined to be loners, but all of us need at least some connection to other people and some sense of individuality. Netzach without Hod has no boundaries. It is meddlesome, invasive, and needy; it gives all of itself to others, and it demands all of them in return. At its best, Netzach is loving and supportive, but at its worst, it can become manipulative and codependent. Hod without Netzach, on the other hand, does not understand why anyone or anything other than itself matters. Hod's better qualities are curiosity, independence, and intelligence, but it can also be selfish, cold, and egotistical. It sees only itself. That's not to say that it's sadistic or cruel. It simply lacks the capacity to care.

HEART AND HEAD

The things that are of interest to Hod are internal pursuits: thinking, studying, self-improvement, and the like. Hod's primary interest with the world is being able to dissect and experiment on it, in order to understand it to Hod's own personal satisfaction. To empathetic Netzach, this approach comes across as clinical and sterile, but for Hod, the world exists simply as an object of study. Problems in the world, including problems that affect other people, are mere abstract puzzles; Hod wants to solve them just for the satisfaction of having done so. On the other end of the spectrum, Netzach cares deeply, but it lacks self-awareness. It cannot analyze or strategize, and it doesn't know how to distinguish between how things seem and how they actually are. Its fundamental nature is passion and compassion, and this renders it incapable of dispassionate judgment.

Building on this dynamic, a second way we can define the relationship between Netzach and Hod is as the connection of the heart to the head. The other-regarding nature of Netzach is determined by feeling, and the self-regarding nature of Hod is determined by thinking. This opens up a range of other associations for the two Sephiroth, which aren't as easily seen through the self-and-other lens. Netzach is aesthetic, containing experiences of love, beauty, luxury, and pleasure. Hod is detached, utilitarian, economical, and rational. The great mystery of the Astral Triad lies in harmonizing the two. How do we unite head and heart? How do we keep clarity of thought and depth of feeling, without sacrificing one for the sake of the other?

These two ways of understanding the relationship between Hod and Netzach may seem like they don't quite align. On the one hand, we have the polarity of self and other. On the other, the polarity of head and heart. And while it is certainly true that these can align, it is also obvious that they don't have to. Some emotional concerns are self-interested, and some intellectual concerns are essentially social. We may find beauty and joy in things that have nothing to do with other people, and we can turn sociology and psychology into intellectual disciplines that reduce human interaction to facts and statistics. Yet beauty belongs to Netzach and statistics belong to Hod.

Who Am I?

The key here, which is worth remembering throughout this book, is that "polarity" does not simply mean "opposites." The two poles do not negate each other, but rather strengthen and reinforce each other. They share of a common nature that makes them the same even though they are different; in the fullness of each, we find the seed of the other. Day leads to night, life leads to death (and thence to rebirth), the Goddess gives birth to the God. When we identify a polarity and use it for magic, we are not just saying, "These things are different." We are saying, "These things are different, but somehow the same," and the polarity gives us a deeper insight into their shared nature.

It is no surprise, then, that the various qualities we attribute to Netzach and Hod can overlap and bleed into each other. If they had nothing in common at all, there would be no polarity between them. All polarity is a spectrum, and though we identify poles at the two extremes, there are infinitely many points in between them. The aesthetic appreciation we feel for something that no one else sees is in one sense Netzach and in another Hod, as is the scientific study of the connections that bring people together. Identifying the polarity lets us see the complex and often paradoxical ways in which these things are connected, and allows us to make something new out of their union. Whenever we talk of polarity, look not only for the difference, but also for the sameness: What is the spectrum on which the poles lie?

With Netzach and Hod, the commonality, the fundamental question that both Sephiroth ask, is: "Who am I?" The answer to that question is complicated, because people are complicated. We are at once unique and alike, alone and together, thinking and feeling, restrained and decadent—Hod and Netzach.

Meditation on Netzach and Hod

This meditation will help you feel the interplay of magical energy between yourself and someone you love, using small objects to represent the two of you. By feeling this energy, you will get a better understanding of the polarity of Netzach and Hod. Read through the instructions beforehand so that you can perform this meditation without having to refer back to the book.

You Will Need

- a small object that represents you: a compact mirror, a photograph of yourself, or even a slip of paper with your name on it
- a small object that represents someone you love: a picture of the two of you together, a gift they gave you, or maybe a piece of jewelry they wear
- a quiet room with no distractions, where you can meditate undisturbed.

Instructions

Holding the first object in your left hand and the second object in your right hand, find a comfortable position to sit or lie down. Breathe deeply and quiet your mind. Relax your body and find your center. Remain there for as long as you need to, until you feel calm and collected.

When you are ready, notice the object in your left hand—the object that is *you*. How does it feel? Is it heavy or light? Hard or soft? Rough or smooth? Explore it completely with your hand, forming a mental image of it. Then, try to sense the magical energy in the object. Is there a color you associate with it? Does it tingle in your hand like electricity? Does it feel solid and steadfast? Or maybe it's dynamic and flowing? What are the defining features of the magical energy you feel?

Take as long as you need to explore that object completely. The energy you feel in it is your energy; it is who you are. Now turn your attention to the object in your right hand, and repeat the process. Examine it physically at first, and form a clear mental image of it. Then, examine it energetically. Identify the magical energy of this object, of the person you love. What are the ways it is similar to your own energy? What are the ways it is different?

Finally, bring your hands together, and hold both objects over your heart. Take a moment just to hold them. Feel their energy. How does that energy change when you have both of them together, versus when you sense each one on its own? How are you each, individually, altered by the bond of love that you share?

COMMUNITY IN WICCA

As a religion, one of Wicca's secondary functions is to provide people with a community. Its primary function is, without a doubt, the worship of the Gods and the performance of magical and seasonal rites, but there is also a sense in which one of the most important things religion does is to bring people together. This goes for all religion, not just Wicca. Religion fosters a community, and gives people a liturgical framework to mark important social rites of passage like birth, marriage, and death. It provides us with a language with which to celebrate momentous occasions, to grieve our losses, and to help each other through good times and bad. All of these functions are about bringing people together, and therefore all of them are connected to Netzach. The next time you go to a handfasting or a baby blessing, consider how essential love and community are to what we do.

Netzach is even more present for those Wiccans who belong to covens. The old-school folkloric image of the witch is a solitary old woman, a recluse and a hermit, but many modern witches, both Wiccan and non-Wiccan, practice in groups. Each coven is different—some covens know each other intimately and socialize outside of ritual, while others may only see each other for rituals and training—but regardless of the social dynamics of a coven, working magic together forms a bond between people. A coven is a basic social and magical unit, a group of people who come together out of a shared love for each other, for the magic they perform, and for the Gods.

Sharing sacred space is an act of tremendous intimacy and vulnerability. Casting a spell together is doubly so. Group magic requires a singularity of purpose that's difficult to achieve with strangers. Everyone present needs to be of one mind, visualizing the same goal, raising power together and sending it to the same target. The whole group needs to become functionally one unit, a single, cohesive magical entity rather than a loose collection of individual practitioners. Developing that kind of group-mind takes time, patience, and genuine affection for one another. Most people, unless they're inordinately good at sensing magical energy, need some level of connection in order to work effective magic with another person, let alone with multiple people; it's the kind of thing that you really can't fake.

This is one reason that the process of finding a coven takes so much time. Looking for a coven requires building a genuine connection with the people in it, getting to know who they are and what they're like. On some ineffable level, it also requires getting a feel for the extant group dynamic. A newcomer needs to gel with the coveners, not just individually, but as a collective whole. Each group is unique, and there are plenty of groups that are not the right fit for a particular seeker even if they're full of lovely people who like that person and enjoy their company.

Nonetheless, difficult though it may be to find a coven and form a connection, the experience of practicing Wicca in a group can be life-altering. There is something profound about sharing a religious connection, not just with the Gods, but also with other people in one's own community, members of a chosen family. Of course, not all Wiccans work in covens, but that doesn't mean that solitary Wiccans can't or don't experience Netzach as part of their practice. All of the Sephiroth can be expressed in a variety of ways in Wicca; I single out one example, not as the end-all and be-all, but as a demonstration of how we can uncover Qabalistic structure in the things we already do in Wicca. Anything in your practice that connects you to other people and allows you to feel that bond of a magical community carries with it the energy of Netzach.

Ritualizing Netzach: The Coven

The most inspiring experience of Netzach I ever had was completely unplanned. I was at an ordinary esbat rite with my coven, and toward the end of the ritual, a coven sibling said, "Let's all go around the circle and say what we love about each other." To this day, that ritual remains one of the most heart-warming and impactful I have ever attended, and I don't know if I have ever felt more loved or more loving than I felt in that circle.

You Will Need

- a group of people with whom you share a loving bond. This ritual is designed for a coven, but if you are a solitary practitioner, you can still perform it with family or close friends
- a ritual space large enough to accommodate the whole group.

Instructions

Declare the opening of the ritual by saying, "Now is the time for us to love and be loved."

One by one, go around the room and let everyone say what they love about each other person in the ritual. These comments should be personal and specific: anecdotes about shared experiences, descriptions of positive qualities someone has, ways that your life has changed for knowing each person. No one should interrupt, and the speaker should be allowed to go on for as long as they feel is appropriate. While they are speaking, everyone else should be attentive and engaged with their expression of love. If there are regular members of the coven who are unable to attend this ritual, it would be appropriate to speak about the love you feel for them, as well. Once everyone present has had the chance to speak, everyone should embrace or hold hands.

If you do not belong to a coven, you can still perform this exercise. Invite over a group of close friends or family members for dinner. These should be people who all know each other well and care deeply about each other; you should all be a family of sorts, even if you are not connected by blood. Over dinner or after the meal, ask everyone to take a moment to speak about the love they feel for each other. (For those in the United States, Thanksgiving is a great opportunity for an exercise like this!)

This exercise may be as formal or as informal as you like. The point is simply to take a moment and be conscious of the love that you share with the people in your life. Appreciate how much love you feel, and how loved you are in return. That is the essence of Netzach.

Magical Names and Personal Identity

What, then, of Hod? Where Netzach connects us to others, Hod connects us to ourselves. It allows us to know ourselves better, and to strive for self-improvement. In Wicca, all kinds of magical work can be done toward these goals. We can ask the Gods to inspire us, or perform spells for self-confidence or emotional growth. We can use magic to supplement the goals we set for health or career advancement. We can even use ritual and meditation to uncover and heal our past traumas. All of this is related to Hod. Nonetheless, there is one widespread Wiccan practice that stands out to me as exceptionally rooted in the energy of Hod: the choice of a magical name. Magical names are a staple of Wicca, and they serve a variety of functions, but all of those functions relate back to Hod.

On one hand, a magical name is a pseudonym that can be used with other Pagans, so as to keep your legal name secret. There's a rather fantastical myth that back during the "Burning Times," witches meeting in secret would use magical names to conceal their identities, so that if one of them was caught by the Inquisition, they'd be unable to name the others. Setting aside the questionable historicity and internal logic of this story (as if someone wouldn't be able to identify the blacksmith's wife just because she called herself "Willow" instead of "Catherine"?), it is true that Craft names in the modern day can provide a level of anonymity that many of us want or need. During the Satanic Panic of the '80s and '90s, people involved in the Craft risked losing their jobs, having their children taken away, or feeling unsafe in their own homes. Nowadays, there are still places where Wiccans run that risk, and even in more tolerant places, there are a variety of reasons that someone might want to keep their involvement with witchcraft private. I, myself, am writing this book under a pseudonym.

The privacy-preserving power of a magical name is a power of Hod. It insulates us from the eyes of other people and allows us to practice our religion without fear of negative social consequences. The creation of a boundary between the self and the outside world is a magical act, an assertion of individuality and independence. It says that some things are not for others to see. Some things are made more sacred because they are for us alone.

Magical names have a second function that also relates to Hod. They act to affirm our identity within ritual, so that we become a different person than the ordinary, quotidian version of ourselves. "Jack Chanek" is a regular person with a job, bills to pay, and problems to solve, but when I step into ritual space, I don't want to carry all of that with me. I want to be more focused, more devoted to the magical and religious work at hand, so I use a different name—one dedicated to ritual use. With that name, I am no longer Jack, the ordinary person. Instead, I am a priest of the Gods, a witch, and a magician. With my mundane name, I have mundane problems, worries, and doubts, but as soon as I hear my magical name, all of that melts away. I am transformed into a version of myself that is wholly present in sacred space, unburdened by anything outside the bounds of a ritual circle.

Magical names are both expressive and aspirational. In one sense they say, "This is who I am," and in another they say, "This is who I wish to be." In choosing a magical name, we pick out something already meaningful to us. We look for something that expresses who we already are, whether that's a quality we possess, a plant or animal that has personal significance, a deity we worship, a crystal we love, or some other thing that connects to how we see ourselves. We don't choose names out of nowhere, because we want them to have meaning for us, personally; I would never take a name like "Agrimony," because I'm not much of an herbalist, and I don't have much of a connection to agrimony. It's a wonderful, powerful name for the right person, but it's not *me*. The magical names we choose are such that when we step into ritual and begin to use those names, we become more wholly ourselves. We do not want our names to make us into other people entirely.

However, magical names can still help us to aspire to who we want to be. We may pick names expressing qualities that we wish to cultivate in ourselves, helping us to become the kind of people we want to be in ritual and in life more generally. Such names affirm our power and our magic. They shouldn't contradict who we are outright—once again, the goal is to be ourselves, not other people—but they can bring parts of us to the fore and cultivate a ritual persona. Jane Doe might be an accountant whose day-to-day life is not particularly magical, but if she chooses the name Circe, then every time she enters ritual, she leaves her mundane self behind and assumes all of the power and dignity associated with that name. This name isn't antithetical to who Jane really is. Rather, it permits her to give voice to those parts of herself that she wishes to center in ritual. As a witch, taking a magical name is a transformative act that lets someone be who they had always hoped they could be.

This affirmation of identity, both expressive and aspirational, is once again characteristically the power of Hod. Who we are and who we want to be are inextricably connected, and a good magical name manages to convey both at once. In both cases, someone's name is unique to them, something special that they have chosen for themselves. More than anything else, a magical name says, "This is me," and that declaration of selfhood is what Hod is all about.

Ritualizing Hod: A Naming Ceremony

When you have chosen a magical name, you can perform a ritual to formally adopt that identity in circle. If you have previously performed a formal naming ceremony for yourself, you may alter the wording to use this ritual as a reaffirmation of your name.

You Will Need

- a small container of anointing oil prepared before the ritual. I like valerian for something like this, but any herb(s) associated with purification and new beginnings will do
- a wand or athame
- a space to use as an altar. If you do not have a dedicated altar, an ordinary table or shelf is fine. Failing that, you can lay out your ritual implements on a cloth on the ground
- a ritual space you can move around freely.

Instructions

Kneel in front of your altar and meditate for a time on the name you have chosen, and why. Then, when you are ready, say:

"I, [legal name], come before the Lady and Lord tonight to adopt a new name. I shall be known by this name in all my magical endeavors, before the Gods, spirits, and other witches. Be it known, my new name is [magical name]."

Take your wand or athame and write your magical name in the air in front of you. Visualize each letter glowing with brilliant white light.

Place your wand or athame back on the altar, and pick up the anointing oil you have prepared. Anoint your forehead, saying, "May I bear this new name, [magical name], with power."

Then, anoint your left foot, saying, "May I bear this new name, [magical name], with humility."

Anoint your right hand, saying, "May I bear this new name, [magical name], with compassion."

Anoint your left hand, saying, "May I bear this new name, [magical name], with wisdom."

Anoint your right foot, saying, "May I bear this new name, [magical name], with strength."

Anoint your forehead again, this time in silence. (You have just drawn an invoking pentagram of earth on your body.) Then, anoint your chest, just over your heart. Say, "Now I am [magical name]. The Gods have borne witness. So mote it be!"

You may end the rite here if you choose, or you may incorporate the energy of Malkuth into the rite by presenting yourself to the four quarters with your magical name. If you wish to do the latter, take your wand or athame and proceed to the east. Write your magical name in the air as you did previously, and announce, "Mighty element of air! Hear and witness that I am now known as [magical name]!" Then do the same for the other three elements in the south, west, and north, making a final stop back in the east to close your circuit.

Different Names for the Same Polarity

We will see the polarity between Netzach and Hod repeated and magnified as we continue our ascent up the tree. All the polarities of the Tree of Life are echoes of each other, and our understanding of this relationship will help us to comprehend Chesed and Gevurah, Chokmah and Binah, and on the larger scale, the Pillars of Mercy and Severity as a whole. The balance between social and individual, love and indifference, aesthetic and intellectual will play out in a variety of ways, but one of the great mysteries of Hermetic Qabalah is that all of these polarities are somehow expressions of the same inner truth. Keep this in mind, and circle back to it, as we start to delve into the larger, more abstract polarities that give the tree its structure.

For now, we have talked enough about the division. Let us now turn our attention to their synthesis in Yesod.

Journal Prompts

- The central question of this chapter was "Who am I?" Take this as a freeform journaling prompt and answer it however feels right to you. You can do free word association, draw a picture, or write longform. Once you have finished, read through what you've written and identify areas where your self-description is more Netzach or more Hod.

- How does your practice connect you to other people? Do you have a coven? Pagan friends? Do you go to festivals or participate in online forums? How can you become more conscious of Netzach in all these areas?

- What does your magical name mean to you? Why did you choose it? Write about the version of yourself that your name expresses.

CHAPTER 4

THE ASTRAL TRIAD: YESOD

Having discussed the division, we now come to the recombination. When the tension between Netzach and Hod is resolved, they combine to produce Yesod, the ninth Sephirah. Qabalists translate the Hebrew word יסוד as "Foundation," but as with Netzach and Hod, this name actually does very little to help us understand the symbolism of the Sephirah. The name "Foundation" suggests solidity and an unchanging nature, but in fact, Yesod is exactly the opposite. It is protean, mysterious, and in a state of constant flux.

Where Malkuth is the visible world, Yesod—the Sephirah immediately above Malkuth on the tree—is the invisible world. We know it by a variety of names: the otherworld, the underworld, the spirit world, the astral plane. All of these are Yesod, and it is from Yesod that the Astral Triad gets its name. For this reason, witches are already quite familiar with Yesod. Much of the magical work we do takes place there. Astral projection, mediumship, hedge crossing, and any work with non-corporeal spirits are all, to some extent, works of Yesod.

Yesod is the domain of dreams and intuition. It is a shifting, inconstant landscape, where something can be two contradictory ways at once. The rules of the ordinary world, of Malkuth, don't apply in Yesod. Time is not linear. There is no strict progression from cause to effect. Even space cannot be mapped the way it can in Malkuth; we can all remember dream experiences where we cross an ocean within seconds, or where we're trapped in a labyrinthine landscape that changes as we try to navigate it. Yesod is a Sephirah where the rules of the mundane world don't apply. Nothing is logical, nothing is predictable, nothing is what it appears to be on the surface.

Because of its fluid nature, Yesod can never properly be understood by reading about it in a book. The act of writing crystallizes an idea, makes it solid and graspable. The words on this page are the same for every person who picks up this book. They never change, no matter who is reading or when. Yesod, however, is in a state of perpetual change. It is not the same for any two people, nor is it consistent even in the experience of one person. Any attempt to define Yesod, to pin it down and hold it under a microscope, will miss out on some part of its essence, because the simple act of describing it changes its nature.

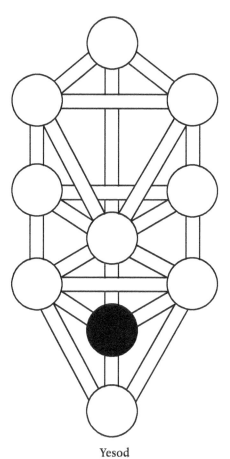

Yesod

Myth and Symbol

Rather than words and definitions, the language of Yesod is the language of dreams, symbols, and metaphor. Where a book will describe transformation and change, Yesod will show you a butterfly. A picture is worth a thousand words, but in Yesod, it is worth so much more than that; images and symbols can convey a depth and complexity of meaning that mere words never will. For this reason, all forms of divination, which involve interpreting meaning from abstract symbols of one kind or another, belong to Yesod. So do myths and fairy tales, which occupy a paradoxical space of true-and-not-true.

Is it actually, literally true that Loki turned into a horse and was impregnated? Well, yes and no. There is no such thing as literality in Yesod. It did happen, in a time that was not a time and a place that was not a place: somewhere far, far away. When we tell myths, our concern is not with the biology of how someone could possibly shapeshift and then give birth to an eight-legged horse; to think of the story in those terms would be reductively literal. It happened, or it didn't, or maybe it both did and didn't. That detail doesn't matter, and if we were to focus on it, we would be utterly missing the point. What does matter is the symbolism, the deeper meaning of the story, which could never be expressed in any other way. The universe is a great, big, confusing place, full of contradictory truths, and sometimes those truths don't fit into the structure of the world that we can comprehend. Yesod gives us an oblique glimpse of the truths that don't make sense, the contradictions and the paradoxes, by expressing those truths through the language of symbols.

When we journey to Yesod, we must leave behind our expectations about the nature of reality. We must be willing to accept the uncertain, ever-changing nature of the astral plane, where a thing can be both true and not true, where in one moment something exists and in the next moment it never existed at all. We have to learn to accept the world of dreams and visions—and everything that comes with it—as reality. To cross into Yesod is to surrender certainty and embrace the mystery of something larger than we can ever understand.

EXERCISE: SCRYING

Scrying is a form of divination that involves relaxing your conscious mind and passively allowing symbolic images to filter into your consciousness. As such, it is a perfect way to open yourself up to the energy of Yesod.

You Will Need

- a scrying mirror or a dark-colored bowl filled with water
- a candle
- a quiet room with no distractions, where you can scry undisturbed.

Instructions

Light the candle and position it so that you can see the reflection of the candle flame in the water or the mirror. Unfocus your eyes. Relax your breathing. Clear your thoughts. Think of a question you want answered, and say, "In this reflection of a flame, I seek a reflection of the truth. May it show me [your question]."

Gaze into the reflected flame and allow your mind to wander. Begin to notice shapes and images dancing on the surface of the water. Allow the images to come and go, moving freely through your mind. Don't try to pin them down or hold them. Just let them rise into existence and fall out of it again. You may see many images, or just one; some images may even disappear and then reappear.

Continue gazing into the reflected flame until you feel you have received your message. Then say, "I have found what I sought. I go now in gratitude for what I have been shown." Extinguish the candle, then write down all of the images and symbols you saw during your scrying. Take some time to interpret them. What does each symbol mean individually? What do they mean when you take them all together? The skill of interpretation may take some practice to develop; don't be discouraged if your first few attempts are confusing and unclear.

WHERE HEAD MEETS HEART

Yesod's paradoxical nature is precisely what allows it to resolve the tension between Netzach and Hod. The language of symbolism speaks to both the head and the heart, if we allow it to. Symbolism and metaphor are at once universal and deeply personal. Anyone who reads tarot knows that after a time you build up two sets of associations for each card: the "official" ones and the personal ones. The former come from books and discussion with others; they are the shared symbolic language of the tarot, which allow two different readers to look at a card and share a rough understanding of what it means. Everyone knows that the Two of Cups deals with companionship and love. But there is also a second set of more personal interpretations, depending on the artwork in the deck you use, previous readings you've done, or your own gut intuition. Reading tarot, or any other divinatory system, requires both the personal and the shared symbolism. The symbolic language of Yesod is at once fully rooted in Hod (the self) and Netzach (the other).

Likewise, Yesod is associated with the faculty of intuition, which unites the thinking and feeling aspects of Hod and Netzach. Intuition is not properly categorized as either rational or emotional. It is some third thing, which comes from the union of the other two. Intuition is what guides us when the head and the heart come into sync with each other, when they stop trying to drown each other out and instead work together in concert. When we make decisions based on intuition, we can't explain exactly why we do what we do. We simply know, on some inexpressible level, that it is right. We have no intellectual doubts, nor emotional reservations.

Importantly, Yesod is not just a haphazard admixture of the energies of Netzach and Hod. It is something greater, something new produced by their union. All synthesis, all creation out of polarity, results in something greater than the sum of its parts. Yesod takes the two extremes of a polar spectrum and unites them, not by mixing a little bit of each, but by affirming the totality of both of them and bringing them together to result in something new.

MEDITATION ON YESOD

This is a guided meditation that will help you to leave your body and travel briefly to the astral world of Yesod. Visiting the astral is a skill that takes time to develop, so don't worry if you struggle with it at first; the more you perform this or similar meditations, the easier they will become. Before beginning this meditation, record yourself reading the instructions aloud so that you can listen to them while you are on your journey.

You Will Need

- a quiet room with no distractions, where you can meditate undisturbed.

Instructions

Lie on your back in a dark room with all the doors closed. Breathe deeply and evenly, and clear your mind. Find a sense of serenity and calm. Inhale, and as you exhale, feel your body start to get lighter. Inhale again; exhale again. With each breath, you feel lighter and lighter. You are dizzy and weightless. The physical world is falling away from you. You are floating and free. In your mind's eye, form a picture of the room you are in. Visualize every detail: the color of the walls, the floor, the furniture. Notice your own body, lying supine, and watch your chest rise and fall with each gentle breath.

Become aware that the body you see is separate from you. You are elsewhere in the room, looking at that body. Where are you? Are you floating above your body? Standing next to it? Take a moment to look down at yourself. Note the clothes you are wearing—are they the same as the clothes on your physical body, or different? Also notice a silver cord wrapped around your waist, with one end leading away and tying you back to your physical body. Tug gently on this cord, and feel the connection between you and your physical self. Nothing can sever that tie, and whenever you want to return to your body, all you have to do is follow the cord.

Turn away from your body and find the door leading out of the room. Walk over to it, reach for the handle, and gently open it. As you step through the door, you find yourself standing on a pier extending out into the ocean.

It is nighttime; the crescent moon shines above, surrounded by glimmering stars, and a thin veil of mist is draped over the waters. Smell the salt spray of the waves. Hear them gently lapping against the shore and the wood surface of the pier. Walk forward, into the mist, until you come to the end of the pier. There, you find a small rowboat tied up, bobbing up and down on the waves.

Kneel at the edge of the pier and dip your hand into the water. Feel the gentle shock of the cold water against your fingertips. You see a flash of silver under the water's surface, as a fish darts away from the ripples made by your hand. As it swims away, its tail breaks the surface of the water, and you hear a gentle splash. Sit down and dangle your feet into the water, letting the cool current swirl around them. You may wish to return to this spot another time, get into the boat, and see where it takes you, but for now, you rest here, at the edge of the great unknown. The mist thickens and envelops you, catching the moonlight with a gentle silver glow. Look into the mist, and you'll start to notice faint shadows and shapes taking form. Concentrate on them, and they'll become clearer, sharper, images emerging from the fog. What do you see? What do these images mean? What are they telling you?

After a while, the images will begin to blur and fade, until they are gone altogether. The mist thins again, and you catch a glimpse of the stars up above. Stand up and take one last look around yourself. It is time to leave this place. Walk back up the dock to the door through which you came. Walk back through the door and close it behind you. You find yourself back in the room where you started your meditation. Notice all the details about the room: the walls, the floor, the furniture. See your body, exactly where you left it, breathing slowly and evenly.

Gradually, allow this mental image to dissolve. You no longer see the room, and yourself within it. Inhale; exhale. As you exhale, notice that you are starting to feel heavier. With each breath, you feel heavier and heavier, more and more physical, more connected to material reality, until you realize that you are back in your body. When you feel totally grounded, open your eyes and find yourself back in the ordinary world.

Different Perspectives on the Sephiroth

The astute reader will notice a disconnect between the way I write about Yesod and the way I've discussed Netzach and Hod. I described the latter two primarily as personal qualities, parts of the individual psyche. In contrast, I have presented Yesod not merely as something psychological, but as another plane of existence, the otherworld where spirits reside and where myths and legends take place. What gives? Are the Sephiroth psychological, or are they alternate planes?

The truth is, they're both, and much more besides. Netzach and Hod are other worlds unto themselves, just as Yesod is; Yesod is a part of the psyche, just as Netzach and Hod are. The Sephiroth are multifaceted. In introducing them, I have endeavored to pick out the facets that are the most relatable and the easiest to understand, but we should never forget that the other facets exist. Thus, although I describe Yesod as a separate world, removed from the physical, it is also present in this world and within the human soul. Yesod is not just the otherworld. We find it in our dreams, in our intuition, in every part of us that is perplexing and contradictory. Somehow, through Yesod, these things are all the same. They are points of access that give us entry to the same divine emanation.

There is an entire plane of existence that is just Netzach, and one that is just Hod, but it is difficult for us to conceptualize what, exactly, such worlds would look like. As we progress up the tree, the forces we encounter become bigger and more abstract, and by consequence, they become harder for us to understand without filtering them through our own concepts and experiences. It is easy to see Malkuth as the physical world, and it is even easy enough to talk of the world of spirits and dreams, but what would the "world" of Netzach look like? How can we even begin to visualize that? Without physical or psychological points of reference, Netzach in the abstract is all but impossible to wrap our minds around—and the challenge only gets greater with the higher Sephiroth.

To understand the Sephiroth, then, it is often necessary to look for them in the world we know, to find the ways that they manifest in ourselves or our environment. Remember that the Sephiroth connect to and flow through each other. No Sephirah is ever entirely without the energy of the others, and we find glimmerings of each reflected in every other. Thus, we can understand Netzach, Hod, and Yesod in part through the ways they show up in this world, and in ourselves, and in our magical rites and our understanding of the Gods. All of these things are aspects of the energy of each Sephirah. So long as we remember that there is a greater whole uniting them, there is nothing wrong with understanding that whole through smaller aspects. The true nature of the Sephiroth is bigger than us, too big for us to understand in their totality. We can only ever understand them in part, through an interpretive lens. The more lenses we learn how to use, the more complete our picture, but it will never be one hundred percent, and that's okay. That's part of the mystery of trying to explore the Divine.

THE SEPHIRAH OF WITCHCRAFT

This leads us to an important point. When we talk about working with the Tree of Life, it is easy to feel like you are expected to have a complete understanding of all ten Sephiroth, as if you should be constantly journeying up and down the tree and having awe-inspiring visions that lay bare the true nature of reality. There's so much going on in Qabalah, and part of why people get so discouraged is that they feel like they'll never master it all. Here's the truth, though: no one ever masters it all. The higher Sephiroth are simply beyond human comprehension. We can talk about them in abstract terms, tie them to more relatable and familiar concepts, but we can never know them unfiltered and in their entirety. That's as it should be. Anyone who claims to understand everything about the Tree of Life is full of hot air, because the tree is meant to hint at levels of reality beyond our grasp.

The increasing difficulty of exploring the higher Sephiroth is sometimes denoted on the tree as a "veil" above Netzach and Hod, separating the Astral Triad from the Moral Triad. It is easy to know Malkuth, Yesod, and even Netzach and Hod, but as we move up out of the Astral Triad and explore the higher mysteries of the Tree of Life, the natures of the Sephiroth will become more and more obscure, more veiled, and harder to know in their entirety. One of the great lessons of occultism, of any mystery tradition, is that for all we learn, there will always be something we can't learn. To borrow terminology from Chapter 2, no mortal has ever lifted the veil of Isis, and no mortal ever will. There must always be something hidden, veiled, unknown, and unknowable. That is the nature of ultimate reality.

For the practical purposes of witchcraft, it's enough to get to Yesod. If you can achieve a strong, intuitive grasp of this Sephirah—if you can *know* it with the ease with which you know Malkuth—then you are equipped with the psychic and magical skills you need in order to be a successful and competent witch. It's still important and worthwhile to study the higher Sephiroth, but cut yourself some slack if you find them harder to access. That's normal. Having any grasp of the Sephiroth whatsoever is an extraordinary achievement, and there is plenty of time for you to build up more complex, layered interpretations of the Sephiroth as you study. The best way to learn each Sephirah is by starting with a very simple concept and elaborating on it until we begin to see it with greater depth and complexity. The more time we spend doing so, the easier it will be for us to understand them. Be patient with yourself as you study; understanding will come in time.

The two Sephiroth that are closest to the manifest world, and therefore the most important for us to understand, are Malkuth and Yesod. If you have a good handle on just those two, you're already well on your way to being a successful Qabalist. These are the Sephiroth that figure most prominently in witchcraft and practical magic. Any act of sympathetic magic works by connecting the two. Magic establishes a symbolic connection, and symbolic connections are the domain of Yesod. When I place a photograph of a friend under a lit candle to help heal that friend's illness, I am speaking the language of Yesod. I am declaring, "This photograph is like my friend; therefore, it is my friend. What happens to it happens to them." That sympathetic link belongs to Yesod. To cast any spell, simple or complicated, I elevate my consciousness into the astral world and perform a ritual action there, in order to effect change in the physical world. I am bridging the gap between Yesod and Malkuth.

In many ways, the essence of witchcraft is in that liminal space between Malkuth and Yesod. What we do as Wiccans, both religiously and magically, is to lift ourselves up out of the physical world, conduct ritual in the other-world, and then bring the results of that ritual back with us when we return to the mundane. It is for this reason that, for the purposes of witchcraft, we don't need to be able to cross into the "worlds" of the higher Sephiroth the way that we cross into the world of Yesod. All we really need to do is raise our consciousness above Malkuth; for the practical purposes of spellwork, bringing our consciousness to the astral is just as effective as bringing it higher up the tree.

Yesod and Sacred Space

No part of Wiccan ritual more perfectly encompasses that journey to Yesod (and back) than casting a magical circle. The Wiccan circle is a descendant of magical circles used by ceremonial magicians throughout the history of Western magic. It establishes a boundary between the ordinary and the sacred, enclosing us in a liminal space that is set apart from the flow of day-to-day life. Within the magic circle, the laws of the mundane world don't apply. Everything is laden with new symbolic significance. A cup ceases to be merely a cup, becoming the womb of the Goddess; a dish of salt is transformed into the essence of elemental earth. Especially when we do spellwork, one thing becomes another: A poppet becomes a person, a knotted cord becomes a tethered storm, a set of scribbles on a piece of paper becomes the embodiment of a wish. Time goes wonky, and you may conduct a ritual that feels like it lasts for ages, only to discover that it only took twenty minutes. All of this is to say that when we cast a circle, reality takes on a new quality: the slippery, symbol-rich, changeable quality of Yesod.

This altered nature of reality facilitates magical work. While it's certainly possible to perform magic without casting a circle (and when a spell needs to be done urgently, we do it whether or not we have the time and resources for a full circle), magic is significantly easier to do when we can bring ourselves to a place where reality is fluid. It's easier to exert an influence on the world, especially a magical influence, when the nature of the world itself is so much less fixed. Thus, we cast a circle, which severs our ties to the material plane and lifts us up the Tree of Life into Yesod. Once the circle is cast, everything within it has been moved from Malkuth into Yesod, thus making it easier for us to perform the ritual or magical work of the occasion.

This may seem to contradict what I said in Chapter 2: that Wiccan theology affirms the material world as sacred, and Wiccan ritual makes us present in the world rather than removing us from it. The reason for the apparent contradiction is simple: Wicca does both. Yes, Wicca absolutely holds that this world is holy, and that the Gods are to be found here with us rather than sitting in judgment somewhere on high. But at the same time, Wicca is a mystery religion; we are aware not just of the Divine as it manifests in the world, but also of the existence of something else. We do not aspire to a spiritual life at the expense of our connection to this world, but neither do we live a fully material life at the expense of the spiritual. Witches, and especially Wiccan witches, are walkers between the worlds, at once belonging to the astral and the material.

To this effect, once we cast the circle and put ourselves in Yesod, we then call the quarters, bringing Malkuth into our sacred space as well. Wiccan ritual, then, has one foot planted in Yesod and the other foot in Malkuth. We occupy the liminal space between the two Sephiroth. Our witchcraft is a perpetual dance wherein we pull ourselves out of Malkuth, cast spells and invoke the Gods in Yesod, and then bring the blessings of the Gods (and the effects of our spells) back into Malkuth—and then start the whole thing over again. Our ritual space, the circle of Yesod overlaid with the quarters of Malkuth, reflects that delicate interplay of the two Sephiroth as it is expressed in Wiccan practice.

Ritualizing Yesod: Cast the Circle

Bring Yesod into your rituals by casting the circle each time with the intention of separating yourself from the material world and conducting your rite in the liminal space of this Sephirah. If you have another script that you regularly use to cast your circles, you may use that instead of the one I've provided here.

You Will Need

- a lit censer
- a small bowl of loose incense
- a small bowl of water
- a small bowl of salt
- a wand or athame
- a space to use as an altar
- a ritual space you can move around freely.

Instructions

Take your wand or athame and proceed to the east of your ritual space. Holding your tool at chest height, walk deosil around the space, drawing the perimeter of your magical circle. As you walk, project energy through the tip of your wand or athame. Visualize a searing white light coming out the end of your tool and cutting you away from the rest of the world. The light extends over your head and below your feet, enclosing your space in all directions. As you draw the circle, say:

In peace and in love, the circle is cast:
The world of the spirits, where future meets past.
The world of humanity now falls away
In a space beyond space, between night and day.
Within this circle, our spirits are free;
In the names of the Gods, so mote it be!

As you finish casting the circle, see it glowing all around you, above and below, with intense light. Feel the shift in the air as you are surrounded by energy and separated from the material world. Then, slowly, let the light start to dim, until you can't see it any longer, although you can still feel the energy of the circle holding you inside.

Now, you may finish the circle by bringing the four elements into it. Place your hand over the bowl of incense and say, "Element of air, I bless and consecrate you so that you may make this circle holy." Bless the censer (fire), water (water), and salt (earth) in turn. Put the incense into the censer; mix the salt and water. Take the salt water and asperge the perimeter of the circle, starting in the east, and then take the censer and perfume the circle as well. When the circle is cast, you may complete the opening of your ritual by calling the quarters (see Chapter 2).

When it is time to end your ritual, after you have dismissed the quarters, take your wand or athame and go to the east. Walk deosil around the circle and trace the perimeter with your magical tool, projecting energy through it. Visualize the circle dissipating, the boundary between yourself and the ordinary world slowly melting away. Say:

> *Our rites are ended. We bid farewell*
> *To the powers that aided in our spell.*
> *Transformed and renewed, but yet the same,*
> *We return to the world from which we came.*
> *Merry we met and merry we part,*
> *And we carry the circle within our hearts.*

Initiation into the Mysteries

A final note on Yesod. I said earlier in this book that the Qabalistic work expressed by the Tree of Life, the journey between the pillars of Mercy and Severity, is an initiatory path of sorts. It delivers an experiential revelation of divine power and of the presence of the Gods in the world. Yesod is the first Sephirah we encounter on that journey, as we set out from Malkuth in our pursuit of wisdom. It is the beginning of our esoteric pursuit.

In that sense, Yesod is the Sephirah concerned with all forms of initiation. Transformative experience, and specifically transformative experience that initiates us into occult knowledge, occurs in Yesod. This is true of formal initiations, like the sort of initiation ceremony someone might undergo when they join a coven, but it is also true of individual mystical experiences. If I have a vision of the Goddess that ends up setting me on a new path, that doesn't confer any status, titles, or degrees on me; it is not a formal initiation bestowing membership in any group or tradition. Nonetheless, it is still an initiatory experience of sorts, insofar as it has a transformative effect on me, my relationship to the Gods, and my life. That transformation can never be taken away from me.

All initiatory experiences take place, in some sense, in Yesod. Likewise, each time we visit Yesod, that visit should change us somehow. It should leave us with something more than we had before, a new perspective or a fuller sense of ourselves and our place in the world. To put it differently: every encounter with Yesod is an initiation of sorts. Every night when we fall asleep and begin to dream, we are undergoing an initiatory ordeal that prepares us to face the following day. Every time we cast a circle and invite the Gods to ritual, we are re-initiating ourselves into their mysteries. The initiatory experience of Yesod is constant and ever-renewing.

JOURNAL PROMPTS

- Keep your notebook next to your bed. Every morning, immediately upon waking up, write down what you remember of your dreams the night before. What common themes do you notice? Which symbols and images obviously pertain to things going on in your mundane life, and which ones seem deeper in meaning?

- Have you ever seen a ghost? Had a precognitive dream? Encountered the otherworld in some other way? Write about numinous experiences you've had that could connect back to Yesod.

- Select your favorite myth or fairy tale and identify the key symbols in it. What are the images that stand out? Where else have you seen these images? Have you encountered them in your own life? Do you find them in your divination system of choice? Write about what these symbols mean to you and how you might interpret them in different contexts.

CHAPTER 5

THE MORAL TRIAD:
CHESED AND GEVURAH

We come now to the Moral Triad, which amplifies the polarities we saw in the Astral. Where the Astral Triad was fundamentally personal, dealing with the boundaries between self and other, the Moral Triad is fundamentally transpersonal. It deals with who we are collectively, with our sense of justice and morality. Thus, the fourth and fifth Sephiroth are Chesed and Gevurah, whose Hebrew names (חסד and גבורה, respectively) are translated by Qabalists as "Mercy" and "Severity." From them, the Pillars of Mercy and Severity take their names.

Chesed and Gevurah represent two different kinds of collective identity, two different views about how society should be organized. Chesed is passive, gentle, and forgiving. Gevurah, on the other hand, is strident, harsh, and punitive. The fundamental question of the Moral Triad is, "What is justice?" Chesed answers that justice, properly understood, is found in kindness, charity, altruism, and compassion. From Gevurah, we receive the answer that justice is found in order, discipline, accountability, and law. Chesed is the lenient, forgiving good cop; Gevurah is the hot-headed, disciplinarian bad cop. They work together to implement justice.

In the polarity of Chesed and Gevurah, we see a magnification of the polarity between Netzach and Hod. Chesed is expansive in much the same way Netzach is. It is oriented toward understanding and forgiving others—but it does so at the expense of establishing and maintaining boundaries.

Too much Chesed without the counterbalance of Gevurah is a doormat. It becomes permissive, weak, and obsequious, unable to stand up for what is right because it is too busy accommodating and making excuses for people who do what is wrong. Chesed is compassionate and giving, but it is also conflict-avoidant and easily cowed. At the other end of the spectrum, Gevurah is constrictive and restrictive in similar ways to Hod. It draws boundaries and maintains them at all costs, requiring control and structure. Without Chesed, however, Gevurah becomes tyrannical and despotic, so obsessed with maintaining its narrow vision of what is right that it scorches the earth and destroys everything that doesn't fit that vision. Gevurah can be self-righteousness and commitment to a cause, but it can also be anger, violence, and entitlement.

Crucially, as with the Astral Triad, we need both ends of the spectrum. It is easy—perhaps especially so for Wiccans—to associate the severity of Gevurah with brutality and oppression, and to think that we should be all love and light. But Gevurah has essential positive qualities, without which our society would collapse. It is the Sephirah of accountability, both personal and collective. It keeps us on task and focused, and it holds us to our word; when we say we're going to do something, Gevurah is what makes sure we actually do it. Yes, it can be stringent and demanding, but that's necessary sometimes. Gevurah provides us with structure, rules, and order, all of which help us to make sense of the world around us and to regulate our collective action.

Chesed is undisciplined. It is relaxed and peaceful, eager to believe the best of everyone and to provide second chances (and third chances, and fourth chances) when we make mistakes. This can easily slip into complicity or negligence, but it comes from a good place. More than anything else, Chesed is benevolent. On its own, it can be ineffectual and passive, but the reason it is passive is that it maintains the belief that people are basically good. We don't need correction or order, according to Chesed, because we will always end up acting out of our better natures if we're just given the opportunity to do so.

As a metaphor at the broadest societal level, Chesed is diplomacy and Gevurah is the military. Diplomatic operations are wonderful when they work, and can make the world a genuinely better place, but they often fall flat when their idealistic goals are undermined by ineffectual governments, unrealistic expectations, and a lack of structured incentives for all parties to comply. Military institutions are highly structured and can be ruthlessly efficient, but left unfettered they can become bloody and cruel. A state needs both energies, in some measure, in order to function.

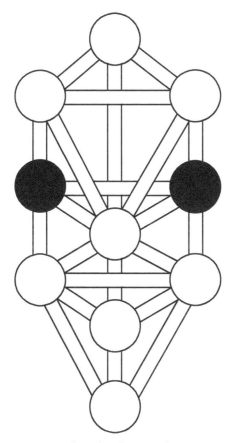

Chesed and Gevurah

GUIDING OUR ACTION

We see the polarity of Chesed and Gevurah at the smaller scale, as well. Think about parenting. A parent needs to have a good measure of Chesed: kids have to make mistakes in order to learn the lessons that the adults in their lives have already learned, and those mistakes need to be met with compassion, understanding, and forgiveness. When a child screws up, they need to understand that making mistakes is okay, and that they are still loved. At the same time, a parent has to be an authority figure, and that requires Gevurah. Someone has to enforce bedtime, make sure children eat their vegetables, and see to it that homework gets done. Sometimes, that job involves being the bad guy and acting as a disciplinarian.

Chesed and Gevurah even help us to regulate our own lives. Gevurah gives us structure and routine; it is the reason we get out of bed, go to work, exercise, and so on. Anything we do that requires discipline and willpower, anything we hold ourselves to because we think it's good, even if we don't want to do it, belongs to Gevurah. If you quit smoking, or make a New Year's resolution, you are setting a goal and making yourself accountable for accomplishing it. That's an act of Gevurah. On the flip side, Chesed is the natural human disposition to clemency. Anything you do out of altruism—giving to charity, volunteering your time, even just offering to help a friend who's moving into a new apartment—comes from Chesed. Any time we turn the other cheek, let go of a wrong that has been done to us, or act from a sense of kindness and a wish to see the suffering of others alleviated, we are manifesting Chesed. This also applies to self-compassion. When we stop nit-picking ourselves and move on from our past mistakes, we are directing the mercy of Chesed inward, toward ourselves.

The Sephiroth of the Moral Triad can serve as a lodestar for questions of morality and right action. Whenever we feel conflicted and unsure of ourselves, whenever we are unsure of what we should do, we can stop and consider the issue in terms of Chesed and Gevurah. Ask yourself, "If I were acting just on Chesed, what would I do in this situation? And if I were acting just on Gevurah?" Notice which direction your first impulse leans when you find yourself in conflict with others. Are you the sort of person whose first response is to get angry and indignant? Or do you roll over and avoid conflict?

Different people need different things in their lives, and the right course of action for one person may well be wrong for someone else. Some people are too timid, too meek, and need a great deal of Gevurah. Others are too inflexible and unforgiving, and need a dose of Chesed. Each person must learn for themselves how to balance the energies of these two Sephiroth. How can you maintain the integrity of what feels natural and right to you, while still bringing in some of the complementary Sephirah's energy to balance your response? How can you stand up for yourself without losing sight of the other party's perspective, or make allowances for someone else's failings without giving up on the fair treatment you know you deserve?

Meditation on Chesed and Gevurah

One of the best ways to connect to Chesed and Gevurah is to look for mercy and severity in your own behavior. This meditation will take you through a recent argument or conflict, and will show you how the balance of these two Sephiroth can affect the way that disagreements play out. Read through the instructions before performing this meditation.

You Will Need

• a quiet room with no distractions, where you can meditate undisturbed.

Instructions

Sit or lie comfortably and find your center. Focus on your breathing until your mind is clear and you feel calm and collected. Now, think back to a recent argument or conflict you had. Replay it in your mind, remembering what you said and how others reacted. Remember the emotions that this conflict dragged up for you. Allow those emotions to pass freely through your mind, without judgment and without experiencing them again to their full extent. You are not reliving this conflict, you are watching it from afar, observing what was said and done. Take note of how you felt, but keep yourself removed, as if you are watching someone else say, do, and feel these things.

Ask yourself why you behaved the way you did. Were you reacting to something that someone else said or did? Was it really about something else entirely, which you were projecting onto this conflict? Did you escalate or deescalate the situation? If you could go back and do things differently, would you?

Imagine the conflict again, from the beginning. This time, tell yourself, "I will act entirely out of mercy. I will turn the other cheek." Imagine the argument playing out in its entirety, but this time, you make different decisions. Everything you say, everything you do, is motivated by pure compassion. You do not raise your voice. You do not express anger at the ways you have been wronged. You simply wish the best for your interlocutor.

Replay the conversation a third time, and now tell yourself, "I will act entirely out of severity. I will demand justice." Imagine how the argument would go if you refuse to yield at all, if you refuse to make any concessions whatsoever. You stand your ground and demand what you think is owed to you. You do not see the issue from anyone's point of view but your own. What happens in this version of the argument?

Now, return to yourself. Think about how the argument actually happened, and ask yourself again whether there is anything you would do differently. Neither pure mercy nor pure severity is likely to be the answer, but are there lessons you can take away from either scenario?

EXPANSION AND CONTRACTION

The polarity of Chesed and Gevurah is complex, and there are many ways of expressing it. We have talked about social and psychological aspects of these Sephiroth: mercy and severity, lenience and discipline, restorative justice and retributive justice, forgiveness and accountability, kindness and impartiality. However, if we broaden our understanding, we can find other ways of seeing this polarity, as well. Chesed is soft, while Gevurah is hard. Chesed is bountiful and generous, while Gevurah is reserved and miserly. Chesed gives, Gevurah takes. Chesed yields, Gevurah resists. Chesed praises, Gevurah critiques. Chesed expands, Gevurah contracts.

All of these qualities are, somehow, expressions of the same polarity that holds these two Sephiroth together. Though we have introduced them as social concepts, and we have understood them as primarily governing morality, there is a greater, more mysterious polarity underlying them. There is a bigger picture here, a higher truth that is only hinted at by the names Mercy and Severity.

Part of the work we have undertaken in studying the Tree of Life is scratching at the surface of this polarity, trying to uncover what's hidden.

THE MORAL TRIAD AND THE GODS

One hidden aspect of that polarity is in the nature of the Gods. The Gods are present throughout the Tree of Life, and we see them in all the Sephiroth, but in the balance of Chesed and Gevurah, we see a peculiar internal polarity that each deity possesses. With very few exceptions, all of the Gods have elements of both Chesed and Gevurah in their personalities. Perhaps the Goddess Nemesis has only Gevurah, or the stories and worship around Kwan Yin might show only Chesed, but for the most part, the Gods express both.

Pagans tend to balk at this concept, because many of us don't want to associate Gevurah with deity. The notion of severity as a divine attribute can feel uncomfortably Christian to many, a fire-and-brimstone God sitting in judgment and threatening to cast his worshippers into hell. That's not what Gevurah is about—or at least, not a healthy manifestation of Gevurah. Regardless, this balance of mercy and severity, of give and take, is essential to religious devotion. We hope for the Gods to be merciful. When we pray to them, we want them to understand what we're going through, feel for us, and intervene to help us with our struggles. While there are certainly times that we might pray to deities with no expectation that they're moved by our suffering, Chesed is a fundamental component of divine grace, because without it, the Gods wouldn't care about us.

But at the same time, the Gods are capable of severity. They don't just give us everything we ask for, simply because we asked. We don't always get what we want. In particular, it's important to note that the Gods usually ask something of us in return. We make offerings to them, we worship them, we devote ourselves to their service. To put it somewhat crudely, we have our end of the bargain to maintain. Our relationship with the Gods is both a give and take, and we see Gevurah in the Gods when they require our worship and devotion. Worship takes *work*. We make offerings, build altars, and conduct elaborate rituals in the service of our Gods. Sometimes, the Gods ask us to do things we don't want to do, or to give up things we would rather keep.

That's the nature of sacrifice: we give up something dear to us and set it aside for the Gods. The part of the Gods that requires that from us is the severe, restrictive, disciplined energy of Gevurah.

Wicca is not a particularly sacrifice-heavy religion. Wiccans don't go in much for self-abnegation. We see nature and everything in it as holy, so our bodies are also holy; we don't deny ourselves material pleasures like food or sex in order to get closer to our Gods, because those pleasures are part of the world we celebrate as divine. Neither do we perform the gruesome blood sacrifices of which witches were accused throughout the Satanic Panic of the late twentieth century. Animal sacrifice is anathema in Wicca, although there are other religions where it plays a meaningful role in uniting worshippers with their Gods.

Nonetheless, there are ways in which we find Gevurah in Wiccan ritual. Any regular and disciplined spiritual practice contains the seeds of Gevurah; examples include meditating once a week, following a ritual calendar, or saying a daily devotional prayer. I was taught to put a vase of fresh-cut flowers on the altar for every ritual, as a sacrifice to the Goddess. Furthermore, I was also trained that the first thing we do after invoking the Gods is to make some kind of offering to them. We don't simply call the Gods and then immediately start making demands. Instead, we show them that they are appreciated and loved, we express our gratitude to them, and we make them feel welcome. We give our devotion to them in order to show that we are dedicated, serious, and committed to their worship.

In religious ritual, then, Chesed and Gevurah show the two directions that love flows in the relationship between us and the Gods. Chesed is the love the Gods feel for us, the acts of beneficence that they work on our behalf. Gevurah is the love we feel for the Gods, and all the ways we commit ourselves to showing that love. This is one of the deeper truths that can be found in the Moral Triad, although it's certainly not the only one: the questions of justice we find in our first-pass examination of these Sephiroth give way to questions of how we give and receive love. Chesed is all the ways that love is effortless, bountiful, and all-forgiving. Chesed shows us that when we love someone, we will do just about anything for them—that loving them and wanting them to be happy is as natural as breathing. Gevurah is all the ways that love requires hard work and commitment. It shows us that we don't only love someone when it's easy. When we really love someone, they're worth putting in effort for, even when it would be easier to cut and run.

Real love requires both Chesed and Gevurah, and the love we bear for the Gods is no different. Thus, we find Chesed in the boons we receive, in answered prayers, and in the sheer ecstasy that comes with direct contact with the Divine. To complement that, we find Gevurah in all the hard work that goes into religious devotion: the sacrifice, the dedication, the dark nights of the soul when we keep praying even though we might want to give up on our religion altogether. Together, Chesed and Gevurah give us access to divine love.

Ritualizing Chesed: Petition the Gods

This ritual draws upon the divine benevolence of the Gods by asking for their aid, using a fire in a cauldron to carry your petitions. Make sure to perform this ritual in a safe, fireproof setting. If you cannot safely light a fire, you can write a variation of this ritual, for example releasing flower petals into the wind on a blustery day.

You Will Need

- a cauldron. I use a cast-iron Dutch oven, but you can also use one of the small handheld cauldrons designed for use as a censer
- 1 cup of Epsom salts if you are using a large cauldron, or ¼ cup if you are using a small one
- 1½ cups of rubbing alcohol for a large cauldron, or 6 tablespoons for a small one
- a long fireplace match or lighter
- a bowl of loose incense
- a fire extinguisher. *DO NOT* perform this ritual without a fire extinguisher on hand. Always practice fire safety
- a heatproof surface to put your cauldron on

Instructions

In the bottom of the cauldron, mix the Epsom salts and rubbing alcohol together to form a slush. To begin the ritual, extend your hands over the cauldron and say:

"I come before the cauldron of the Gods, the cauldron of inspiration. May the holy fire I kindle within it carry my words to the Gods, and may they look favorably upon my requests."

Set fire to the mixture in the cauldron. The mixture will produce a bright, hot yellow flame, and the cauldron itself will get very hot. Now take the bowl of incense in your hands. Take some of the incense and sprinkle it over the flames, saying:

"Great Mother Goddess and Horned Lord of the Hunt, hear my prayers! I come to you to ask for your aid."

You may now make your petitions. With each request, throw a measure of your incense into the cauldron. Visualize the flame carrying your prayers to the Gods as it consumes the incense. When you have finished asking the Gods for help, add a final pinch of incense and thank the Gods:

"Lady and Lord, I thank you for hearing my prayer. My heart is full of gratitude for all the gifts you have given me. Blessed be."

If your cauldron has a lid, you may use it to smother the flame. Otherwise, stay with the fire until it has burnt out. *DO NOT* leave the fire unattended. When the flame is gone, your rite is officially ended.

THE CYCLES OF NATURE

In Wicca specifically, we may also see the Gods manifesting mercy and severity in the cycles of nature. The full moon is the Goddess as we are accustomed to worshipping her, the all-mother who gives birth to new life and who fills us with love and joy, but the Goddess has other faces, as well. She rules over all the phases of the moon, not just when it's full; though we see the bountiful energy of Chesed in the waxing and full moon, the Goddess presides just as much over the contractive energy of Gevurah in the waning and new moon. Just as the moon itself constantly cycles between the two, the Goddess has both faces. She is the gentle mother and the terrible mother.

When we worship her, we worship all of her, and part of her mystery is that she contains both. The archetypal image of the witch is at once the beautiful seductress and the hideous crone, alluring and revolting. She is either the beneficent fairy Godmother or the cannibal living in the house made of candy. She is always at one extreme or the other, never in between, and yet somehow she is both. The same is true for the Goddess. The Goddess of Wicca encompasses both of these aspects. The merciful and the severe, the full moon and the new moon, are both her.

We likewise find the push and pull of Chesed and Gevurah in the cycle of the seasons, although we will have more opportunity to explore that relationship in the following chapter. The mildness of early summer gives way to harsh winter, and the bountiful harvest is succeeded by a fallow period when the earth is still and barren. Think about how this cycle of comfort and hardship connects to the polarities we've already seen expressed on the Tree of Life. The seasons are in a constant ebb and flow of expansion and contraction. Crops grow and die, the days grow longer and shorter, trees flower and then lose their leaves. All of this is a manifestation of the polar forces structuring the Tree of Life. We see Chesed and Gevurah in the cycle of the seasons, and we also find a hint of the larger, deeper polarity we will come to with Chokmah and Binah—the ultimate polarity that gives rise to all others on the tree.

Ritualizing Gevurah: Make an Offering

This ritual is an offering to the Goddess as the Dark Mother, the frightening and severe aspect of the divine feminine. The heart of this rite is the act of making a sacrifice to the Goddess without asking for anything in return.

You Will Need

- a goblet
- a representation of the Goddess. If you do not have a statue, you can use a drawing, a seashell, or even a bouquet of flowers
- a bottle of wine and a corkscrew to open it, if necessary. If you don't drink, use pomegranate juice or grape juice instead

- a jar of honey
- a bottle of vinegar
- a libation bowl
- a spoon for stirring
- a space to use as an altar.

Instructions

This ritual is best performed on a new moon. Place the empty goblet and the representation of the Goddess on your altar. Kneel in front of the altar with your arms outstretched, palms up. Form a mental image of the Goddess. See her in every detail. Then invoke her, saying:

"Great and terrible mother, you who are queen of heaven and earth, I call to you! From your breasts flow the nourishing waters of life and the cold rivers of the underworld. From you all things are born, and to you all things go when the time comes for them to die, for the womb that bears us is also the tomb that inters. The brightest stars in the sky are arrayed in your crown. Blessed Goddess, be present here with me, so that I may adore at your feet!"

Wait a moment and allow the power of the Goddess to wash over you. Meditate in her presence for as long as you desire. Then say:

"Goddess, hear my praises. I am humbled before you. I love you with all that I am."

Open the bottle of wine and fill the goblet. Raise the goblet to the image of the Goddess on your altar, saying:

"I worship and adore all that you are, and I give myself in love for you. I love you with all that I am."

Pour some of the wine from the goblet into the libation bowl. Then stir a spoonful of honey into the wine goblet. Lift it to the image of the Goddess again, and this time say:

"I adore you when you are sweet and wreathed in smiles. I love you with all that I am."

Pour into the libation bowl again. Now stir a measure of vinegar into the wine goblet. Lift it to the Goddess image a third time, saying:

"And I adore you when you are bitter and full of tears. I love you completely and without reservation. I love you with all that I am, and tonight, I ask nothing in return."

Empty the goblet into the libation bowl. You may remain in the ritual space for as long as you like, and you may sing, dance, read devotional poetry, or make other offerings as you see fit. Now is *not* an appropriate time to pray for anything, nor to do magic. When you are ready to end the ritual, kneel before the altar with your arms outstretched again. Say goodbye to the Goddess:

"Great and terrible mother, you who are queen of heaven and earth, I thank you for attending this rite of worship. Now I bid you farewell, knowing that you have heard my praises and received my love. Blessed be!"

Once the ritual is concluded, take the libation bowl outside and pour your offerings upon the earth.

A QUESTION OF JUSTICE

We have talked about Chesed and Gevurah as different interpretations of justice and as aspects of the Gods. They naturally come together, then, and lend themselves to the interpretation of these Sephiroth as aspects of divine justice. They are the crook and flail of Osiris: Chesed is the gentle guiding tool of the shepherd, and Gevurah is the whip used by the farmer to thresh the grain from the chaff. When we understand the Sephiroth this way, it is easy to feel like every event in our lives is fated by the Gods, as if everything is a reward or punishment meant to mete out justice. But that's really not the worldview of Wicca. Our Gods don't punish. They may encourage us to be better, and give us ideals to aspire toward, but a morality based purely on reward and punishment is antithetical to the Craft.

Moreover, it's important to understand that not everything that happens to us is the expression of some greater divine justice. Chesed, without the balance of Gevurah, can be inclined to the belief that everything in the world happens for a higher good, that even our suffering is secretly a blessing of some kind. That's not the case. Sometimes, the world is cruel, and bad things happen, no matter how much we pray to the Gods to intercede. There are times that the Gods don't (or can't) protect us from harm. When that happens, it's not our fault, nor is it the Gods testing us or trying to teach us a lesson. Sometimes, there is no lesson to be learned, no higher purpose. Some things that happen to us are, well, just things that happen. They're not necessarily acts of divine justice. This is one of the hardest lessons of Gevurah: that suffering happens, and it's not sent by the Gods in order to help us learn. There may well be lessons we can find in suffering, ways we can choose to change and grow because of it, but the events themselves did not happen for that purpose. We do ourselves a disservice when we refuse to acknowledge the reality of suffering and instead gloss over it with platitudes about everything happening for a reason.

JOURNAL PROMPTS

- How does the polarity of Chesed and Gevurah compare to that of Netzach and Hod? What are the similarities and differences you notice?

- Which of these two Sephiroth comes more easily to you in your own moral choices? Write down some ways you can bring the energy of the other one into your behavior.

- Draw a visual representation of the polarity of Chesed and Gevurah. What images would you use to show the relationship between them?

CHAPTER 6

THE MORAL TRIAD: TIPHERETH

If you look at the tree, you'll notice that there are paths connecting Tiphereth to every other Sephirah except for Malkuth. Tiphereth is the keystone that holds the whole tree together. This Sephirah maintains perfect harmony, not just between Chesed and Gevurah, but between all the Sephiroth. Tiphereth is where all the energies of the Tree of Life converge and balance each other. The meaning of Tiphereth is all about equilibrium, harmony, and all things being in their proper place and serving their proper function.

The Hebrew name for this Sephirah, תפארת, is translated as "Beauty." Here we should understand the word "beauty" not to mean superficial aesthetic appeal, but rather something deeper and more innate. It is the kind of inner beauty that comes from truth and authenticity. A beautiful life is a life well lived, and a beautiful person is one who lives in accord with their highest ideals. Someone might look like a supermodel, but if their inner world is in disarray, they do not have the beauty of Tiphereth. When we are out of balance and overwhelmed, when we have too much of one Sephirah within us and not enough of the others to complement it, we are disconnected from Tiphereth. Beauty is what we find when we manage to bring ourselves back into balance. It is the sense of peace and equanimity that comes when we live our lives well.

In ancient Greek philosophy, particularly the philosophy of Aristotle, we encounter the concept of *eudaimonia*, a word that has no exact translation into English but is best described as "flourishing."[7] Eudaimonia is the end goal of ethics. It is the state we strive for when we try to live a good life—whatever, exactly, that means. No one has ever been able to provide a satisfactory definition for what constitutes a good life and what leads to eudaimonia. Any conditions we try to define end up proving insufficient, and the exact nature of the good life slips through our fingers when we try to hold it up for examination. Eudaimonia cannot simply be happiness, because there are people who struggle with depression and other mental illnesses, but whose lives are nonetheless full of love and kind acts. Nor is it a simple measure of the amount of good we put into the world, because someone with limited means may still lead a good life even without changing the world drastically. Moreover, eudaimonia isn't just a reflection of our inner moral characters; a bad person who does a lot of good things might still be praiseworthy for their actions, even if their character is decrepit.

Hundreds of thousands of pages have been penned about what qualifies as a flourishing life, a life worth aspiring to. It is the central question of moral philosophy, though it is phrased in many different ways. For our purposes here, I'll just say that still, after all this time, no one really knows. We can't define eudaimonia to everyone's satisfaction, though there are certainly people who have tried. It seems to be the sort of thing that we know when we see it, even if we can't explain exactly what comprises it. It is some combination of all these qualities, in ratios that can't be exactly fixed. Striving for a good life involves working toward our own happiness, toward performing good actions in the world, toward developing our own moral character, and more besides. All of that, combined, is Tiphereth.

Put another way: Tiphereth is what makes life worth living. If we can live a life that makes us fulfilled—the sort of life where, looking back on all the mistakes we've made and all the bumps in the road we've traveled, we wouldn't go back and do things differently even if we could, because we've ended up in the right place—then we have learned the central lesson of Tiphereth. That lesson will look different for everyone, because we all have different lives, but the

---

7. Aristotle, *Nicomachean Ethics*, Book I, chapter 4.

feeling of having found one's place in the world will be the same. The sense of belonging and inexplicable *rightness* is Tiphereth's hallmark.

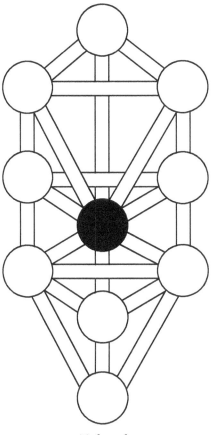

Tiphereth

THE CENTER OF EVERYTHING

Tiphereth sits at the center of all things. It is the axis on which the world turns, the sun sitting at the center of the universe. Without it, everything else would fall into chaos and disarray; the unifying power of Tiphereth is what holds the cosmos together. Just as the planets would spin off into nothingness without the gravitation of the sun to maintain the arrangement of the solar system, the differences between the other Sephiroth would tear them apart if it weren't for Tiphereth uniting them. If we think of the Tree of Life as a map of the universe, then Tiphereth is literally and figuratively at its center. Everything else, every emanation of divine power we find on the tree, orbits around Tiphereth.

In this sense, Tiphereth also expresses the synthesis that comes from reuniting the opposite ends of a polar spectrum. It is not only the union of Chesed and Gevurah, it is the union of every polar pair on the Tree of Life: Netzach and Hod, Chokmah and Binah, even Kether and Malkuth; Tiphereth is the place where they all conjoin. Tiphereth is the power of conjunction itself, the thing that results from dividing two poles and then bringing them back together. No matter what polarity we identify, Tiphereth sits at its center. The act of resolving the tension between the poles, the alchemical transmutation of *this* and *that* into something new and greater, is the essence of this Sephirah, and it is the core mystery of the Tree of Life.

This leaves an open question: How is Tiphereth specifically the union of the other two Sephiroth in the Moral Triad? How does it unite Chesed and Gevurah? As with Yesod, the answer is that it manifests the fullness of both Sephiroth at once, rather than taking some of each and commingling them. Tiphereth creates order, and in that sense it is like Gevurah, but its lawgiving function is not authoritarian and dogmatic. Instead, it is tempered by the mercy of Chesed, so that the order we find in Tiphereth is the sort of harmony that feels serene, natural, and inevitable. In order to achieve balance—in order to find eudaimonia and live a good life—we must be at once merciful and severe. The tides of the universe both ebb and flow, expand and contract, give and take. Tiphereth is not the law we impose on the world, but rather the natural law that comes from everything acting in perfect unity. It is the universe brought into balance.

Tiphereth is also at the focal point of things on a personal, psychological level. It sits at our center; it is the part of ourselves where we feel comfortable, calm, and collected. When we meditate, we begin by bringing ourselves into balance, finding tranquility and harmony; in fact, what we are doing is finding Tiphereth within ourselves. From there, we are able to access whatever energies we wish, just as we can travel to the other Sephiroth from Tiphereth. Meditation at the beginning of a ritual is often a twofold process of both grounding and centering. We establish not only a sense of wholeness within ourselves, but also a connection to the earth. This means that when we go into ritual and perform spellwork or invocation, we are drawing power from two sources: our own center (Tiphereth) and the material world (Malkuth). Thus, our magic comes at once from ourselves and from the imманent power of the Gods.

Exercise: Finding Balance

One of the easiest ways to encounter Tiphereth in the world is to look for the literal center of gravity of various objects. The simple act of bringing something into physical balance will help attune your consciousness to the central Sephirah.

You Will Need

- a pencil
- an array of other objects to balance. I recommend trying with a saucer, a basketball, and a hardcover book.

Instructions

Take the pencil and find the halfway point on its shaft. Try to balance it on your finger at that point, feeling the weight distributed evenly on either side. It might take you a couple of tries to get it right, but eventually you'll find the central point. Be still. Hold that balance for as long as you can. Try to go a full sixty seconds without letting the pencil drop. If that's easy for you, try two minutes, then five.

Now try balancing the other objects you've chosen. Each time, focus on finding the central point around which the object's mass is evenly distributed, then balance it for as long as you can.

As a further step, you may try this exercise with your own body. Balance on one foot, with the other foot braced against the trunk of your leg and your hands folded together in the center of your chest. This is the Hatha Yoga pose known as *vriksasana*, or "Tree Pose." Breathe deeply and find your center of gravity. See how long you can hold this pose.

Tree Pose

THE AXIS MUNDI

In the previous chapter, we discussed how the polarity of Chesed and Gevurah can be seen in the cycles of nature: the full and new moon, summer and winter, and so on. If we think in these terms, then Tiphereth is the unity that holds the cycle itself together. It is the progression from the new moon to the full, from summer to winter—and back again. Tiphereth is wholly present at all points in the cycle, because it *is* the cycle. It is the power that binds the two poles together concordantly, so that they work together as parts of a unified whole rather than competing with each other for dominance. It is the *axis mundi* upon which the world itself turns.

Cyclicality, and therefore Tiphereth, is fundamental to Wicca in a variety of ways, but one of the clearest is in the Wheel of the Year. We celebrate the changing of the seasons, revering autumn and winter just as much as spring and summer. We don't only thank the Gods for the light, warm, pleasant times of the year; we also honor the dark, cold, harsh times, the fallow periods, taking them as an opportunity to turn inward and introspect. We value the light sabbats and the dark sabbats in equal measure, and crucially, we value the turning of the wheel itself. Each sabbat we celebrate is a ritual occasion unto itself, but they also all connect to each other. They form a closed circuit, with energy constantly flowing through it.

Thus, the energy of the seasons is drawn from Beltane through Midsummer and into Lammas, and so on around the wheel until it comes back to Midsummer. It never stops, because each sabbat pushes that energy further along, maintaining a delicate balance that would be interrupted if the wheel ever stopped turning. This flow of energy is driven by the polarity between each sabbat and its counterpart on the opposite side of the wheel, and Midsummer reflects Yule just as Beltane reflects Samhain. And as the cycles repeat, the seasonal energy returns to the same place on the Wheel of the Year, and the whole thing is begun anew. Midsummer of this year is not just a frozen moment in time, nor even just part of a circle connecting the other sabbats over the course of one year. It is part of an infinite cycle of magical energy that flowed through Midsummer of last year and will flow through Midsummer of next year and the year after, until the end of time. Although we perform each sabbat as a unique ritual at a particular moment of time, the whole Wheel of the Year is, itself, one extended rite. The Wheel of the Year is one ritual, without beginning and without end. The unity that binds it all together is Tiphereth.

THE DYING AND RESURRECTING GOD

In Wicca, one common way to interpret the cycle of the seasons is as the life cycle of the Horned God. The God is born at Yule, grows and matures during the spring, and reaches the height of his power at Midsummer; then, he starts to weaken and wane, dying at one of the harvest festivals and return-ing to the underworld to await rebirth. Meanwhile, he has met and made love to the Goddess, who is impregnated and will give birth to him again at Yule, when the cycle begins anew. There are many, many ways to interpret the Wheel of the Year, and even among Wiccans who use some version of this myth, there is an extraordinary amount of variation in the details; I've seen people say that the God is slain at Midsummer, or that he dies at Lammas, at the Autumn Equinox, or at Samhain. It sometimes feels like someone or other has interpreted every single sabbat as the death of the God. Moreover, there are plenty of Wiccans for whom this mythological framework simply doesn't resonate, and they don't structure their seasonal ritual observances around it. That's totally legitimate, but I'm going to use the myth here, because it allows us to connect the Wheel of the Year back to Tiphereth in an elegant way.

Christian Cabalists associated Tiphereth with the symbolism of the dying and resurrecting God. In Christianity, of course, this God is Christ, but later Qabalists expanded the imagery to include a whole host of world mytholo-gies. Stories like Odin hanging on the World Tree for nine days in order to learn the secrets of the runes, or Osiris being slain by his brother and brought back to life by Isis, contain a central theme of death and resurrection, and are therefore associated with Tiphereth. That same motif is present in the myth about the Wheel of the Year. The Horned God of Wicca is perpetually dying and being reborn. He is a God of both death and resurrection, and his mythos focuses on the two as part of an eternal and harmonious cycle. He is life and death (growth and harvest, mercy and severity…You get the idea) brought together and made one. He is Tiphereth.

We likewise see Tiphereth in the Goddess, who unites the phases of the moon, but the symbolism of this Sephirah is clearer with the God because of the myth of his death and rebirth. The Goddess never dies. She waxes and wanes, but she is eternally present, unlike the God who dies, travels to the underworld, and then is brought to life again.

Why is this motif of the dying and resurrecting God so relevant to our discussion of Tiphereth? Because it perfectly shows how Tiphereth unites the energies of Chesed and Gevurah. I said in the previous chapter that Chesed and Gevurah represent two different ways of relating to the Gods. Chesed is the boons we receive from them, the things we ask and the ways we hope they will intercede on our behalf to make our lives better. Gevurah is the sacrifices we make, the commitments we hold ourselves to, and the ways we are expected to give to the Gods instead of unilaterally demanding things of them without ever offering anything in return. In broad strokes, Chesed is divine benevolence and Gevurah is the demand for sacrifice.

The dying and resurrecting God of the Wheel of the Year is special because he experiences both. He does not just demand sacrifice; he undergoes it. Just as Odin hangs on the World Tree as a sacrifice so that he can learn the secrets of the runes, the Horned God's death during the harvest season is a sacrifice that allows the cycle of the seasons to remain in harmony. The God experiences sacrifice from our perspective, performing it rather than receiving it, when he gives up his own life. He thus experiences the severity of Gevurah for himself, and he subsequently experiences Chesed when he is born at Yule and grows out of the harshness of winter and into the mild spring. In the eternal cycle of death and rebirth, the God undergoes both Gevurah and Chesed, and that is why he is able to unite them in Tiphereth, holding together the whole Wheel of the Year.

Because of this symbolism, Tiphereth is also the Sephirah where the hope for rebirth lies. Yesod is the land of the dead, the spirit world where we meet the shades of the recently departed, but the greater mystery of death—what lies beyond—is in Tiphereth. As we pass away from this world, we rise up the tree into Yesod, and thence to the promise of resurrection given by Tiphereth. In a Wiccan context, then, we can understand Tiphereth as the Summerland where the dead find peace and restoration, and where they wait until they are ready to be reborn into this world. Just as Tiphereth rules over the cycles of the natural world, it rules the cycle of birth and death across a soul's incarnations. It is the central axis around which all things revolve, even the mysteries of life and death.

Meditation on Tiphereth

This meditation is designed to help you find your own psychic center. It can be combined with the meditation on Malkuth (see Chapter 2) as a grounding and centering exercise, or it can be used on its own. Record yourself reading the instructions aloud and listen to the recording the first few times you perform this meditation; eventually, you will find that you no longer need the recorded instructions.

You Will Need

- a quiet room with no distractions, where you can meditate undisturbed.

Instructions

Stand with your feet shoulder-width apart, your shoulders relaxed, and your hands comfortably at your sides. Focus on your posture; imagine a cord strung from the ground, up through your body, coming out the top of your head and extending vertically into the sky. Stretch your spine and raise your hands all the way up over your head before lowering them back down.

You are wholly here, in this moment, in yourself. Collect all the stray thoughts that are wandering through your head, the bits and pieces of your day, your obligations, and your conversations with other people. Bring everything back to the center. Breathe in. Breathe out.

Notice a faint tingling sensation at your extremities. Your fingers, your toes, the top of your head. Let that sensation grow and begin to spread. It moves up your arms, along your wrists, forearms, and elbows. It comes up your legs, through your ankles, calves, and knees. It flows down through your head and neck. The tingling spreads through your entire body, eventually meeting at a point in the center of your chest. Then, gradually, starting from your extremities, it begins to fade. The sensation leaves your fingers and toes, your wrists and ankles, your head and neck, until the only place you still feel it is that point in the center of your chest.

Feel all of your consciousness drawn into that central point. This point is the core of your being. It is the spark of life, the soul that unites all the different thoughts, feelings, and actions that make you up as a person. This, what you are feeling right now, is the essence of who you are. Take a moment to hold the awareness of your center. Then, allow the feeling to dissipate as you end the meditation.

THE MYSTERY OF CAKES AND WINE

We see Tiphereth spanning the rituals that make up the Wheel of the Year, but we can also find it within each individual Wiccan rite. In Wiccan ritual, as everywhere else, Tiphereth sits at the center, in the blessing of cakes and wine. Cakes and wine is the heart of Wiccan ritual practice. This simple act is one of the most deep and symbolically rich ceremonies in all of Wicca. All of Wiccan theology and symbolism, everything that we do as witches, comes together in this one moment. To understand cakes and wine is to understand all the mysteries of Neopagan religious witchcraft.

Like all the best mysteries, it's incredibly simple on the surface. You'll see something like this at just about any public Wiccan ritual. A goblet, representing the womb of the Goddess, is filled with wine. The high priestess or someone else acting as a representative of the Goddess then holds the cup, while the high priest or some other representative of the God blesses the wine by inserting his athame into the cup. Just as the goblet is the womb, the athame is representative of the God's phallus; when they are brought together, the Goddess and God are joined in a symbolic act of sexual union.

At first glance, then, cakes and wine is straightforward (hetero)sexual imagery. It replicates the process of sexual reproduction by which everyone was born, and it honors the Goddess and God as the mother and father of all living things. The goblet, as the Goddess's womb, has been fertilized by the sexual conjugation of the Gods. It is blessed with life-force, the animating principle that pervades all nature. The polarity of Goddess and God, the division between the two, has been reconciled by their union, creating the potential for new life. We then take that blessed wine and use it, in turn, to bless a plate of bread or cakes. We libate some of the wine, and offer some of the cakes, in thanks to the Gods who are the source of all life, and then we drink and eat to partake of their blessings.

To limit this symbolism to sex, however, is painfully reductive. There's so much more to the Gods than penis and vagina, and the symbolism of sexual reproduction is only a surface-level expression of a much deeper truth about the polarity between them. The Gods are bigger than us, so big that any box we try to fit them into will inevitably be too small; although the language of sex and gender can help us begin to express who and what the Gods are, we must not mistake it for their essence. There is a greater mystery lying behind the symbolism of cakes and wine, which cannot be reduced to sex between a cisgender, heterosexual human couple. It includes that symbolism, to be sure, but it is also something more. We will have the opportunity to complicate this imagery somewhat in the following chapter.

Cakes and wine, as the focal point of Wiccan ritual, expresses the culmination of the Gods' relationship. It is the point where they love and become one. When we conjoin the cup with the athame, we are ritualizing the sacred union not just of sperm and egg, but of all polarities. Lover and beloved, self and other, heaven and earth, Gods and humanity. Cakes and wine is where they all come together. It is the most powerful, fundamental moment in Wiccan ritual, containing the secret of division, reunion, and generation. The greatest mystery of Wiccan theology is laid bare during cakes and wine, where the opposite ends of a polar spectrum are brought together in an act of creation. That moment of unification, which manifests the energy of Tiphereth, is the heart of Wicca.

Moreover, the rite of cakes and wine can be made to reflect the symbolism of death and rebirth. Wine, or any fermented drink, has undergone death and resurrection. Grapes have been harvested from the vine, mashed, and drained of their juice, effectively being killed. But then that juice is given new life as yeast ferments its sugars and transforms them into something new. Likewise, bread is made with flour that has been reaped and ground down, but then brought back to life by the process of leavening. The food and drink that we bless contain within them the cycle of life, death, and rebirth, all held together by Tiphereth. This symbolism can be maintained even for those who don't drink alcohol: instead of wine, use raw cider, which still has the potential to ferment. Alternatively, you can use fruit juice and stir a spoonful of raw honey into the cup; the yeasts in the honey make the drink "alive" in the proper sense, and give it the potential for fermentation and the symbolism of new life.

The symbolism of this ritual is completed by the act of libation. The Gods have bestowed their blessings upon us, and we give back to them in an act of thanks. In this moment, we are simultaneously giving and receiving, brought into a reciprocal communion with the Gods that is neither entirely about them blessing us nor about us worshipping them. It is both. Love is flowing in both directions, from us to the Gods and from the Gods back to us. Thus, the ceremony of cakes and wine unites the energies of Chesed and Gevurah, bringing us together with the Gods in Tiphereth. In cakes and wine we find that the Gods love and become one, and their love creates new life—underscoring the mysteries of life and death, and the promise of rebirth. Moreover, we commune and become one with the Gods. This is the central religious symbolism of all of Wicca, and as such, it is the perfect expression of Tiphereth in Wiccan ritual.

Ritualizing Tiphereth: Bless Cakes and Wine

The blessing of cakes and wine is the point where all the energies of Wiccan ritual come together. If you are working in a coven, this ritual should be performed by two people together; if you are solitary, you may place the cup on the altar and bless it alone.

You Will Need

- a goblet filled with wine or an appropriate substitute
- a plate of bread or cakes, suited to the number of people in the ritual—a whole loaf of bread is unnecessary if you're the only one in the circle
- an athame
- a libation bowl
- a space to use as an altar

Instructions

Place the plate of cakes on the altar. The two participants should hold the cup between them, and should take a moment to feel for each other energetically, forming a magical bond. Together, they say:

"In the beginning, all things are one."

Then one person should take the cup, while the other picks up their athame. The athame-bearer says:

"But without division, there can be no union. Without difference, there can be no love. And so it is told that the Horned Lord is born from the one, made separate from the Goddess so that he may love her."

The athame-bearer poises the tip of their athame over the cup. The cup-bearer says:

"And she loves him in return, and from their love the world is born, for love is the secret that unites all things."

The athame-bearer lowers their athame into the cup, then removes it and uses it to sprinkle some of the blessed wine onto the plate of cakes, while the cup-bearer says:

"And now we partake of that mystery, for by love we are made one with the Gods just as the Gods are made one with each other. Blessed be!"

Pour some of the wine into a libation bowl along with one of the blessed cakes. Then each person in the circle may drink the wine, eat some of the cakes, and offer their thanks to the Gods.

OTHER POLARITIES BETWEEN THE SEPHIROTH

Thus far, we have spoken of Tiphereth as the unity that comes from conjoining the two halves of a polarity. Although the greater polarities of the Tree of Life are those expressed by the pillars and the triads, there is a smaller polarity manifested between any two Sephiroth that are connected on the Tree of Life. Chesed and Hod sit across from each other on the tree, with Tiphereth bridging between them; the same goes for Gevurah and Netzach. Even within the Pillars of Mercy and Severity, we can use Tiphereth as a mediating point to pass between two Sephiroth: we can move through Tiphereth from Netzach in order to reach Chesed, or through Tiphereth from Hod in order to reach Gevurah. For *any* two Sephiroth on the Tree of Life, we can find a polar relationship between them, and delving into this relationship helps us to understand the Sephiroth individually. We can see each Sephirah in a new light by taking the time to examine the connections between them.

However, Tiphereth can also be at one end of a polar spectrum. It doesn't always have to be in the center. Because Tiphereth connects to eight of the other nine Sephiroth, there are eight different polar spectrums that each contain Tiphereth itself as one of their two poles. Thus, there is a polar spectrum between Tiphereth and Yesod, between Tiphereth and Hod, and so on. Each of these individual polarities expresses the unique relationship between those two Sephiroth, exposing aspects of them that we might not otherwise have seen. Because Tiphereth sits at the center of the Tree of Life, it can form a polar relationship with *any* Sephirah. Thus, it forms the center of an eight-spoked wheel, where each spoke is a polarity connecting it to another of the Sephiroth.

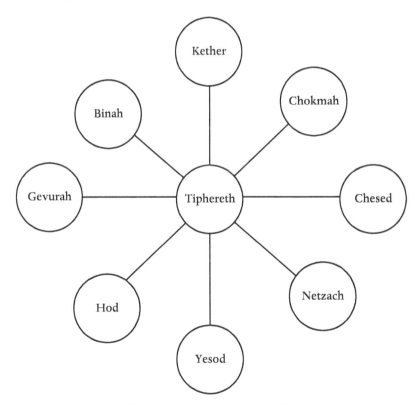

Tiphereth at the Center of the Wheel

The relationship between Tiphereth and any other Sephirah is like the relationship between an orchestra and the individual musicians who comprise it. Tiphereth is the place where the voices of all the other Sephiroth meet, and it contains all of them within itself. Its purpose is not to drown out the individual Sephiroth, but to amplify and intensify them with supporting voices. It highlights the specific, unique qualities that each Sephirah contributes to the Tree of Life—without which, the harmony of the whole would be incomplete. Working with the polarity between Tiphereth and another Sephirah is like listening to an ensemble piece and singling out a particular instrument. Ask yourself two questions. First, *how does this contribute to the greater whole?* And second, *how does the rest of the ensemble*—that is to say, the rest of the tree—*highlight the strengths of this individual component?* In this way, the polarities between Tiphereth and the other Sephiroth can give us a deeper, richer understanding of the whole of the tree and of each Sephirah individually.

There is even a connection to be discovered between Tiphereth and Malkuth. Malkuth is divine energy made manifest in the material world; Tiphereth is the principle of underlying harmony that is revealed when the material world is stripped bare. Between them, serving as the resolution of the two poles, lies Yesod, the world of dreams. On our way up the tree, Yesod helps us to lift our consciousness out of the material plane so that we may become aware of Tiphereth; in the other direction, the shifting, symbol-rich world of Yesod gives form to the sublime balance of Tiphereth, cloaking it in myth and metaphor so that it can be revealed to us.

The dynamic of Tiphereth, Malkuth, and Yesod is a division-and-recombination polarity much like the ones we saw in the Astral and Moral Triads. These Sephiroth are arranged on the Tree of Life in a vertical line, not a triangle, but they express the same polar dynamic. Malkuth and Tiphereth give us the division, and then Yesod gives us the recombination. The world of spirits, symbols, and intuition unites manifest reality in Malkuth with the beauty at the heart of the universe in Tiphereth, just as it unites self-awareness in Hod with our connection to others in Netzach.

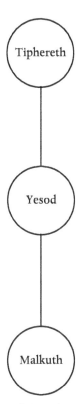

Tiphereth-Yesod-Malkuth

All of this can seem complicated and overwhelming, I know. If it's too much to handle right now, walk away from it, read the rest of this book, and then circle back and reread this chapter once you've explored the whole Tree of Life. The point of introducing all these polarities is not to confuse you, but rather to show you how interdependent the Sephiroth are. Remember, no Sephirah can be understood in isolation. An essential part of what they are is their connection to each other. Tiphereth is defined by how it centers the rest of the Sephiroth; Malkuth is defined by how it grounds the tree. The Tree of Life is a cohesive, dynamic whole, not just an aggregation of isolated parts, and so each Sephirah must be understood relationally. As we turn now to the Supernal Triad, we come at last to the most fundamental relationship on the Tree of Life, the one that lends its nature to every other polarity we have discussed: Chokmah and Binah.

Journal Prompts

- What does the good life mean to you? How do you hope to live your life, and by what metric do you measure success? What are the times when you've felt totally fulfilled?

- What does the motif of death and rebirth mean to you? How does it relate to your religious practice and your understanding of the Gods?

- Look through the scripts of rituals you have performed in the past. What is done right in the middle of the ritual? What is the central act around which everything else pivots? In light of what we have said about Tiphereth, what does that say about this part of your ritual?

CHAPTER 7

THE SUPERNAL TRIAD: CHOKMAH AND BINAH

Passing up the Tree of Life toward the Supernal Triad, we encounter a void where it seems something is missing. The Supernal Triad sits at a remove from the rest of the tree; there is a great big blank spot between it and the lower Sephiroth. This empty space is known, rather melodramatically, as the Abyss. It is home to the "missing" eleventh Sephirah, Daath (דעת, pronounced *DAH-aht*), the name of which means "Knowledge." Much like the veil between the Moral and Astral Triads, Daath shows us that part of the tree is unattainable to us; as well as we might come to know the ten Sephiroth, there will always be something else, something further, the knowledge of which is hidden from us. There is an empty spot on the Tree of Life, a visual reminder of the things we do not and cannot know.

There's other symbolism associated with Daath, much of which is explicitly biblical; "Knowledge" is what's absent from the Tree of Life, because of the story of the Garden of Eden. For our purposes in this book, we will leave that symbolism aside. As far as we are concerned, the most significant feature of Daath is its absence. It is defined by its inaccessibility, and by the Abyss that is left in its place.

To reach the Supernal Triad, we have to cross the Abyss. We have to traverse that great expanse of empty space, and this serves as an important visual and energetic reminder of a truth we discussed in Chapter 3: the farther up the Tree of Life we go, the harder the Sephiroth are to understand. Attuning to Malkuth is a level of mindfulness that we can all achieve; learning to shift our consciousness into Yesod requires a great deal of work and patience. For most of us, just getting to Yesod is the work of a lifetime. We may be able to talk about the other Sephiroth and to conceptualize them on some level, and yet never fully understand them. And remember, that's okay! For the purposes of witchcraft, we're able to accomplish just about everything we need, simply by moving from Malkuth to Yesod and back again.

Some people, who dedicate decades of study, meditation, and ritual magical practice, will rise further up the tree than Yesod and shift their consciousnesses fully into one of the higher Sephiroth. These are the sorts of people who are larger than life, who seem to radiate divinity: bodhisattvas, saints, artistic geniuses, and so on. To make it as far up the tree as Tiphereth is to attain enlightenment, or at least what most of us think of as enlightenment, and getting that far takes a lifetime, even multiple lifetimes, of dedication. Almost no one, if anyone at all, reaches a state of consciousness higher than the Moral Triad.

Once again, I want to emphasize that *that's okay*. Our goal in studying the Qabalah is not to cast off the shackles of the earthly world, become beings of pure consciousness, and remove ourselves to Kether. Our goal is much, much humbler than that. We can use Qabalah to aid in our understanding and worship of the Gods, to help us in our magic, and yes, to elevate consciousness—but we need not overreach ourselves with that aim. Any amount of transcendence achieved means that our time has been well spent; if we can get as far as Yesod, and then have a basic grasp of what's going on higher up the tree, we have succeeded.

All of this is to say that as we cross the Abyss, we reach a part of the Tree of Life that no one will ever be able to fully comprehend. The Supernal Triad deals with the level of ultimate reality, and as long as we are finite beings who belong to the material world at the bottom of the tree, we will never be able to know the true nature of reality. We will never be able to draw back the veil of Isis and see what lies beyond. The best we can do is hint at it, using shadows and reflections to try and give ourselves a sense of what the real thing looks like.

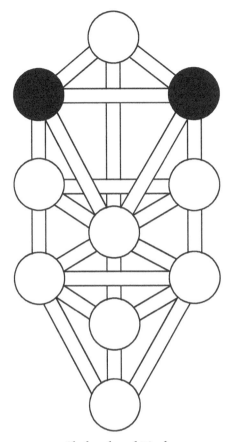

Chokmah and Binah

FORCE AND FORM

And so we come to the second and third Sephiroth, Chokmah and Binah. They are the ultimate pair, the polarity that lends its nature to all others on the tree. Polarity on the Tree of Life begins with Chokmah and Binah, and all other polarities—such as those on the Moral and Astral Triads—are descendants of this pair. If we can understand Chokmah and Binah, we have understood the entire Tree of Life.

Chokmah rests atop the Pillar of Mercy, and the Hebrew name חכמה means "Wisdom." Meanwhile, Binah tops the Pillar of Severity, and its name, בינה, translates as "Understanding." Neither of these English names is particularly illustrative of what these Sephiroth are all about, but Chokmah and Binah are also much more helpfully referred to as "Force" and "Form," respectively. It is for this reason that the Pillars of Mercy and Severity are sometimes also known as the Pillars of Force and Form, taking their names from the Sephiroth of the Supernal Triad rather than from Chesed and Gevurah.

What, exactly, do the terms "Force" and "Form" mean? Chokmah is energetic and expansive. It is powerful, spontaneous, and undirected, a pure explosion of divine energy. It is absolutely unlimited, and it contains the potential for anything at all, but it is also wild and chaotic. Like an electrical charge building into a bolt of lightning, it has infinite energy but no shape, no fixed presence in the world. Binah, on the other hand, is material and contractive. It is the vessel that limits and contains the energy of Chokmah, giving it form and confining it to a singular state of being. It harnesses the raw, chaotic power of Chokmah and binds it to a purpose, a shape, a presence in the world. If we think of Chokmah as building electrical charge, Binah is the lightning rod that grounds it, pulling that energy down to a particular point.

Binah is the divine vessel, which holds the energy of Chokmah and alters its nature in so doing. Just as water takes on the shape of the container it's poured into, Chokmah takes the shape given to it by Binah. Where Chokmah is dynamism and activity, Binah is stasis and inertia. Chokmah *does*; Binah *is*. The force of Chokmah animates and gives life to the form of Binah; the form of Binah gives being and substance to the force of Chokmah.

Another way to put it is to say that Chokmah is energy and Binah is matter. They both pervade the universe, but Binah restricts Chokmah and gives energy something to act upon. After all, energy without matter can't do anything. It needs some object to interact with. Likewise, matter without energy would be static and unchanging. The gravitation between objects with mass draws them together, so in a world with only the matter of Binah and none of the animating energy of Chokmah, the whole universe would collapse in on itself and form a singularity, much like the state that things were in before the Big Bang. Likewise, energy is responsible for the expansion of the universe, both at the moment of the Big Bang and continually for the past fourteen billion years. If the universe were only energy and no matter, it would explode outward, expanding unchecked until it dissipated in all directions and there was nothing left. What holds the fabric of the universe together is the presence of both matter and energy, of Binah and Chokmah.

Binah is what causes things to be, and Chokmah is what causes things to change. If we alter our language somewhat, rather than thinking of them as matter and energy, we can think of them as space and time. Extension in space is what gives things shape, substance, and some level of fundamental nature. It's what allows them to exist in the world. Extension in time, on the other hand, is what allows those objects to change: something can be big at one point in time and small at another, black and then white, alive and then dead. Without time, there is no way for change to occur. Something can't be simultaneously black and white. However, without space, nothing would exist in the first place in order for that change to take place. An object has to exist, has to have a presence in the three-dimensional world, before it can change from one way of being to another.

Gender, Sex, and What's Beyond

Perhaps one of the simplest and most relatable ways to talk about Chokmah and Binah is simply to say that Chokmah is active and Binah is passive. Chokmah fills Binah, and Binah receives Chokmah. Discourse of this kind often conflates the polarity of active and passive with sexual and gendered imagery, identifying Chokmah as male and Binah as female. We should be careful about this language; the idea that men are sexually active and women are sexually passive is, itself, a reductive holdover from a patriarchal view of women as inert objects for men's pleasure and procreation, rather than people with their own desires and agency. In fact, *everyone* involved in sex, for pleasure or for reproduction, is an active participant, and a gestational parent is far more than just a receptacle for impregnation. Nonetheless, there is a sense in which this language can be a helpful metaphor for Chokmah and Binah if we contextualize it appropriately and remember that the reality of sex, gender, and sexuality is far more complex than this simplified picture. Chokmah is like an ejaculation, a spurting forth of creative potency. Binah is the womb that receives that ejaculation, contains the egg that is fertilized by one of its sperm cells, and gives the resulting embryo form so that it can become new life. Seen in this way, sexual reproduction comes from the union of force and form.

However, it would be a grievous error to think that all Chokmah and Binah amount to is an elaborate metaphor about sex. Sexual reproduction is one way that force and form can be understood, but the principles themselves are so much greater than that. Chokmah and Binah are typically assigned biological imagery having to do with phallus and womb, for the ease of our understanding, but they are beyond sex. They are cosmic principles that manifest throughout the universe. To say that the fundamental nature of reality reduces to penis and vagina is hubristic beyond measure. Rather, we must flip the script and say that the imagery of phallus and womb is one specific metaphor that we use to try to make a larger reality comprehensible, and that it necessarily falls short of the whole truth.

Moreover, we should be careful to disentangle the biological symbolism of phallus and yoni from social, magical, or energetic questions about gender: man and woman, priestess and priest, and so on. Gender and sexuality are complicated. The polarity of Chokmah and Binah doesn't neatly align with the categories "man" and "woman" any more than it does with penis and vagina. Everyone has both Chokmah and Binah inside of them, manifesting in different ways and to different degrees. Everyone is vocal and assertive at some times and soft and receptive at others. Once again, gendered language can be a point of entry for us to begin to make Chokmah and Binah more relatable and understandable, but we err if we assume that all men are paragons of forceful Chokmah and all women are made in the image of form-giving Binah. It would be sophomoric to claim there is a one-to-one gendered correspondence to these Sephiroth. There is always something greater going on, and we lose sight of the truth when we simplify it too much.

Remember that every polarity is a spectrum, and there are infinitely many points between the two poles. Gender is not a straightforward division of men and women; there are people who fall at various points along that spectrum, and even people whose gender identities don't fall between those poles at all. There are men with vaginas, women with penises, and people who are neither men nor women. Biological sex isn't a binary division, either, and a substantial number of people have disorders of sexual development or are intersex—that is to say, they exhibit both male and female primary or secondary sex characteristics. In fact, at an estimated 1.7% of the global population, there are more intersex people on the planet than there are redheads.[8] To simply say Chokmah = penis = man, and Binah = vagina = woman, misses out not only on the complexity of these Sephiroth, but also on the complexities of sex and gender in human life. Similarly, to equate Chokmah and Binah with sexual reproduction ignores everyone in the world who has same-sex attraction or who has sex for any reason other than procreation. Things just aren't that simple.

Don't get me wrong, sex and gender can be useful metaphors to try and grasp at the nature of these Sephiroth that are fundamentally beyond our reach. Most of us can easily conjure up cultural associations around gender: stereotypes of femininity as passive and nurturing, of masculinity as active and aggressive, and so on. This language can be helpful, because at the very least it gives us *something* through which to understand this polar relationship. But we must always remember that the language we choose is limited, and the universal principles we are trying to describe are not. Any way that we talk about the higher Sephiroth will necessarily be insufficient, because these Sephiroth are beyond our capacity to know and describe. Let us not make the mistake, then, of relying on the crutches of sex or gender and forgetting that there is something far greater and more mysterious at work.

Chokmah's nature is always to grow, expand, and alter. Binah's nature is to contain, constrict, and preserve. This language should be familiar from previous chapters. I have already talked about the polarity of expansion and contraction, particularly in the context of Chesed and Gevurah. Here, we see that expansion and contraction is, at bottom, the domain of Chokmah and Binah. The ways that Chesed and Gevurah are respectively expansive and contractive are reflections of this higher polarity, pulling the qualities of the Supernal Sephiroth down into the Moral Triad in order to manifest that polarity on a more limited, more personal scale. The energy of Chokmah

8. Melanie Blackless, et al. "How Sexually Dimorphic Are We? Review and Synthesis," 159.

flows throughout the Pillar of Mercy, and Binah flows through the Pillar of Severity. Both Chesed and Netzach are shadows of Chokmah, and on the other side of the tree, Gevurah and Hod are shadows of Binah. The interplay of Chokmah and Binah is the ultimate principle that governs the Tree of Life.

Meditation on Chokmah and Binah

This meditation uses the flow of water between two containers to help you feel the interplay of force and form. Read through the instructions beforehand so that you understand the purpose of the exercise, and then perform the meditation in silence.

You Will Need

- two identical vessels, each of which can fit comfortably in one hand. Bowls or cups are ideal
- water to fill one of the vessels
- a quiet room with no distractions, where you can meditate undisturbed.

Instructions

Begin by filling one of the vessels with water, then sit in a comfortable position with both containers in front of you. Breathe deeply. Ground. Find your center. Take the empty vessel and begin to examine it with your hands. Get a feel for the shape of it, the weight, the texture. Explore it with your mind until you know every square inch of it. Form a replica of the bowl in your mind. Clear away all other thoughts. There is only this vessel. It is the beginning and end of the world, the beginning and end of yourself.

Now take the other vessel and slowly pour the water from it into the first one. As you do so, allow your mental replica to fill with water as well. Feel the water change course as it makes contact with the vessel, limited and shaped by the boundary of its container. Feel that limitation giving form to the water, taking something moving and changeable and bringing it to a place of stillness. Invest your mind completely into the form of the vessel.

When you have poured out all of the water, wait until it has adapted fully to its form. It has stopped moving entirely, and there is no disturbance on its surface. Gradually, shift your consciousness from the vessel to the water it contains. Instead of focusing on the edges of the vessel, the ways that it constrains the fluid within it, focus on the water itself. Dip a finger into the water and stir, feeling the flow of a miniature current building as you agitate it. Experience the dynamism, the inherent changeability of the water. Feel how it wants to move. Clear away all thoughts except for the water.

Now pour the water back into its original vessel, and as you do so, let your consciousness flow with it. Feel the force of change as it flows freely, fluid and mutable. Feel the sheer joy of motion. Pour the whole of your consciousness into the water, and allow yourself to be swept away by the energy of that movement.

Repeat this exercise several times, pouring the water back and forth, feeling both force and form.

THE GODS UNVEILED

It is easy to understand how Chokmah and Binah relate to Wicca. Simply put, they are the Gods. The polarity of force and form is the heart of who the Wiccan Gods are. The Great Mother Goddess gives form and manifestation to the world. Much like Binah, we tend to represent her as a woman, and we use the imagery of a fertile womb and nourishing breasts to describe the way she gives life to the world. She is certainly all of that, and there is beauty and power in the iconography of the Goddess as the mother of all living things, but she is also something more. There is something mysterious and unknowable to the Goddess, a greater reality that lies behind the faces by which we know her. In a sense, she is immediate, embodied, and personal—the Goddess made immanent in the fabric of the universe itself—but in another sense, she gives expression to a transcendent principle that lies perpetually out of our reach. We saw the first face of the Goddess in Malkuth, as Isis Veiled. Here, in Binah, we encounter the second face, as Isis Unveiled.

Binah, then, is the true nature of the Goddess, as she exists when we draw back the veil of the material world. Binah is the part of the Goddess that we may hint at and describe, but that we can never really know, because she lies beyond the world of our perception. She gives form and manifestation to the force of the God as Chokmah, and the polarity between them drives the creation of the universe. We know her as the mother of the universe, and indeed, one of the names sometimes given to Binah in Qabalah is the "Supernal Mother," but that language is only a limited expression of what she really is. The Goddess as Binah transcends motherhood. She is greater than gender and sex, greater than the whole of the universe and anything within it. She is antecedent to all creation, a first principle that grounds the possibility of existence for all things.

As the Goddess is Binah, so the Horned God is Chokmah. With him, too, we have already seen a lesser face, just as we saw the lesser face of the Goddess in Malkuth: we encountered him as the dying and resurrecting God of Tiphereth. In Tiphereth, we found the God as a seasonal deity who presides over the cycles of the universe, who maintains harmony in the manifest world, and who keeps the promise of rebirth beyond death. In Chokmah, we find the hidden face of the God, stripped bare of these more concrete aspects. This is the raw force of the God. The God as Chokmah is the Lord of Change, who dances the universe into creation. He is the leader of the Wild Hunt, untamed and untamable, caught up in a constant pursuit and unable to stop or rest. He is the primordial lover who adores the Goddess and impregnates her. He is all of these things, and more.

Where the Goddess as Binah is the first principle of manifestation, the God as Chokmah is the first principle of liberation. Everything that is energetic and transcendent, everything that provides a release from this world, belongs to him. Thus, sex and all other ecstatic experiences are ways we can connect to the God. So, too, is death; sex and death are both intimately tied up with the energy of the God, even as Chokmah. The God who presides over change and release is both the Lord of Love and the Lord of Death. While birth is a manifestation into this world, giving us form and material presence, death is a liberation from it. Death removes us from our bodies, releasing us from physical incarnation. The form given to us at birth is concrete and enduring, and we have the same bodies for our entire lives. In contrast, the force of death is transformative and freeing. Thus, the mystery of birth is given to us by the

Goddess as Binah, and the mystery of death is given by the God as Chokmah. When they unite, the cycle of reincarnation is brought into existence.

Wicca has little in the way of mythology and no official creation story, but we may think of the Big Bang, and the beginning of the universe, as the creation of the Gods. Billions of years ago, before the universe began, all the primordial stuff that now makes up our universe was condensed into a singular point. There was no time, no space, nor matter or energy. There was just this one point of being. And then, all of a sudden, everything exploded outward. The universe expanded in a massive rush of energy, extending along the dimensions of time and space, and as it cooled, it formed matter, organizing into atoms and molecules, stars and planets. We can understand this as the story of the Supernal Triad, and by extension, the story of the Gods. In the beginning, there is only one thing, all-encompassing and undifferentiated. This is Kether, which we will discuss in the next chapter. Then out of Kether comes force and form. The expansive energy of Chokmah, the God, is what sparks all change and initiates creation. The contractive energy of Binah, the Goddess, shapes Chokmah, constrains it, and makes it manifest into the universe that we know.

Ritualizing Chokmah: Invoke the God

Bring Chokmah into your circle with an invocation of the Wiccan God as the primordial force that animates the universe. This invocation should be dynamic, energetic, and forceful to suit the nature of the God.

You Will Need

- a representation of the God. If you don't have a statue, you can use a drawing, a piece of antler, or a pinecone
- a wand
- a space to use as an altar
- a ritual space you can move around freely

Instructions

Place the representation of the God on your altar. Take your wand and raise it above your altar, invoking:

"Horned Lord of life and that which lies beyond, you who pervade and precede all things! Transformer, creator, destroyer! Be present in this circle. Come down among us and fill us with your ecstasy. O great God of the unknown, be with us so that we may adore you!"

Lifting the wand high above your head, begin to dance clockwise around the circle. If there are other people present for the ritual, they should dance around the circle as well, and you may all join hands if you choose. The dance may be as simple or as complex as you like; a basic grapevine step is easy to maintain with a group. While you are dancing, everyone should build energy by clapping, chanting, or using a musical instrument like a rattle or tambourine. If your mobility is impaired and you cannot dance, raise energy by chanting in place and waving your arms if possible.

Feel a whirlpool of energy starting to build up around you. As it builds, use your wand to focus that energy. Visualize all the power in the circle coalescing around the tip of your wand, like cotton candy around a paper cone. Keep the dance going until the power builds to a peak, and you feel like your circle cannot possibly contain any more. Then come back to your altar and, if necessary, signal for everyone to stop chanting and clapping. Draw all of the power from the circle into the tip of your wand, then lower your wand and touch it to your representation of the God. Allow the magical energy to flow out of your wand and into the figure on the altar, imbuing it with the power of the God. Say:

"We welcome you, mighty God, with love and praise. Receive our adoration."
Immediately make an offering of some kind.

A PARADOX ON THE TREE

There is a puzzle at the top of the Tree of Life. Chokmah is traditionally considered male, and Binah is considered female; by extension, the Pillar of Mercy is masculine and the Pillar of Severity is feminine. But if we look at the lower Sephiroth on these pillars, they exhibit qualities at odds with the stereotypes of their assigned genders. On the masculine Pillar of Mercy, we have yielding, compassionate Chesed and loving, community-oriented Netzach. On the feminine Pillar of Severity, we have strident, commanding Gevurah and rational, self-interested Hod. It seems that the qualities on the Pillar of Mercy are more stereotypically feminine than masculine, and vice versa for the Pillar of Severity. What are we to make of this?

For starters, it's helpful to remember that stereotypes are not reality. Femininity is not inherently tender and nurturing, any more than masculinity is inherently dominant and individualistic. These pictures of male and female qualities are cultural constructs, and ideas about what is typically masculine or feminine have changed drastically over the course of human history. What unites the Sephiroth on either pillar is not gender, but something more abstract and less limited to human culture: each pillar is pervaded either by force or by form. All the Sephiroth of the Pillar of Severity are form-giving. Gevurah gives form through law and discipline, and Hod gives form through intellectual inspection and rational categorization. Likewise, the Sephiroth on the Pillar of Mercy are force-giving. Chesed and Netzach are united by an outpouring of energy, the same unrestrained overflowing that we find in Chokmah.

In this sense, if we consider force masculine and form feminine, we may call Chesed and Netzach male and Gevurah and Hod female. Even so, we should remember that gender is a different polarity from the one that unites force and form, and the two spectrums do not line up perfectly. Force is neither exhaustively nor exclusively male, and form is neither exhaustively nor exclusively female. Consequently, the Sephiroth beneath Chokmah and Binah are also never going to be perfectly describable in gendered language.

There is also a second way we can look at the dynamics of gender on the Tree of Life, should we choose to. We can think of the gender polarity as swapping poles, so that the top of each pillar has an opposite gender to the Sephiroth beneath it. Thus, we may conceive of Binah as feminine but see Gevurah and Hod, with their respective energies, as masculine—and vice versa on the Pillar of Mercy.

What's the point of thinking about the tree in this way? Well, it amplifies the polarities between the Sephiroth, and allows energy to flow in new and interesting ways. Remember, polarity generates magical power. So far, we have looked at a number of polarities between Sephiroth on the Pillar of Mercy and ones on the Pillar of Severity. Each of the three triads on the Tree of Life completes a magical circuit that allows energy to flow between the right-hand pillar and the left-hand pillar. We have also talked about other polarities, such as the relationship between Malkuth and Kether (or, for that matter, Tiphereth), which draw energy up and down the middle pillar. What we have not talked about is the polar flow of energy within either of the outer pillars. What kind of energetic circuit moves energy up or down the left-hand or right-hand path?

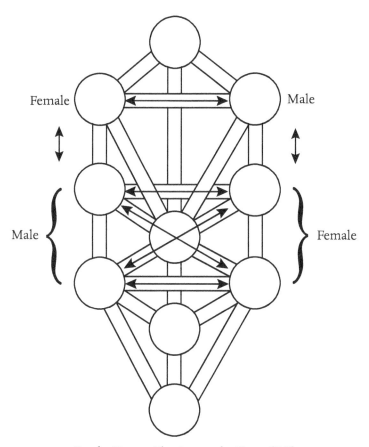

Gender Energy Flowing on the Tree of Life

One way to answer this question is to explore the polarity between the top of the pillar and the bottom, much as we did when we talked about the relation between Kether and Malkuth. There is a polar tension between Chokmah and Netzach, which finds its resolution in Chesed; on the other side of the tree, we find a similar dynamic with Binah, Hod, and Gevurah. In both cases, the Moral Triad serves as a bridge between the cosmic, transpersonal energy of the Supernal Triad and the psychological, inescapably human energy of the Astral Triad. The principle of division and recombination is present everywhere we look on the Tree of Life.

The other way to answer the question of how energy flows on the outer pillars is to talk in terms of gender. If Chokmah is traditionally masculine, but we think of the Sephiroth beneath it as feminine, then there is a polar circuit built up between them; energy flows between it and them, just as energy flows between it and Binah. The same is true on the Pillar of Severity. The language of gender polarity won't resonate with everyone, and that's okay. Polarity is big and complex, and manifests in so many more ways than just gender (or, for that matter, sex), so if talking about gender polarity in the Sephiroth doesn't aid in your understanding of them, don't worry about it. There are plenty of other lenses through which the flow of divine power through the Tree of Life can be viewed. But for those who do draw on gender polarity in their magical practice, this can be a helpful way to think about how power flows down from the Supernal Triad to the lower Sephiroth.

Ritualizing Binah: Invoke the Goddess

Binah is the Goddess as the giver of form. Bring her into your circle by invoking her into the form of a representation you have prepared for her.

You Will Need

- a representation of the Goddess
- a space to use as an altar

Instructions

Sit or kneel in front of your altar, holding a representation of the Goddess in your hands. Close your eyes and breathe deeply. Whisper under your breath:

"I invoke you, gracious Goddess, into the circle I have prepared in your honor. I invoke you, gracious Goddess, into the circle I have prepared in your honor. I invoke you, gracious Goddess …"

Keep repeating this simple invocation, and as you do so, allow your body to sway back and forth. Repeat the invocation until you have lost track of time and you have no sense of how long you have been sitting in place. Clear your mind of all thoughts other than the words of the invocation. Once you have reached that state of timelessness, feel the Goddess entering your ritual space. The representation of her you are holding gradually grows heavier as its form is solidified by her presence. It is as if the whole of the universe is condensing into this one object, held between your hands. All of space, all of the stuff from which the earth and stars are made, is brought into your circle, into your representation of the Goddess. You find yourself more present in your body, more aware of the joy that comes with being alive and incarnate. The Goddess is coming. The Goddess is here.

When you feel that the Goddess has fully entered into the object you prepared for her, raise it to your lips and kiss it. Say:

"Welcome, mighty Mother, and blessed be!"

Immediately make an offering to the Goddess.

Working with Alternate Polarities

There are countless ways that polarity can be brought into Wiccan practice. Much of traditional Wicca is structured around gender polarity, which often gets conflated with sexuality, fertility, and biological characteristics. This is, in part, because Wicca emerged at a point in the mid-twentieth century amid broad cultural assumptions that everyone practicing it would be cis, heterosexual, and fertile. Thus, early Wiccans had little reason to tease these concepts apart and think about ways that polarity could be meaningful independently of them.

As we have seen throughout this book, polarity is so much more complicated than that. There are so many ways that polarity manifests on the Tree of Life, and countless other polarities that could be explored beyond the tree. If gender polarity or polarity associated with the symbolism of heterosexual reproduction doesn't work for you, try leveraging one of the other polarities we've seen on the tree. Think about things in terms of force and form, of liberation and manifestation—or, if that's too abstract and you want something more approachable, try descending the tree and working with the polarity of self and other instead. The Tree of Life is many, many things, but it is first and foremost a map that shows us how to explore the magical universe and the magic within ourselves. The various polarities of the tree are ways to do exactly that.

There is a sense in which all polarities on the Tree of Life are one polarity, in which Chokmah and Binah contain the essence of all the others. But even if they are all facets of the same ultimate truth, that does not negate the existence of the different facets. Explore each polarity on its own, and see what it has to offer you. The lessons you get from walking between Netzach and Hod may connect to the lessons you get from walking between Chesed and Gevurah, but each journey will nonetheless have something unique to offer you.

Journal Prompts

- List all the polarities we have discussed so far on the Tree of Life. What unites them? In what sense are they all the same? Conversely, what sets them apart from each other?
- What do force and form mean to you? If you had to explain this polarity to someone else, what kind of language would you use? What metaphors would you apply?
- What makes the Sephiroth of the Supernal Triad different from the others we've discussed so far?

CHAPTER 8
THE SUPERNAL TRIAD: KETHER

At long last, it is time for us to discuss the top of the Tree of Life: the first Sephirah, Kether. This is the beginning point of all creation, the One-ness that is the source of everything. Kether is the Sephirah farthest removed from the material world—and because of this, we can never quite reach it. It exists beyond time, beyond space, beyond anything we can possibly know. No human being will ever have a complete and perfect understanding of Kether, because it exists beyond human understanding. However, we can at least talk about it in general terms and get a rough idea of what this Sephirah is. Even if we'll never shift our consciousness all the way into Kether, we can move ourselves in that direction, and—on rare occasions—we can catch the briefest glimpse of the ultimate truth contained in the first Sephirah.

Kether is at once full and empty, containing the latent potential of all the qualities of all the other Sephiroth, but not manifesting any of those qualities. The seed of Kether is present in all of the Sephiroth, because Kether is the original font of divine power from which all creation flows forth, but Kether itself is unattainable and incomprehensible. It contains the possibility, the potency that emanates and gives rise to the other Sephiroth on the tree, but Kether itself has no qualities. It is undifferentiated, like the universe before the Big Bang.

This is the paradox of Kether, that it is simultaneously everything and nothing. It is everything, because everything comes from it. Every Sephirah, every emanation of divine energy into the universe is just an expression of the power that is already in Kether. Yet at the same time, Kether is nothing. It is not the force of Chokmah, nor the form of Binah, nor the harmony of Tiphereth; by being all of the Sephiroth at once, it manages to be none of them, because the qualities that distinguish them from each other are negated when they're all made one in Kether. Kether is absolute oneness, undifferentiated, undivided, and unchanging. It is a state of pure stasis.

When all things are one, they effectively do not exist. In Kether, there's no way to identify one thing, or one person, without lumping the whole of the universe in with it, because nothing has any property that is not shared by everything else. There is no color, no shape, no motion, no light, no sound, no mass—nothing but all-encompassing Oneness. There is not even any language with which we can describe Kether, because the nature of language is to define, to give words for things that are *this* and not *that*. Kether makes no distinction between *this* and *that*. It is both of them at once, and it is neither, because they are one and the same. In the world of Kether, the division between *this* and *that* is empty and meaningless, a mere illusion of the lower Sephiroth, which falls away when we finally ascend to the top of the tree.

As we ascend the tree, then, Kether is the final revelation we strive for. It is the unity that pervades all of the Sephiroth. This unity is, as with Chokmah and Binah, ultimately beyond us, and the best we can do is to hint at it and describe it with analogy; the nature of Kether is such that if we truly understood the Oneness at its heart, *we* would no longer exist. The experience of Kether is the absolute dissolution of the ego, the transcendence of everything that makes us separate from anything else. So long as we still have awareness of ourselves, or of any kind of differentiation in the world around us—so long as we look into the world and see multiple things and people, rather than just a swirling mass of all-pervading sameness—we can never truly know Kether.

Rather, Kether is the experience of divine sameness, of everything-and-nothing, that comes with absolute transcendence. As we ascend the middle pillar of the Tree of Life, Malkuth is the material world we inhabit now, Yesod is the spirit world populated by ghosts and visions, and Tiphereth is the Summerland where we find the promise of rebirth and reincarnation. Kether is the top of that pillar, the final culmination of the process of incarnation, death, and reincarnation. From Tiphereth, if we are reincarnated, we return down to Malkuth, but there is another direction we could go: up the tree, to Kether. If we follow the middle pillar all the way to its summit, we achieve not reincarnation, but transcendence. Kether is where we get off the merry-go-round, so to speak. It is removal from the cycle of death and rebirth, where instead of reincarnation, we find dissolution. In Kether, the individual soul is dissolved and returned to the Infinite, to the original source of all things.

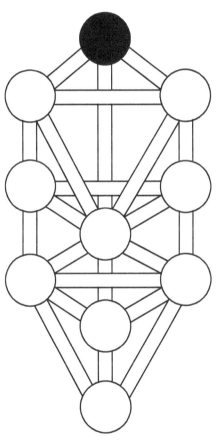

Kether

EXERCISE: A VOW OF SILENCE

We can never really experience Kether, but we can approximate it in some ways. One such way is with a vow of silence.

You Will Need

- one hour of time when you won't be disturbed. Make sure any family or roommates know not to try to speak to you during this time

Instructions

Spend one hour in absolute silence. Do not speak, write, sign, or communicate with anyone in any way. Don't listen to music or watch TV. Don't read anything. Don't do anything to try to break that silence, externally or internally. Allow yourself to dissolve into it.

If that feels easy, repeat it again the next day. Try for a whole week: be silent for one waking hour of each day. Don't journal about your experiences, or try to voice them or formulate clear thoughts about them. The nature of this experience is necessarily beyond your ability to articulate. Just appreciate the silence for what it is.

THE THREE NEGATIVE VEILS

Kether is the top of the Tree of Life, but that does not mean that there isn't anything beyond it. In fact, Qabalistic tradition describes three "negative veils" of existence beyond Kether (not to be confused with the veil between the Astral and Moral Triads). These are not Sephiroth, and they don't represent emanations of divine power the way the ten spheres of the tree do. Rather, they represent the mystery of what lies beyond. The veils are named Ain (אין, pronounced *AIN* as in "rain"), Ain Soph (אין סוף, pronounced *AIN SOAF*), and Ain Soph Aur (אין סוף אור, pronounced *AIN SOAF OAR*): "Nothingness," "Infinity," and "Limitless Light." They represent what came before everything, before even the singularity of divine power that is Kether.

If Kether is the moment before the Big Bang, the three veils are what came before that. While we don't have any deep intuitive grasp of the universe before the Big Bang, we can at least theorize about it, constructing hypotheses and mathematical models. But whatever came before that? We just don't know. Not only do we not know, we can't even speculate. Ain, Ain Soph, and Ain Soph Aur are placeholders on the Tree of Life, signifying that there is *something* beyond the tree, but that it cannot be described beyond our supposition of its existence. They are an acknowledgement that there is probably more to reality than what we see on the Tree of Life, but that we have no sense of what that might be.

There is little to be said of the three negative veils, so I will largely pass over them in silence here. By the time we reach the Supernal Triad, we have already pushed ourselves to the limit of human comprehension. The veils are in place as a reminder that even the outermost limit of what we can cognize is in no way the limit of the universe. There is so much beyond Kether, and perhaps even beyond Ain Soph Aur.

It is as if we, in Malkuth, are in a hedged-in garden, trying to learn everything we can about the world. We can easily learn about the things in the garden, and maybe we can even cross the hedge for a brief visit to what lies immediately outside (that is to say, Yesod). Over the top of the hedge, we can see some things in the far-off distance; we'll never really know everything about those far-away Sephiroth, but we can at least begin to describe them. However, we can't see what lies beyond them, below the horizon. We can infer that there's something there, but we will never have any idea of what it is.

It is easy for us to understand Malkuth, because it is *here* for us to touch and examine. The higher up the tree we go, the farther away the objects are, and the harder they are for us to make out and describe in accurate terms, although careful study and meditation can act as a sort of telescope that makes them easier for us to see. Kether is the farthest thing we can make out, and we can only describe it in the most general of terms, even with the help of a telescope. Ain, Ain Soph, and Ain Soph Aur are the names we use when we want to mention things that are even farther away than Kether, hidden below the horizon where we can't see them at all.

We'll never know anything about them, not even the small amount that we can know about Kether. They are defined to us only by the fact that they are unknown. Nonetheless, we're confident that there is something on the other side of the horizon—that the world doesn't just disappear. So, we give that unknown territory a name, like medieval cartographers writing "Here be dragons" where uncharted territory appears on our maps. The names of the negative veils are placeholders, allowing us to gesture in the general direction of what lies beyond.

Meditation on Kether

This meditation is all about emptying yourself and suspending your ego-consciousness. Try to find the silence and stillness within yourself, where there is no conscious thought, no sense of the passage of time, and no differentiation or division. Read through the instructions in advance and perform this meditation in complete silence.

You Will Need

- a bathtub
- a blindfold (optional)
- a time when you can bathe in silence, with no distractions or disturbances

Instructions

Draw a bath for yourself. The water should be about skin temperature, so that when you soak in it, you don't notice it being either warm or cold. It should have no additional oils, scents, or bubbles—just a plain tub of warm water. Once the bath is ready, close the door of your bathroom, turn off all lights, and get into the tub. You should be in total darkness, or the closest you can get to it. If you like, you can add to the sensory deprivation by using a blindfold.

Close your eyes and allow your body to relax. You should be comfortable and calm. In the water, your senses start to slip away. You do not see anything. You do not feel anything other than the water against your skin, and as you begin to relax, it becomes harder and harder to tell where your body ends and the water begins. You are floating, free and easy. You are out of time, out of place. You are everywhere and nowhere at once. There is no sound but your gentle breathing. As your breathing slows and you relax further, even that sound starts to fade away.

Continually empty your mind. Any time you notice a thought intruding, release it. Take a deep breath in, and when you exhale, allow that thought to leave you. If you notice that you are starting to feel uncomfortable, you may gently shift your position, but then relax again, releasing your muscles and letting go of your senses. Your awareness of yourself, and of the world around you, begins to dim. You are full; you are empty. You are everything and nothing at once. Continue to relax, dissolving more and more into this state of peace.

When you feel you are ready, slowly come back to yourself. Notice the sound of your breathing, the soft ripples on the surface of the water as your chest rises and falls. Wiggle your fingers and toes, and start to notice where your body ends and the outside world begins. Think your magical name, then say it aloud, allowing the sound to hit your ears. Open your eyes. You are yourself, present once again in the world.

THE ORIGINAL SOURCE OF ALL THINGS

In the previous chapter, we said that Chokmah and Binah can be understood as faces of the Wiccan Gods. If that is the case, then Kether is what lies beyond the Gods and what exists prior to them. It is the wellspring of divine power from which the Gods themselves pour forth. This raises an important theological question: Does the Tree of Life presuppose monotheism? If there's one single source of divine power, which is placed above the Sephiroth we identify with the Wiccan Gods, does that mean that the Tree of Life presumes one supreme monotheistic deity? Isn't that fundamentally incompatible with the pluralistic worship inherent to Wicca?

In Jewish Kabbalah, of course, the answer would be yes. Kabbalah is monotheistic, because Judaism is monotheistic, and all of the Sephiroth are seen merely as different domains or aspects of the one God. In Hermetic Qabalah, however, the answer is more complicated. Hermetic Qabalah is not intrinsically monotheistic the way that Kabbalah is, and it incorporates a good deal of Pagan myth and symbolism, such as the many dying-and-resurrecting Gods associated with Tiphereth. It lends itself easily to a polytheistic theology, Wiccan or otherwise. In Hermetic Qabalah, we need not see Kether as signifying a monotheistic creator deity.

The reason for this is that Kether is not personified. Because Kether has the potential for all the qualities of everything else on the tree, it effectively has no qualities whatsoever. It has no personality, no distinguishing features. We cannot, therefore, worship Kether or treat it as a deity; it is something altogether different, beyond the Gods. Kether doesn't care about us, doesn't hear or answer our prayers, because Kether doesn't perceive us as beings that exist outside of or separate from it. From the point of view of Kether, everything just is Kether. Everything is the same as everything else, nothing changes, and there is no personality, thought, or desire. There is just infinite, all-encompassing sameness.

Understood in this way, Kether is nothing like a God. We can't worship it, because it has no qualities for us to praise. We can't pray to it, because it won't perceive our prayers, let alone answer them. We can't write stories or tell myths about it, because it doesn't do anything. It simply is itself, changeless and eternal. Kether does not properly number among the Gods. It is, rather, the thing that lies beyond the Gods, the quintessential nature that unites them all. Kether is the quality that all the Gods have, the thing in virtue of which they are divine.

Kether is divinity itself, pervading all the Gods and all the Sephiroth on the tree. Rather than being a separate deity, then—something worshipped above the rest of the Gods—it is the essence of all deities, the undefinable divine power that is shared by all Gods regardless of their other attributes. Kali is not Mercury, and Odin is not Oshun, but all of them are divine, and because they are divine, they all partake of Kether. When Qabalistic texts list deities who might be associated with Kether, they are often primordial creation deities, faceless and set apart from the rest of their pantheons, like Ptah or Brahma. Kether is the source of everything, and it is present in everything, because every part of the created universe is divine.

Thus, all of the Sephiroth, all of creation, all of the deities of every pantheon, are full of the divine power of Kether. Everything flows from one source, and is part of the same current. Even we partake of Kether; the Tree of Life reflects the human soul just as much as it reflects the structure of the magical universe, and our own souls are a pouring-forth of divine energy just as the universe around us is. We are part of the all-encompassing Oneness that is the universe seen through Kether.

However, just because we belong to the pervasive unity of Kether does not mean there are no differences between us. I am not you. We are different people, with different histories, personalities, and bodies. We think and do different things from each other. There is a cosmic sense in which we're all connected, because everything is one with everything else, but in a much more immediate sense, that connection between us doesn't erase the things that make us unique. The same is true for the Gods. There is a sense in which the Gods are all connected, in which they are all united in the tapestry of some great divine unity, but that unity does not erase the differences between them. It does not mean that all the different Gods are, in fact, just one monotheistic deity. There is a way that they are united and there is a way that they are distinct and unique; the former does not negate the latter.

In Wicca, then, Kether is the origin of the Gods, the wellspring of power that has existed since before the beginning of the universe and that will continue to exist for all time. It is the Oneness from which everything comes. But oneness—sameness—is boring. It's sterile and unchanging. In order for there to be any creation, in order for the energy of Kether to manifest into the universe that we know, that One has to divide. There has to be difference between one thing and another, or else the universe is trapped in eternal, uniform stasis, where nothing changes from one state to another because there are no states to speak of. So in the Qabalistic story of the creation of the universe, One becomes Two: Kether becomes Chokmah and Binah, the God and the Goddess, the original polarity. And from them, the rest of the universe is born.

Ritualizing Kether: An Opening Ritual

This opening rite honors the spark of divinity that precedes the Gods, and it acts out the first moment of creation on the Tree of Life. Perform it at the start of your ritual, before the circle is cast.

You Will Need

- unlit candles placed at the four cardinal points of your ritual space. I prefer for them all to be white, but you may also choose elemental colors based on the cardinal directions: yellow for air, red for fire, blue for water, and green for earth
- three unlit candles for the altar: one for the Goddess, one for the God, and one for their source. The Goddess and God candles may be any color you like, but the third candle should be white
- a matchbook or lighter
- a space to use as an altar
- a ritual space you can move around freely

Instructions

Place the God candle on the right-hand side of your altar, the Goddess candle on the left-hand side, and the white candle between them. Ground and center. Then, strike a match and say:

"Before all things, there is light."

Light the central candle. Say:

"At the beginning, light is everything, and everything will be light at the end. But light cannot see itself, cannot know itself, when it is all. Light alone has nothing upon which to shine. Let light divide! Through division, let there be creation!"

Light the God candle from the central candle, saying:

"Lord of the Sun, you who were born so that you might love the Great Goddess, I kindle this light in your honor."

Then light the Goddess candle from the central candle, saying:

"Lady of the Moon, all-loving and first-beloved, I kindle this light in your honor."

Take the central candle and walk deosil around your ritual space to the east. Light the east candle, saying:

"From Goddess and God, light spreads to the east."

Then do the same in the south, west, and north. Return briefly to the east to complete your circuit, then walk back to your altar and place the candle back in its central position. Say:

"May the light of the Gods shine within all things."

You may now proceed to cast the circle and conduct the rest of your ritual.

DESCENDING THE TREE

When we have worked our way to the top of the Tree of Life, there is still one task that remains to us: we must find our way back down. Unless we are somehow transcending our physical forms and all the earthly needs that come with them, we have to live our everyday lives in the manifest world of Malkuth. We don't have the luxury of rising up to Kether and then remaining there for the rest of our lives. We have to eat, sleep, work, and interact with friends and family. We travel, watch bad reality TV, and go shopping. All of these activities take place in Malkuth.

Our goal, not just as Qabalists but as Wiccans, is not to rise up out of Malkuth and never return. As I said in Chapter 2, we are not trying to escape our lives; we celebrate incarnation and our presence in the world. The goal, then, is to ascend the Tree of Life, gain wisdom from the higher Sephiroth, and then bring that wisdom back down the tree in order to use it in our everyday lives. We want to use the Tree of Life for practical purposes, not just to elevate our consciousness, but to make our lives better, to make us better people, and to help those around us. In other words, every time we ascend the tree, we have to go back down, and take what we found down with us.

In our discussion of the Sephiroth, we have followed a modified version of the Path of the Serpent, tracing the ascent of consciousness from Malkuth to Kether. It is important that we also follow the Path of the Flash, the order of creation emanating from Kether to Malkuth. As magicians, we move in both directions, seeking to liberate our consciousness in the higher Sephiroth and to manifest divine power in the lower Sephiroth. Otherwise, we risk becoming armchair magicians—the sort of people who *think* really hard about occultism and magic, but who never actually *do* anything with it. If we follow only the Path of the Serpent, and don't complete the magical circuit by descending the tree again with the Path of the Flash, all our magical study is ultimately reduced to self-involved navel-gazing.

Notice that this ebb and flow of raising consciousness and then returning to the material world is already inherent to what we do in witchcraft. It is precisely what we discussed in Chapter 4: witches cross over into the otherworld, perform ritual or magic there, and then return to the mundane world and bring the results of that magic with them. The process of walking between the worlds of Malkuth and Yesod for the purpose of magic is a scaled-down version of ascending and descending the tree.

Of course, bridging consciousness into Yesod is much easier than climbing all the way to the top of the Tree of Life. We can't simply go to the world of Kether the way we can travel to the spirit world. However, through study, ritual, and meditation, we can begin to acquaint ourselves with the energies of the higher Sephiroth. In the next chapter, we'll look at various symbols and correspondences that can be used to bring the Sephiroth into ritual and magic, which will help us both to understand them and to manifest their energies for practical purposes. The more time you spend with the Sephiroth—the more often you work your way up the Tree of Life and back down again—the better you will understand them.

Always keep in mind that our goal is not to achieve a perfect understanding of the tree, because such a goal would be unattainable. Rather, we want to learn as much about the tree as we can, in order to bring ourselves into contact with the Divine and to supplement our spellwork and ritual with the energies of the Sephiroth. While no one can ever attain perfect knowledge of the Sephiroth, you can certainly get to know them well enough for those purposes.

I challenge you to reread the chapters of this book, or of any other book on the Qabalah, in order from the top of the tree to the bottom. How do the relationships between the Sephiroth look different when we start from the top of the tree? Shift your point of view so that you're starting with ultimate oneness, and then follow the sequence of emanations to get to the manifest world. How does this change your perspective? When we start with the Supernal Triad and work our way down the tree, we can no longer view Chesed as a scaled-up version of the energy of Netzach, nor Binah as a scaled-up version of Gevurah. In the order of ascension, each triad expanded on the energies of the previous one, making them more abstract and more universal. In the order of emanation, however, each triad distills the energies of the previous, making them more concrete and more particular.

This may seem like a trivial point, but it's important. Exploring the Sephiroth in a different order can drastically alter your understanding of the relations between them, and even of their individual energies. No Sephirah exists in isolation. Their natures are all altered by the connections between them. Following those connections from point B to point A, rather than from point A to point B, can show you a side of the Sephiroth that you wouldn't have otherwise seen. Take the time to work through these chapters in a different order, starting with Kether and then working down to Chokmah and Binah, Chesed and Gevurah, Tiphereth, Netzach and Hod, Yesod, and finally Malkuth. Meditate, takes notes, and really work through the tree from top to bottom. I promise, if you take the task of descending the tree seriously, it will enrich your understanding of all of the Sephiroth.

Journal Prompts

- Has there ever been a time when you felt totally peaceful and at one with the world around you? Write about that experience.
- What are some ways you can see the energy of Kether manifested in the world? In the other Sephiroth? What are the images or experiences you would associate with the highest Sephirah?
- Write one keyword for each of the ten Sephiroth. What is the word that best encapsulates your understanding of each Sephirah's energy?

CHAPTER 9
THE FOUR ELEMENTAL WORLDS

I n Chapter 2, we discussed the four elements as they appear in Malkuth, the manifest world. Now that we have finished our ascent of the Tree of Life, we return to the elements, because while they are most notable in Malkuth, they are present throughout the tree. Remember, the elements are not just physical air, fire, water, and earth. They also preside over different areas of life and ways of being: thinking, desiring, feeling, and acting. These qualities of the elements manifest not just in Malkuth, but in every Sephirah of the tree. What we think about Hod is different from how it makes us feel; what we want in Chokmah is not necessarily the same as how we act in it. The elements have a special place in Malkuth as the physical world, but they pervade the whole of the Tree of Life. Thus, we come to the four elemental worlds of the Qabalah.

At first glance, the idea of the four worlds is simple: each of the Sephiroth manifests in four different ways, corresponding to the four elements. Throughout this book, I have spoken about different ways the Sephiroth can be interpreted. They are simultaneously alternate planes of reality, faces of the Gods, psychological qualities within ourselves, and features of the material universe we inhabit. Some are easier to understand through one lens versus another (Malkuth is obviously physical, while Netzach and Hod are deeply psychological), but every Sephirah manifests in all of these different ways. The elemental worlds help to make that clear: they show us different perspectives we can have, and approaches we can take, in understanding the Tree of Life. They are different ways of being for the Sephiroth.

Introducing the Four Worlds

The names of the worlds are:

Atziluth (אצילות, pronounced aht-zee-LOOT), the world of fire

Atziluth, the Archetypal World, is sometimes also called the World of Emanation. This world corresponds to fire, and it is the purest, most abstract spiritual manifestation of the Sephiroth. The nature of fire is to change, to transmute and transform, and Atziluth shows us the dynamic, transformative power of the tree. Atziluth is the experience of coming face-to-face with the divine power of a Sephirah and being fundamentally changed by that experience, walking away a different—and hopefully, a better—person. This is the pure, undiluted, undifferentiated energy of each Sephirah, and as such, it can be exceptionally difficult to wrap our minds around, particularly with the higher Sephiroth.

Briah (בריה, pronounced beh-REE-yah), the world of water

Briah is the World of Creation. The watery world of Briah shows us a side of the Sephiroth that cannot be properly explained using words. Briah is the part of the Sephiroth that must be felt, rather than thought about. It is transpersonal, larger than our individual psyches. Briah is about the big universal emotions that unite us all, experiences of love or justice, things that are too big to put into words. It is the feeling of being in the Sephiroth, getting out of our own heads and encountering a wordless outpouring of divine energy.

Yetzirah (יצירה, pronounced yet-zee-RAH), the world of air

Yetzirah is known as the World of Formation. It corresponds to elemental air, and consequently it connects to everything in our heads. The way we think about the Sephiroth, the way we theorize them, belongs to Yetzirah. So, too, does any interpretation of the Sephiroth as parts of the human soul or psyche. Yetzirah shows us the Sephiroth within ourselves: Chesed and Gevurah in Yetzirah are our own capacities for mercy and severity, Yesod in Yetzirah is our own dreams and intuition, and so on.

Assiah (עשיה, pronounced ah-SEE-ah), the world of earth

Finally, we come to Assiah, also called the Material World or the World of Action. Corresponding to the element of earth, it shows us the ways that the Sephiroth manifest in the world. Anything we can point to, any concrete example we can give of the Sephiroth in the world around us, is in Assiah. Assiah expresses what the Sephiroth *do*. When I say that science belongs to Hod, I am referring to Hod in Assiah. When we talk of Tiphereth as the sun at the center of the solar system, or as the center of gravity in any physical object, we are conceptualizing Tiphereth in Assiah. This world is the most immediate, well-defined, and graspable of the four.

The four elements will be familiar to most Wiccans, so they should serve as a helpful point of access to the Sephiroth. For each Sephirah, you can ask yourself, "What is airy about this Sephirah? What is fiery about it?" And so on. If you notice that when you're working with a particular Sephirah, you can only identify qualities relating to some of the elements and not others, that tells you which elemental worlds you need to work on exploring in order to deepen your relationship with the Sephirah.

Visualizing the Worlds on the Tree

You will likely notice parallels between the way I introduced the Sephiroth and the order of the four elemental worlds. The higher up the tree we go, the more abstract our language becomes, as we try to wrestle with bigger, more universal concepts in the higher Sephiroth. Thus, the language we use to describe Malkuth largely belongs to Assiah, while the Sephiroth of the Astral Triad are easily described in psychological terms relating to Yetzirah; by the time we get to Chokmah and Binah, we are viewing the Sephiroth almost entirely through Briah, describing them as cosmic principles that must be felt, rather than talked about. And when we finally get to Kether, even that does not suffice, and we have to fall back on the language of Atziluth. It is for this reason that the Tree of Life is sometimes represented as divided into four sections corresponding to the four elemental worlds: Malkuth corresponds to Assiah, everything from Yesod through Chesed corresponds to Yetzirah, Chokmah and Binah to Briah, and Kether to Atziluth. Alternatively, the Supernal, Moral, and Astral Triads may be seen as corresponding to Atziluth, Briah, and Yetzirah, with Malkuth as Assiah at the bottom of the tree.

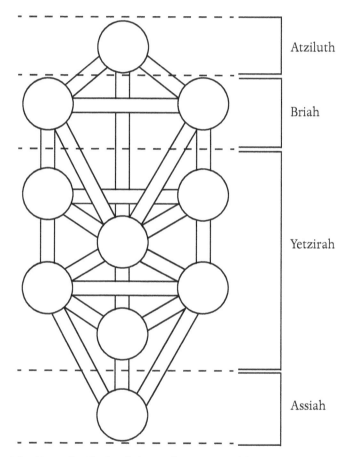

The Tree of Life, divided into the Four Worlds

This way of viewing the tree can be helpful, to a certain extent, because it shows us the hierarchy of the four worlds and reminds us that as we progress farther up the Tree of Life, concrete language starts to fail us and we have to understand the Sephiroth in increasingly abstract terms. However, this conceptualization is only useful up to a point. It neglects to show that all ten Sephiroth exist across all four worlds. Malkuth is not only in Assiah, any more than Chokmah belongs exclusively to Briah. Just because it is easier for us to view certain Sephiroth one way, rather than another, does not mean that those Sephiroth are limited to one way of being.

Another common way to represent the Tree of Life is to say that there are actually four separate trees: the tree in Assiah, the tree in Yetzirah, the tree in Briah, and the tree in Atziluth. These trees are linked together, so that the top of one is the bottom of the next. Thus, the Kether of Assiah is the same as the Malkuth of Yetzirah, the Kether of Yetzirah is the Malkuth of Briah, and the Kether of Briah is the Malkuth of Atziluth. You can work your way all the way up to the top of the tree in one world, only to find that the whole of the next world is still laid before you.

There is something rather beautiful in this description of the four worlds. It captures the feeling that the work of exploring the Tree of Life is never truly done, and that as soon as we think we've understood everything about the tree, we discover that there is more to learn even about the Sephiroth that are most familiar and accessible to us. Furthermore, it shows an important affinity between Kether and Malkuth. The first Sephirah and the last Sephirah are echoes of each other, and each contains a seed of the truth found in the other. What we learn in Kether helps us to understand Malkuth in a new way, and what we experience in Malkuth grounds the knowledge we can have of Kether. Making these Sephiroth the hitching points for four elemental Trees of Life helps to illustrate that connection.

Yet another way of thinking about the four worlds is to overlay them all on top of each other, so that there is only one Tree of Life and each Sephirah on that tree is understood to simultaneously exist in all four worlds. The advantage of this image is that it accurately shows how each Sephirah manifests in every elemental world at once. Separating the worlds out into four distinct Trees of Life gives the impression that our experience of the Sephiroth in Assiah is necessarily separate from, and prior to, the other three worlds, but that's not the case. We often experience the Sephiroth in a number of different ways at once. Moreover, in some cases, it may be easier for us to understand a Sephirah in a higher world than in a lower one; we may connect to

Binah in Briah much more easily than to Binah in Assiah. It's not actually the case that we first experience Binah in Assiah, then in Yetzirah, and then finally in Briah and Atziluth. The reality is much more messy and complicated than that.

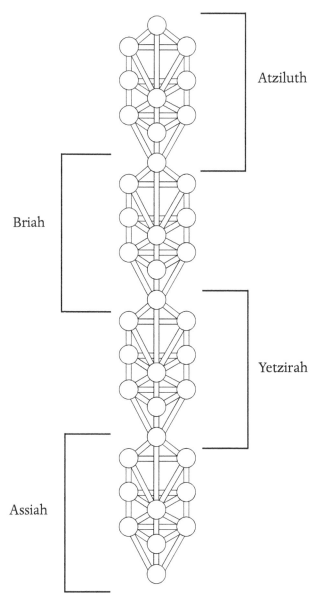

Four Elemental Trees of Life, linked together

All of these different visual representations capture some part of the truth about how the Tree of Life exists in the four elemental worlds. None of them captures the entirety of the truth. A consistent lesson throughout this book is that the true nature of the Tree of Life is larger than us and impossible for us to comprehend in its entirety. Any attempt to define and categorize it will get some things right, but will miss out on others. The best way to understand the four worlds is to take all of these different approaches together, and to understand that each of them leads us to one facet of the truth about how the worlds relate to the Sephiroth.

Meditation on the Four Worlds

Choose a Sephirah to work with for this exercise; I recommend starting with one near the bottom of the tree. This meditation will help you experience the energy of that Sephirah in all four elemental worlds. Prior to starting the meditation, record yourself reading the instructions so that you can listen to them while you meditate.

You Will Need

- a quiet room with no distractions, where you can meditate undisturbed.

Instructions

Close your eyes, clear your thoughts, and take deep, even breaths. Ground and center. Focus on the Sephirah you've chosen. Think about all the various aspects of it, all the concepts and feelings you associate with it, all the ways it appears in the world and in your life. Visualize the name of the Sephirah, written in your mind in brilliant white letters. Say the name of the Sephirah out loud.

Turn your thoughts to all the ways this Sephirah manifests in the material world. Think about the physical expressions of its energy, the objects you would associate with it, and the ways you would bring it into the world through direct action. Focus on all the earthy qualities of the Sephirah. Say, "This is how [Sephirah name] *acts.*"

Now focus on all the Sephirah's airy qualities. Gather together all the thoughts, words, concepts, and definitions you've used to understand it. Let the words tumble through your mind, one after the other in quick succession. Say, "This is how [Sephirah name] *thinks.*"

Thirdly, let yourself feel the emotional effect of the Sephirah. Consider all its irrational, sensitive, intuitive features, the things that are easy to experience but hard to put into words. Say, "This is how [Sephirah name] *feels.*"

Last, let the energy of the Sephirah consume you, overwhelming you and filling you up until there is nothing else in your range of experience. Let the letters of the Sephirah's name glow brighter in your mind. Feel the potential that this energy has to change you, to alter who you are and how you exist in the world. Say, "This is how [Sephirah name] *transforms.*"

When you are ready, let that feeling subside. Work your way backwards through the elements, focusing in turn on how the Sephirah feels, how it thinks, and how it acts. When you feel grounded in yourself once more, allow your focus to dissipate, and let your mental image of the Sephirah's name begin to fade. Open your eyes.

The Order of the Elements

There is one important difference between the elemental worlds on the Tree of Life and the elements as we're used to seeing them in Wicca: the order of their progression. As we saw in Chapter 2, the progression of the elements in Wicca usually follows the order of the quarters. We start with air in the east, then fire in the south, water in the west, and earth in the north. With the four elemental worlds, however, the order of progression is different. These worlds are in a hierarchy with Assiah (the world of earth) at the bottom, then Yetzirah (the world of air), Briah (the world of water), and finally Atziluth (the world of fire) at the top.

Air   Fire   Water   Earth

The Order of the Elements in the Four Quarters

Fire   Air   Water   Earth

The Order of the Elements from Active to Passive

Earth   Air   Water   Fire

The Order of the Elements in the Four Worlds

The reason for this change is that the order of the elemental worlds alternates between active (or, if you prefer gendered language, "male") and passive ("female") elements, building the polarity between them. The arrangement of the elemental worlds thus puts fire, the most active element, at one end of the spectrum, and it puts earth, the most passive element, at the other. In between them come air (which is active, but not as active as fire) and water (which is passive, but not as passive as earth). However, rather than arranging the elements simply from most active to most passive, we switch the placement of water and air, so that the order of the worlds alternates active-passive-active-passive.

This creates a battery of sorts, which circulates energy between the active and passive poles in much the same way that electrical energy flows in a current between the alternating positive and negative poles of an electrical circuit. If there were two active elements (or two passive ones) next to each other in the arrangement, this polarity wouldn't exist, and the energy wouldn't flow in quite the same way—just as an electrical circuit doesn't work if you try to build it with two batteries whose positive ends touch.

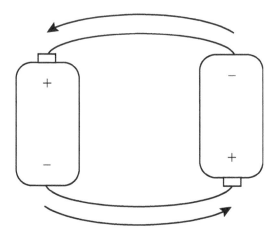

An Electrical Circuit with Poles + − + −

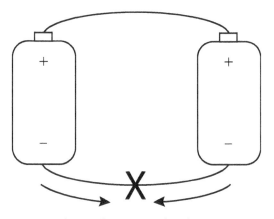

An Electrical Circuit with Poles + + − −

This order of the elements may be unfamiliar and uncomfortable to Wiccans who are used to working with air-fire-water-earth. If that's the case for you, don't worry about it too much. Both ways of assigning a sequence to the elements have longstanding histories and justifications, and they're each appropriate in different contexts. You should feel comfortable continuing to call the quarters in the order and with the elemental correspondences that you already use. For practical purposes, the earth-air-water-fire ordering of the elements is something you only need to use when you're explicitly working with the four elemental worlds on the Tree of Life.

THE TAROT COURT CARDS

There is, however, one place we see the order of the elemental worlds that might be familiar to you, and that's in the elemental correspondences of the court cards in a tarot deck. In the Rider-Waite-Smith tarot deck, there are four court cards in each suit: the king, the queen, the knight, and the page. These correspond elementally to fire, water, air, and earth, blending the elemental attribution of their rank with that of the suit to which they belong. Thus, the King of Pentacles is a personality combining elemental fire (the king) with elemental earth (pentacles). The Queen of Pentacles is a personality combining water with earth, and so on. The order of these elemental correspondences comes from the order of the four worlds of the Qabalah: kings are Atziluth, queens are Briah, knights are Yetzirah, and pages are Assiah.

At this point, we should stop for a brief historical aside, because there has been a great deal of confusion about the hierarchy of the court cards. In the Rider-Waite-Smith deck, the order of the courts from top to bottom is king-queen-knight-page. However, Arthur Edward Waite adapted the structure of his tarot deck from the specifications of the Golden Dawn, which are responsible for the Qabalistic correspondences we know today. In the Golden Dawn, the court cards (from top to bottom) are named the knight, queen, king, and knave. The knight was the top of the hierarchy, corresponding to Atziluth and fire; the king was the second from the bottom, corresponding to Tiphereth and air.

To further add to the confusion, each individual card in the Golden Dawn system had its own titles and honorifics. The Golden Dawn Knight of Pentacles, for example, is called "The Lord of the Wide and Fertile Land: The King of the Spirits of Earth." Meanwhile, the Golden Dawn King of Pentacles is called "The Prince of the Chariot of Earth." Thus, the knight of the suit is called a king, and the king of the suit is called a prince! This is true across all four suits. The Knight of Cups is "The Lord of the Waves and the Waters: The King of the Hosts of the Sea," while the King of Cups is "The Prince of the Chariot of the Waters."[9]

---

9. S. L. MacGregor Mathers, *Book T: The Tarot*.

Knight? King? Prince? What's going on with these titles? How are we to make any sense of them? Which card is which?

The key is to look at the hierarchy. The Golden Dawn order of the court cards, from top to bottom, is knight-queen-king-knave. The Rider-Waite-Smith order is king-queen-knight-page. Thus, the Rider-Waite-Smith king and the Golden Dawn knight are both assigned to Atziluth and the element of fire, while the Rider-Waite-Smith knight and the Golden Dawn king are assigned to Yetzirah and the element of air. Why Arthur Edward Waite decided to swap these cards is unclear. Perhaps he simply thought that the king should rank higher than the knight, or maybe the reason is that he was publishing his tarot deck for a general audience who were not initiates of the Golden Dawn, and he didn't want to give away all of the order's secrets. "It's an initiatory blind" is always the excuse people fall back on when something doesn't make sense to them, and we'll see momentarily how problematic that excuse can be, but in this case, it may actually be the truth. At any rate, no one has been able to definitively prove Waite's reasoning.

Just to put a cherry on the top of the sundae, there's yet another mainstream tarot deck with different names for the court cards. Aleister Crowley's Thoth tarot is a child of the Golden Dawn system, but his cards are named the knight, queen, prince, and princess. As the knight is at the top of the hierarchy, it corresponds to Atziluth and fire, just like the Golden Dawn knight. The Thoth prince, with the third rank in the deck's hierarchy, corresponds to Yetzirah and air, along with the Golden Dawn king and the Rider-Waite-Smith knight. For ease of reference, here are the court cards of all three decks laid side by side:

World	Element	Golden Dawn	Rider-Waite-Smith	Thoth
Atziluth	Fire	Knight	King	Knight
Briah	Water	Queen	Queen	Queen
Yetzirah	Air	King	Knight	Prince
Assiah	Earth	Knave	Page	Princess

THE MINOR ARCANA

The four elemental worlds appear in tarot in a second crucial way. They are the basis of the four suits of the minor arcana: wands (fire), cups (water), swords (air), and pentacles (earth). Each card in the minor arcana, ace through ten, is assigned to one of the ten Sephiroth manifested in one of the elemental worlds. Thus, the Ace of Wands is Kether in Atziluth, the Two of Cups is Chokmah in Briah, and so on down the tree.

The court cards are also assigned to the Sephiroth, although we should note that these correspondences are independent of the elemental correspondences listed above. Rider-Waite-Smith kings (the knights in the Golden Dawn system) are assigned to Chokmah, and queens are assigned to Binah. Rider-Waite-Smith knights (the Golden Dawn kings) are assigned to Tiphereth, and pages (Golden Dawn knaves) are assigned to Malkuth. Thus, the king and queen are the supernal faces of the divine masculine and feminine, the primordial force-form pair, corresponding to the ultimate natures of the God and Goddess. Meanwhile, the knight and page are a lesser, more accessible pairing in Tiphereth and Malkuth. They capture something of the relationship between the king and queen, but in a more concrete, manifest way—just as the dying-and-resurrecting sun God of Tiphereth is a more familiar face of the force God of Chokmah, and the Goddess as Isis Veiled in Malkuth is the manifest counterpart to the Goddess as Isis Unveiled in Binah.

Thus, the minor arcana of the tarot map out all ten Sephiroth across all four elemental worlds:

Number	Wands	Cups	Swords	Pentacles
Ace	Kether in Atziluth	Kether in Briah	Kether in Yetzirah	Kether in Assiah
Two, King	Chokmah in Atziluth	Chokmah in Briah	Chokmah in Yetzirah	Chokmah in Assiah
Three, Queen	Binah in Atziluth	Binah in Briah	Binah in Yetzirah	Binah in Assiah
Four	Chesed in Atziluth	Chesed in Briah	Chesed in Yetzirah	Chesed in Assiah

Number	Wands	Cups	Swords	Pentacles
Five	Gevurah in Atziluth	Gevurah in Briah	Gevurah in Yetzirah	Gevurah in Assiah
Six, Knight	Tiphereth in Atziluth	Tiphereth in Briah	Tiphereth in Yetzirah	Tiphereth in Assiah
Seven	Netzach in Atziluth	Netzach in Briah	Netzach in Yetzirah	Netzach in Assiah
Eight	Hod in Atziluth	Hod in Briah	Hod in Yetzirah	Hod in Assiah
Nine	Yesod in Atziluth	Yesod in Briah	Yesod in Yetzirah	Yesod in Assiah
Ten, Page	Malkuth in Atziluth	Malkuth in Briah	Malkuth in Yetzirah	Malkuth in Assiah

EXERCISE: THE MINOR ARCANA AND THE FOUR WORLDS

Work through the energies of the Sephiroth in the four elemental worlds by looking at the tarot cards corresponding to them. These cards can provide a new and helpful perspective on each Sephirah as it manifests across the four worlds.

You Will Need

- a tarot deck
- your journal or notebook (optional)

Instructions

Choose a Sephirah to study, and remove the cards corresponding to that Sephirah from your deck. Lay them side by side, in elemental order. Now take one card at a time and examine it. Think about the energy of this card, and the divinatory meaning it has. How do you interpret this card when it shows up in a tarot reading? What personal meaning does this card have for you, which might not be found in any tarot books?

Now connect all of those meanings, connotations, and associations to the energy of the Sephirah in the elemental world represented by this card. If, for example, you're looking at the Ace of Wands, how does the meaning of the card help you to gain insight into Kether in Atziluth? Repeat this process with the remaining cards. I encourage you to write your thoughts and findings down in your journal.

THE ELEMENTAL TOOLS OF WICCA

As we discuss the four suits of the tarot, we touch upon a second historical controversy that we should pause to address. The symbols of the minor arcana correspond to the four elemental weapons used by the Hermetic Order of the Golden Dawn: the fire wand, the air dagger, the water cup, and the earth pentacle. The Golden Dawn system of magic did also use a sword, in addition to the air dagger, but it wasn't considered an elemental tool; rather, as a sign of power and domination, it corresponded to Gevurah. These four elemental tools formed the basis of much of Golden Dawn ritual practice, and particularly any magic working with the elements.

Modern Wicca inherited the Golden Dawn elemental weapons, and just about any Wiccan ceremony you attend will feature a wand, an athame, a cup, and a pentacle. In most Wiccan practice, moreover, these four tools are still considered elemental, and are used in a variety of ways to summon and direct the powers of the elements. However, some Wiccans swap the elemental associations of the dagger and the wand, choosing to align the wand with air and the athame with fire. This is often due, in part, to an erroneous belief that wand-as-air and dagger-as-fire were the original Golden Dawn correspondences, and that Arthur Edward Waite switched the elemental associations of the suits in order to protect Golden Dawn initiatory secrets when he published his tarot deck.

If you use these swapped elemental correspondences, by all means, do what works for you. I am not in the business of telling other people that there is a right way and a wrong way for them to do their magic. However, I would like to take a moment to clear up this historical myth.

It is well documented that in the Golden Dawn system, the wand was a weapon of fire and the dagger was a weapon of air. This is noted in Israel Regardie's magnum opus *The Golden Dawn*, which is a compiled publication of internal Golden Dawn documents that were not made available to non-initiates of the order.[10] Moreover, the personal magical tools of the poet William Butler Yeats, who was a member of the Hermetic Order of the Golden Dawn, are on exhibit at the National Library of Ireland in Dublin.[11] These were the tools that he used in his magical operations with the order, and they were not made available to the public until after his death. I've been to the National Library and seen Yeats's tools for myself, and I can personally attest that his wand is unmistakably tipped with a flame and his dagger is painted with the name of the archangel of the element of air. There can be no question that in the original Golden Dawn system, the wand was fire and the dagger was air.

So where did the Pagan community get the idea that the elemental correspondences should be swapped? It comes indirectly from an occult author named Francis King. In his 1976 book *Techniques of High Magic*, King decided to switch the correspondences of the dagger and the wand. For reasons that have been lost to history, he gave this switch a veneer of historical legitimacy by claiming that the altered correspondences were the true, secret elemental associations used by the Golden Dawn, and that wand-as-fire and dagger-as-air were initiatory blinds used to deceive the general public.[12] This lie was then unknowingly picked up by Janet and Stewart Farrar in their seminal work *The Witches' Way*,[13] and from there it made its way into the broader Wiccan and Pagan community.

Once again, let us emphasize that if wand-as-air and athame-as-fire is what works for you, you should go with it. Those correspondences are neither more nor less legitimate than the original Golden Dawn ones, so long as they work

---

10. Israel Regardie, *The Golden Dawn: A Complete Course in Ceremonial Magic*, 320–22.

11. National Library of Ireland, "The Life and Works of William Butler Yeats."

12. Francis King and Stephen Skinner, *Techniques of High Magic: A Handbook of Divination, Alchemy, and the Evocation of Spirits*, 60.

13. Janet Farrar and Stewart Farrar, *A Witches' Bible: The Complete Witches' Handbook*, 252.

for your magic and give you the results you want. Regardless of which correspondences you use, though, it is helpful to understand where they came from and what their history is.

Ritualizing the Four Worlds: Revisit Circle Casting

In the circle casting procedure provided in Chapter 4, you first cast the circle once with your wand or athame, but then you finish it with the four elements. One way to interpret this second step is that you are bringing the energy of Malkuth into the circle, but you do that later anyway when you call the quarters. A second way to understand what you are doing at this stage is that you are forming the circle of Yesod in all four elemental worlds.

You Will Need

• all the materials for the circle casting ritual provided in Chapter 4.

Instructions

Cast the circle with your wand or athame as usual. Then consecrate the elements, but instead of consecrating them in the order of the quarters (air-fire-water-earth), try consecrating them in the order of the elemental worlds, from Assiah up to Atziluth. As you circumambulate with your salt water and your burning incense, imagine the circle of Yesod solidifying around you, manifesting in Assiah, Yetzirah, Briah, and Atziluth.

God-Names, Archangels, and Angels

A final word on the four worlds. In Hermetic Qabalah, one of the most important uses of the elemental worlds is theurgic. Each world is associated with a level of divinity, which can be invoked for magical purposes. The Sephiroth in Atziluth are each associated with a different Hebrew name of God. In Briah, each Sephirah is associated with an archangel; in Yetzirah, with a choir of angels. Finally, in Assiah, each Sephirah has an astrological correspondence, a part of the heavens over which it presides. There is a hierarchy between these divine powers: the God-name of the Sephirah in

Atziluth has dominion over the archangel of that Sephirah in Briah, who in turn commands the choir of angels in Yetzirah, who control the astrological power of the Sephirah in Assiah.

A common formula for Qabalistic magic is to invoke the power of a Sephirah in all four worlds, drawing power down from Atziluth into Assiah so that you can manifest it to your magical ends. You invoke the appropriate Hebrew name of God and ask God to command the relevant archangel. Then you ask the archangel to command the relevant angels, you ask the angels to command the planet (or other astrological correspondence), and finally, you use the astrological power you have invoked, directing that power into your spell.

This is an extraordinarily powerful and efficacious way to do magic. It is also alien to most Wiccans, who work with Pagan deities rather than angels and archangels. Because this is a book for Wiccans, and we are concerned primarily with how Qabalah works for Wiccan ritual, I will not go further into the names of God, the archangels, or the angels of the Sephiroth. Simply put, that's not the kind of magic that most of us do. I will discuss astrological correspondences in the following chapter, but that is as far as we will go with this subject, and I mention it here only because an introduction to Qabalah would be grievously inadequate without at least touching on it. Should you wish to explore the use of these divine names, they are listed in Appendix II.

Journal Prompts

- How do you understand the four worlds of the Tree of Life? What energy does a Sephirah in Briah have that is not expressed by that same Sephirah in Yetzirah, and so on with the other worlds?
- Which way of visually representing the four worlds on the Tree of Life makes the most sense to you, and why?
- For each Sephirah, write down a few keywords for how its energy manifests in each of the four worlds.

CHAPTER 10

CORRESPONDENCES
OF THE SEPHIROTH

Having concluded our thematic examination of the Sephiroth, we may now embellish our understanding of the Tree of Life using a variety of magical correspondences, which can aid in spellwork or in theurgy. Qabalah is infamous for its tables upon tables of correspondences, which give it a reputation for being dry, academic, and inaccessible. Plants, animals, gemstones, magical tools, Pagan deities, and names of angels, archangels, and demons have all worked their way into the Qabalah, and it can be overwhelming to even begin to try and understand all these layers of magical symbolism. Where do we even start?

Don't be discouraged. Remember, by this point, you already have a general understanding of what the Sephiroth are, and which energies on the tree belong where. That's the most important thing. The elaborate correspondences are simply a way of enriching your extant understanding of those energies. By giving you more images and symbols that you can associate with the Sephiroth, these correspondences help you to establish a magical connection to them, or to gain a new perspective on some aspect of a Sephirah's energy that you hadn't considered before. The correspondences are here to help you, not to hinder you.

Number and Shape

As a simple, straightforward example, let's think about number and shape. There are ten Sephiroth, numbered in the order of emanation from the top of the Tree of Life to its bottom. Each Sephirah corresponds magically to its number in that order:

1. Kether
2. Chokmah
3. Binah
4. Chesed
5. Gevurah
6. Tiphereth
7. Netzach
8. Hod
9. Yesod
10. Malkuth

This also means that the Sephiroth correspond to geometric figures with an appropriate number of vertices. The energy of Kether is unextended and indivisible, so we represent Kether with a single point. Chokmah is the initial outpouring of divine energy from Kether, the first separation of one point from another, so we represent it with a line, which may continue indefinitely in either direction. Binah, the third Sephirah, takes the raw power of Chokmah and constrains it into a definite form; it shapes the line of Chokmah into a triangle, the smallest possible polygonal shape (and which corresponds to Binah's magical number, 3). From there, each subsequent Sephirah corresponds to a shape with the appropriate number of sides, either a polygon (-gon) or a star (-gram):

1. Kether: Point   •
2. Chokmah: Line   ——
3. Binah: Triangle   △

4. Chesed: Square ☐

5. Gevurah: Pentagon or Pentagram ⬠ ✮

6. Tiphereth: Hexagon or Hexagram ⬡ ✡

7. Netzach: Heptagon or Heptagram ⬡ ✧

8. Hod: Octagon or Octagram ◯ ✹

9. Yesod: Nonagon or Enneagram ◯ ✹

10. Malkuth: Decagon or Decagram ◯ ✹

See? Qabalistic correspondences really aren't as frightening as they're made out to be. The idea behind these correspondences is that you can use them as a symbolic short-hand to evoke the energy of a particular Sephirah. If you're performing a ritual action associated with Chesed, you can immediately strengthen the connection to Chesed by performing it four times. If you're leveraging the energy of Binah, you can add to that energy by drawing a triangle to symbolize the Sephirah. All Qabalistic correspondences, including those based on number and shape, are opportunities for you to establish and strengthen a symbolic, sympathetic connection to the power of a desired Sephirah.

Suppose you wanted to do a simple magical affirmation to bring love into your life. Why not make a connection to Netzach, through the number seven? Every morning, when you wake up, look in a mirror and say "I love and I am loved" seven times in a row. If you focus your intention through the Qabalistic symbolism of the number seven, you have cast a simple and efficient Qabalistic love spell. Congratulations! You're now a Qabalistic magician.

Exercise: Adding Number to Ritual

The rituals provided in this book are designed to show you how Qabalistic energy manifests in Wiccan practice, without overloading you with complicated Qabalistic symbolism. Now that you are more familiar with the Tree of Life, look back through those rituals and consider the ways you could enrich them with more explicit Qabalistic correspondences. Start out simple, with number correspondences.

You Will Need

- No supplies are necessary for this exercise, but I encourage you to perform the altered ritual you have written. If you do so, you will need the appropriate materials for that ritual

Instructions

Pick a ritual from this book or a ritual that you commonly perform in your own practice. How would you alter that ritual in order to incorporate the number of the Sephirah (or Sephiroth) it connects to? Perhaps for Yesod, you could cast a circle with a nine-foot diameter. Or for Hod, rather than anointing yourself in the shape of an invoking pentagram, you could choose eight different points on your body to anoint, adjusting the wording of your ritual accordingly. Get creative! There's no wrong way to bring Qabalistic numerological symbolism into your rituals, so long as you're making conscious choices intended to connect you to the energy of the Sephiroth.

COLOR

Similarly, it is easy to connect to the Sephiroth through color symbolism. Each Sephirah corresponds to a color, which can be used to visually evoke it in ritual, magic, or meditation. In fact, the Hermetic Order of the Golden Dawn used four different color scales on the Tree of Life corresponding to the four elemental worlds, so each Sephirah had four distinct colors associated with it. These color scales were known as the King Scale (corresponding to Atziluth), the Queen Scale (Briah), the Emperor Scale (Yetzirah), and the Empress Scale (Assiah). However, in practice, only the Queen Scale is still widely used in determining color correspondences for the Sephiroth, so that's the one we will focus on here.

We use the colors of the Queen Scale, because most of the meditative work we do with the Sephiroth gets us up out of ourselves, into the world of Briah, but does not quite bring us to the full, unfiltered experience of the Sephiroth in Atziluth. We are still human, still limited, and so we only use the second-highest color scale as a reminder that the true nature of the Sephiroth is always slightly beyond our reach. These are the colors you will most often see associated with the Sephiroth, and unless you get *deep* into Qabalistic magic, these are probably the only colors you'll ever feel the need to use.

We start at the top of the tree with Kether. As the first source of divine light, Kether's color is pure, white light. It's the color of light when the whole of the visible spectrum is brought together, before it's refracted into distinct hues by a prism.

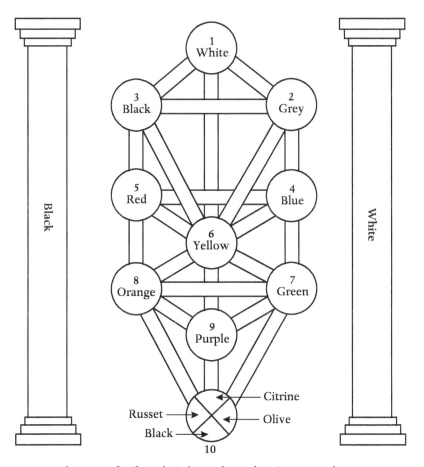

The Tree of Life with Color and Number Correspondences

The Supernal Triad represents the process of that light becoming manifest, being given form and matter by Binah, and the color correspondences of the other two Sephiroth in the triad reflect that. Where Kether is white, unlimited and undifferentiated, the color of Binah is black. It is heavy, solid, and limiting. Blackness gives light shape, by marking out the places where it is not. In between them is Chokmah, which serves as an intermediary step creating the polarity that allows for the oneness of Kether to manifest in the form of Binah. Consequently, the color of Chokmah is grey—halfway between the white of Kether and the black of Binah.

Moving down the Tree of Life to the Moral Triad, the light of Kether splits into the three primary colors: blue, red, and yellow. Peaceful, calm Chesed is associated with the color blue, while dominant, aggressive Gevurah is given the color red. Between them, Tiphereth corresponds to yellow. These correspondences may seem somewhat arbitrary at first, but it helps to follow the structure of the tree and see why they're placed where they are. The Supernal Triad deals simply with shades of light and dark; the other side of the Abyss is too far removed from the manifest world for colors to have any meaning. As we descend across the Abyss into the Moral Triad, we encounter the purest colors of light, from which all other colors are made. We start with the primary colors, and they enable us to produce everything else.

It will be no surprise, then, that as we follow the path of emanation further down the Tree of Life to the Astral Triad, we next encounter the secondary colors. In Netzach, the blue of Chesed and the yellow of Tiphereth combine to form green. On the opposite side of the tree, in Hod, the red of Gevurah and the yellow of Tiphereth form orange. And in Yesod, blue and red meet to make purple. These color correspondences are, themselves, interesting. They suggest that there is a sense in which Netzach contains the energies of both Tiphereth and Chesed, while Hod contains that same energy of Tiphereth colored by Gevurah instead. Likewise, when we look at the color correspondences, we see the energies of Chesed and Gevurah commingling in Yesod, which may provide food for thought on how we understand the ninth Sephirah.

Finally, we arrive at Malkuth. Malkuth has not just one color correspondence, but four, because Malkuth is represented by the quartered circle. Each quadrant of this Sephirah has a different color: citrine, olive, russet, and black. These colors are rough approximations of the intermediate colors that result from mixing the colors of the Sephiroth in the Astral Triad. Draw Malkuth as a circle with an X through it, dividing it into four quadrants. The left-hand quadrant is colored russet, as a combination of the orange of Hod with the purple of Yesod. The right-hand quadrant combines the purple of Yesod with the green of Netzach, producing an olive color. The topmost quadrant combines the green of Netzach and the orange of Hod, resulting in citrine. And, finally, the bottommost quadrant is the black that results from muddling all the colors of the spectrum together—a sort of antithesis to the white of Kether at the top of the tree.

The colors of Malkuth aren't entirely faithful to the secondary colors they're supposed to mix. Orange and purple together do produce russet, and orange and green make something close to citrine, but green and purple combine to make more of a bluish slate grey than an olive color. Nonetheless, the color correspondences of Malkuth fit surprisingly well to contemporary color theory, and we can understand how they're supposed to be produced from the Sephiroth above them. The colors at the bottom of the Tree of Life depend upon, and are generated from, the colors higher up, the same way that the lower Sephiroth are emanations of the energies further up the tree.

There is one final set of correspondences we should mention: the colors of the pillars of Mercy and Severity. These pillars are commonly colored white and black, respectively, as we saw in Chapter 1 with the way they are depicted on the High Priestess card in the tarot. The black color of the Pillar of Severity is easy to understand; it is taken from the color of Binah, which sits atop the pillar. The Pillar of Mercy, however, is colored white—not grey like Chokmah. Chokmah itself is grey to show that it comes after Kether and before Binah in the order of emanations, but the great polarity of the Supernal Triad is between Chokmah and Binah, not between Binah and Kether. The color correspondences of the pillars reflect that relationship. The polarity of light and dark, of force-giving and form-giving, is between the Sephiroth atop the outer pillars, and so those pillars are colored black and white—not black and grey—as a way of showing that ultimate polarity.

Exercise: Adding Color to Ritual

Continue to embellish ritual with Qabalistic symbolism. This time, think about the significance of color and how you can bring the colors of the Sephiroth into your ritual workings.

You Will Need

- No materials are necessary for this exercise, but as with the previous exercise, I encourage you to perform this ritual after you have rewritten it

Instructions

Look at the same ritual you rewrote in the previous exercise, and think about ways that you can bring in the color of the appropriate Sephirah. If you are casting the circle, you could visualize the circle forming out of purple light, instead of pure white light. Or you could use material props, rather than visualizations, to help you connect to the appropriate color: colored candles, an altar cloth, a robe, and so on. As with number, there is no wrong way to do this, so long as you are making your choices mindfully.

Astrology

After number and color, the most crucial set of correspondences for the Sephiroth are the astrological ones. When I tell you that the Tree of Life is a map of the universe, I do not only mean that in an abstract, metaphorical sense. There is also a concrete sense in which the Sephiroth correspond to the different parts of the heavens. Malkuth, naturally, corresponds to the earth; it is where we currently are, the vantage point from which we look out at the rest of the universe and the rest of the Sephiroth. This astrological association is where the symbol of Malkuth as the quartered circle comes from, as the quartered circle is an old astrological symbol for the earth.

Moving upward from Malkuth, the Sephiroth are each assigned a correspondence to one of the seven planets of classical astrology, based on what's known as the Chaldean order of the planets: the order, from fastest to slowest, of their apparent motion across the sky. Yesod, the Sephirah closest to

Malkuth, is assigned to the fastest-moving planet, the Moon, which takes only a month to complete a full cycle through the zodiac. Then Hod is assigned to Mercury, the next-fastest planet. Netzach is assigned to Venus, Tiphereth to the Sun, Gevurah to Mars, Chesed to Jupiter, and finally Binah corresponds to the slowest planet (and the one farthest away from Earth), Saturn.

Moving past Binah, we come to the astrological correspondence of Chokmah, but we find there are no planets left for us to assign to it. Instead of a planet, then, Chokmah corresponds to the wheel of the zodiac itself. It is the primordial division of the sky, not a planet but rather the force that propels the planets in their orbit through the heavens. And Kether is what lies even beyond that, the "primum mobile" of the universe that we cannot divide or categorize. It is all the nebulae that exist at the edge of what we can capture with a telescope, the raw, unformed star-stuff that makes up everything else. It is the outer sphere of the heavens themselves. Thus, the complete set of astrological correspondences for the Sephiroth is as follows:

1. Kether: Primum Mobile
2. Chokmah: The Zodiac
3. Binah: Saturn
4. Chesed: Jupiter
5. Gevurah: Mars
6. Tiphereth: The Sun
7. Netzach: Venus
8. Hod: Mercury
9. Yesod: The Moon
10. Malkuth: The Earth

These correspondences do more than just delineate the structure of our solar system from a geocentric point of view. They also tell us more about each individual Sephirah. The correspondence of Malkuth to the earth is obvious. Astrologically, the earth is the world we inhabit, the place that the celestial forces of the other planets meet and exert their effects. This is exactly what Malkuth is on the Tree of Life. Both Malkuth and planet Earth are our world, the setting for our everyday thoughts, feelings, and actions. They are what we know most intimately, because they are immediately present to us.

Moving up the tree to Yesod, we encounter the Moon, and all the esoteric symbolism associated with the Moon becomes part of the meaning of Yesod. The Moon is associated with dreams and intuition. It is inconstant and shifting, constantly waxing and waning rather than shining as a single, fixed source of light in the sky. Its light is silver and soft, and things seen by moonlight are often less clear than when seen by sunlight. They are blurrier around the edges and easier to mistake for something other than what they are. The Moon represents changeability, reflection, and passage to the otherworld. It is mysterious and full of wonder, and of all the celestial bodies it is the one most classically associated with witchcraft and magic. All of these qualities are also qualities of Yesod, and the connection to the Moon deepens the symbolism we have already discussed with regard to this Sephirah.

We find the same depth with Hod and Mercury. Mercury is the planet of thought, writing, communication, travel, commerce, and science. All intellectual pursuits belong to Mercury. We find these qualities reflected in Hod, along with a few new qualities that help flesh out our understanding of the eighth Sephirah: associations with money, with communication, even with theft and crime. Money and theft are matters of personal material interests, and so they belong to Hod as the expression of self (versus other). Likewise, communication through speech and writing is a social act, but in the domain of Mercury, it is fundamentally an act of self-expression, of making oneself understood. Consequently, it belongs to Hod.

Netzach corresponds to Venus, and here again, the association is easy to see. Venus governs love and relationships of all kinds. Romantic and sexual relationships, yes, but also social and familial connections. Everything that puts us in communion with other people is the domain of Venus, as well as everything that fills our hearts with love and pleasure: art, music, aesthetic beauty, and all kinds of sensual pleasure. The associations with Venus complement the existing associations of Netzach, and provide a further way to understand the energy at the base of the Pillar of Mercy.

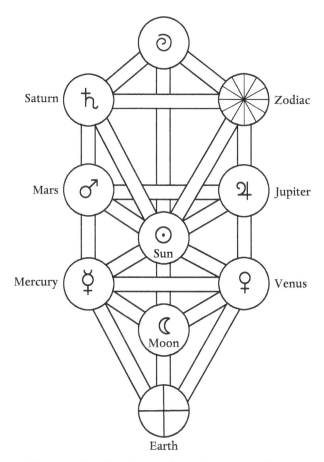

The Tree of Life with Astrological Correspondences

Ascending yet further, we find the Sun in Tiphereth. Just as Tiphereth sits at the center of the Tree of Life, the Sun sits literally at the center of our solar system. It is the unifying body around which the rest of the planets revolve, the most important part of the solar system. Without the Sun as a gravitational center, there would be no solar system; without Tiphereth holding the Sephiroth together, there would be no Tree of Life. Likewise, the image of the Sun corresponds to the seasonal myth of the dying-and-resurrecting God we discussed in the Wheel of the Year. The Sun is what drives the cycle of the seasons, bringing us light at Midsummer and darkness at Yule, and it is the death and rebirth of the Sun that we celebrate when we mark the sabbats.

Moreover, the Sun has other astrological associations that can flesh out our image of Tiphereth. It represents truth, harmony, prosperity, and life.

Gevurah as Mars is yet another easy association. Mars is strict, warlike, domineering, and aggressive—all qualities of Gevurah. Mars has strong connections to the military (after all, Mars is the Roman God of war), and all of Gevurah's best and worst qualities are on full display in military institutions. The drive for order and discipline, as well as the inclination towards anger and violence, are key qualities of both Gevurah and Mars. Beyond these qualities, Mars connects to sexual desire, passion, and honor. We might not previously have associated sex and passion with Gevurah, but through the correspondence to Mars, this Sephirah takes on those properties as well.

The connection of Jupiter to Chesed is probably the most difficult of the astrological correspondences to understand, but it helps to remember that Jupiter is a benefic planet associated with bounty, prosperity, and good fortune. Chesed is the Sephirah that gives us all of these things, encompassing the beneficence of the Gods toward humanity. Every time we catch a break from the universe, every time things go our way, we are experiencing good fortune and divine mercy, the qualities of Jupiter and Chesed. Likewise, when we act out of kindness and charity for others, we manifest the bounteous, all-giving power of Jupiter through our own actions. Jupiter also has associations with wealth, political ascendancy, and career advancement, and so these qualities become associated with Chesed.

At the top of the tree, we find Binah paired with Saturn, the planet of limitation and confinement. Saturn is the slowest and heaviest of the planets, and it rules over everything that weighs us down: work, obligation, even imprisonment. Saturn is the planet that provides us with our limits, and shapes our experience of the world by creating boundaries that hold us in. This can feel oppressive, but it is also necessary. Saturn gives structure and form to our universe. All of these qualities are transposed onto Binah, the Sephirah of form. Through Saturn, we can get a more concrete sense of the things that Binah presides over—not just form in the abstract, but anything saturnine that creates boundaries or shapes something's purpose.

Chokmah is the primordial agent of change, and as such, it is associated with the whole wheel of the zodiac. The zodiac is what alters the energies of the planets, causes them to manifest in new and different ways. It is the first division of the sky, demarcating the vast expanse of the stars into separate, distinct sections with their own imagery and their own meanings. It turns the inscrutable oneness of the universe into something with identifiable parts that change and interact with each other. The zodiac is also a timekeeping device, allowing us to track the movement of the planets through the heavens and measure the solstices and equinoxes. All of this gets folded into our understanding of the energy of Chokmah.

Finally, we are left with Kether, the outer whirlings of the universe. Have you ever looked at pictures from the Hubble telescope, and seen the colossal nebulae where stars are being born? Have you felt a sense of being so infinitesimally small in comparison with the infinite breadth of what lies beyond the stars? That feeling, that sublime awe, is the closest we ever get to a face-to-face contact with Kether. The first Sephirah is the primitive material from which stars and planets are made. We find it out there, in the star-studded blackness of the night sky. But we also find it in ourselves, in all the planets and in everything in the world we know, because everything is made out of star stuff. Kether is everywhere at once.

Enriching Qabalistic Symbolism

These astrological correspondences open us up to a whole world of other associations. Anything with a planetary correspondence is connected, through that planet, to one of the Sephiroth. Cinquefoil, valerian, and parsley are all herbs of Mercury, and therefore herbs of Hod. Tiger's eye and carnelian are crystals associated with the Sun, and therefore with Tiphereth. Silver is the metal of the Moon, so silver jewelry connects us to Yesod. Other correspondences can be leveraged, too; blue crystals and gemstones, through their color, are associated with Chesed. In the magical universe, everything corresponds to everything else. We can take any object in our world and find the ways that it connects to the Sephiroth, through color, number, purpose, or planetary associations. And therefore, everything fits on the Tree of Life. When we start to view the world through the lens of the Qabalah, everything around us becomes Qabalistic. The Tree of Life is a system that lets us categorize the whole of the universe, because nothing exists in isolation. It gives us an infinite store of symbolism we can draw on for the purposes of ritual and meditation.

Revisit the same ritual you've been adapting throughout this chapter. Consider other ways that you could add the symbolism of the appropriate Sephirah to it. For example, you could mix the anointing oil for the Hod ritual out of Mercury herbs—and you could doubly reinforce the connection to Hod by choosing eight different Mercury herbs to blend in the oil. Are there appropriate crystals, metals, or images you could work into the ritual? Is there a particular animal or deity you associate with the energy of that Sephirah, whose aid you might invoke? Add in as much symbolism, in as many different ways, as you like.

THE ASTRAL TEMPLE

One of the most important ways these correspondences can be put to use is in the construction of an astral temple for each of the Sephiroth, which you can visit during meditation. The word "astral" here is a bit of a misnomer; while the astral plane as we have defined it refers to Yesod, the temples you create for the Sephiroth exist fully in the "world" of each Sephirah, from Malkuth to Kether. The more specific and concrete your mental image of the temple is, the stronger your connection to that Sephirah will be. You can visit such a space any time you want to meditate on the Sephirah or reconnect to its energies.

The astral temple has a further, important use in ritual. If you want to conduct a ritual that draws on the energy of a particular Sephirah, one way to do so is to visit your astral temple and perform the ritual there, rather than physically enacting it in the material world. You put yourself in the world of the Sephirah and furnish it with all of the magical tools you would normally use for ritual: an altar, your athame, other magical tools, representations of the Gods, and any particular items or ingredients for the work you want to do. You can then enact your ritual in the astral temple the same way you would do it physically, visualizing each action and sending energy just as you would otherwise.

This is a difficult technique, and it requires a great deal of concentration. You have to be able to hold a consistent mental image of the entire temple, of the tools you're using, and of yourself performing ritual both physically and energetically. The use of an astral temple is an effective and direct way to bring a particular Sephirah into your ritual—or rather, to bring your ritual into a particular Sephirah—but it's an exercise best suited for workings where the primary purpose of the rite is to explore and connect with the Sephirah in question. For most purposes, such as spellwork and religious devotion, a physical ritual space is preferable if one is available to you. That way, you're able to conduct your ritual with one foot planted in Malkuth and one in Yesod, in the liminal space where most witchcraft happens.

Nonetheless, building an astral temple is an invaluable exercise. It sharpens your mental focus and your ability to visualize, both of which are essential skills for magic, and it is one of the most immediate, direct ways to get to know the Sephiroth. The use of astral temples for the Sephiroth is an essential tool for another Qabalistic technique, which we will explore in the following chapter: Pathworking the Tree of Life. By building astral temples for all ten Sephiroth, we can then use meditative techniques to navigate the paths between them, mentally exploring the Tree of Life in a direct, experiential way.

Ritualizing Correspondences: An Astral Temple of Malkuth

The astral temple is a place where you can go in meditation to conduct ritual directly related to your work with a particular Sephirah. This exercise will guide you through the construction of a temple of Malkuth, and in the following chapter we will talk about finding your way to the temple of Yesod; from there, you will have the skills to build the rest of the astral temples on your own. If you like, you can record yourself reading the instructions for this working, or you can simply read through them in advance to give yourself a sense of what to do.

You Will Need

- a quiet room with no distractions, where you can meditate undisturbed.

Instructions

Close your eyes. Imagine yourself standing in the center of a circular room with a high ceiling. The floor is made of smooth marble, divided into four quadrants of four different colors. To your left, it is a deep russet red. To your right, it is olive green. In front of you, it is a bright, vibrant citrine color, and behind you it is a smoky black. The walls are tiled in the same color. The room is lit from above by a bright chandelier holding ten candles. Take a moment to notice the shadows you cast on the floor, and the way the candlelight plays off the stone. Bend down and touch the floor, feeling the cool, firm marble under your fingertips.

Stand up and look around the room. It is empty for now, unadorned except for the chandelier overhead and three doors set into the citrine wall in front of you. Walk around the room and take note of every detail. Look at the grain of each individual marble tile, and notice the size of the tiles and the way they fit together. What shape are they? Do they form a particular pattern?

When you know every detail of the floor tiles, walk over to the three doors and examine them. Don't open them, for now. Just get to know this room. Run your hands along the door frames and gently test the doorknobs, noting what material they're made out of and how it feels in your hand. What color are the doors? How big are they? How far apart from each other are they? Do they have any kind of decoration or embellishment?

Turn to face the center of the room. Examine any further details you might have left unnoticed—the shape and material of the chandelier, the diameter of the room, the color of the ceiling. When you feel you know absolutely every detail of the room, walk back to the center. The candles in the chandelier above your head slowly begin to flicker and dim, until they extinguish altogether and you are left in blackness. Take a deep breath and exhale. Find yourself back in your material body. Open your eyes.

The room you just created is your astral temple of Malkuth. You may return there any time you wish to reconnect to the energy of Malkuth. The next time you return, add furnishings to the astral temple. You could add an altar, a shrine to deities you worship, a collection of magical tools, or anything else you want in your temple. You may also wish to add incense, an oil diffuser, or bells and chimes, to incorporate your other senses. Just take care to consider the appearance, shape, weight, and texture of everything you bring into this space, so that you can see it and feel it perfectly in your mind.

It may take several trips to your Malkuth temple before it is fully furnished to your liking. Once you have the temple set up the way you want, visit it to meditate on the energy of Malkuth. Try visiting this temple and calling the quarters. How does it feel energetically, compared to when you call the quarters in a physical space?

INFINITE CORRESPONDENCES

The purpose of all the correspondences on the Tree of Life is twofold: they help us to understand the Sephiroth better, and they allow us to establish a sympathetic connection to the Sephiroth for magical and ritual purposes. Sympathetic magic operates on the basic principle that whatever is *like* a thing *becomes* that thing. Thus, while we can't easily bring the abstract principle of mercy into our ritual space, we know that lots of more concrete, accessible things are connected to that principle. The color blue, the planet Jupiter, oak leaves, squares, sapphires—all of these things are like Chesed. All of them share, to some extent, in its nature. So when we bring them into ritual, all of them become Chesed, manifesting the energy of that Sephirah in a concrete, graspable way.

The potential correspondences for the Sephiroth are countless. There are entire books of classical correspondences, including ones we haven't mentioned here: mythical creatures, parts of the body, plants, incenses, even diseases. For further research you'll do on your own, Aleister Crowley's book *Liber 777* is the best starting point.[14] It is the definitive source of Qabalistic

---

14. Aleister Crowley, *777 and Other Qabalistic Writings of Aleister Crowley: Including Gematria & Sepher Sephiroth.*

correspondences, consisting of chart after chart filled with different correlations to the Sephiroth. However, remember that there are also personal correspondences available beyond the "official" ones you'll find in books. Many of the correspondences Crowley gives are simply personal innovations that he made based on his own private work with the Sephiroth. You may find that some of these work for you, but as you develop a stronger relationship with the Tree of Life, you will find other correspondences not given by Crowley, based on your own individual understanding of the energies on the tree. Magic is intensely personal, and the same symbols can mean many different things to different people. Think about images, animals, or other symbols that have personal meaning for you, and which you would associate with particular Sephiroth. Maybe you associate doves with peace, and thereby with Chesed. Or maybe you associate peacocks with Tiphereth because Tiphereth is the Sephirah of beauty. These personal correspondences can be just as powerful in your magic. Simply by choosing a symbol and using it in ritual, you connect yourself to the energy of the Sephirah you are representing with that symbol.

When we do Qabalistic magic, it is easy to get caught up in wanting to do things the "right" or official way, but all magic ultimately comes down to what works for you. As you continue to explore the Tree of Life, you will develop your own relationship to the Sephiroth and your own ways of expressing them through symbolism and ritual. That's a good thing. Just as a tarot reader will gradually build up personal interpretations of the cards alongside the meanings they find in books, a Qabalist will develop their own unique, intimate relationship with the Tree of Life. Over time, you will build a personal Qabalah, with your own understanding of the Sephiroth and your own ways of bringing them into your magic. An important part of that is building up your own set of correspondences, alongside the ones that everyone else uses.

Journal Prompts

- Copy out the correspondences listed in this chapter, and research other ones that you might want to use.

- Do some research on herbs, crystals, or other magical items that can be connected to the Sephiroth through color or planetary correspondences. Write down some choice ones for each Sephirah, and think about how they relate to the energy of that Sephirah.

- Write down a number of unofficial correspondences based on your personal understanding of each Sephirah, things you would associate with it but that you haven't found in a book. These could be animals, plants, minerals, deities, or more.

CHAPTER 11
THE PATHS

The Sephiroth are the substance of the Tree of Life, but the paths connecting them are what give the tree its structure. Without the paths, there would be no way for energy to flow between the Sephiroth. The Sephiroth would become stagnant and fetid, like pools of water when they've been cut off from a stream. Without the paths, we ourselves would be unable to ascend the Tree of Life; we would have no means to traverse from one Sephirah to another, no way to come into contact with the higher emanations of the Divine. The Sephiroth exist in constant dynamic interaction with each other, and the paths are what facilitates that interaction. The paths are the stitching that holds the whole Tree of Life together.

There are twenty-two paths connecting the Sephiroth of the Tree of Life. It's worth noting, right out of the gate, that in the history of Qabalah, Cabala, and Kabbalah, there have been a number of different ways of drawing these paths. The version of the Tree of Life you see throughout this book is the standard in Hermetic Qabalah, but for various mystical and theological reasons, Kabbalists and Cabalists have chosen to draw the paths differently throughout history. However, there is one constant: the number of paths on the Tree of Life is always twenty-two, because there are twenty-two letters in the Hebrew alphabet. A medieval Kabbalistic text called the *Sepher Yetzirah* describes God creating the universe through the use of the numbers one through ten (that is to say, the Sephiroth) and the twenty-two Hebrew letters.[15] Together, letter and number allow for the emanations of the tree and the creation of the material universe.

The Paths

THE HEBREW LETTERS

There's a great deal of mystical and theological significance in the connection of the Hebrew letters to the paths on the tree, but as that significance is particular to Judaism, we will leave it aside here. This is one of those aspects of Jewish Kabbalah that, I feel, should remain closed to non-Jewish Qabalists, although there are certainly others who will disagree with me. However, we

15. Aryeh Kaplan, *Sefer Yetzirah: The Book of Creation,* 5.

do still need to know the correspondences between the letters and the paths, because this connection forms the basis of all the other magical correspondences that have built up in Hermetic Qabalah. Assigning Hebrew letters to the paths on the Tree of Life, we start at the top of the tree and work our way down sequentially through the Hebrew alphabet:

1. The letter Aleph (א, pronounced *AH-lef*) is on the path from Kether to Chokmah.

2. The letter Beth (ב, pronounced *BET*) is on the path from Kether to Binah.

3. The letter Gimel (ג, pronounced *GEE-mel*, with a hard G) is on the path from Kether to Tiphereth.

4. The letter Daleth (ד, pronounced *DAH-let*) is on the path from Chokmah to Binah.

5. The letter Heh (ה, pronounced *HEY*) is on the path from Chokmah to Tiphereth.

6. The letter Vau (ו, pronounced *VAHV*) is on the path from Chokmah to Chesed.

7. The letter Zain (ז, pronounced *ZEYE-n*) is on the path from Binah to Tiphereth.

8. The letter Cheth (ח, pronounced *KHET*) is on the path from Binah to Gevurah.

9. The letter Teth (ט, pronounced *TET*) is on the path from Chesed to Gevurah.

10. The letter Yod (י, pronounced *YOOD*) is on the path from Chesed to Tiphereth.

11. The letter Kaph (כ, pronounced *KAHF*) is on the path from Chesed to Netzach.

12. The letter Lamed (ל, pronounced *LAH-med*) is on the path from Gevurah to Tiphereth.

13. The letter Mem (מ, pronounced *MEM*) is on the path from Gevurah to Hod.

14. The letter Nun (נ, pronounced *NOON*) is on the path from Tiphereth to Netzach.

15. The letter Samekh (ס, pronounced *SAH-mekh*) is on the path from Tiphereth to Yesod.

16. The letter Ayin (ע, pronounced *EYE-in*) is on the path from Tiphereth to Hod.

17. The letter Peh (פ, pronounced *PAY*) is on the path from Netzach to Hod.

18. The letter Tzaddi (צ, pronounced *TZAH-dee*) is on the path from Netzach to Yesod.

19. The letter Qoph (ק, pronounced *KOOF*) is on the path from Netzach to Malkuth.

20. The letter Resh (ר, pronounced *RESH*) is on the path from Hod to Yesod.

21. The letter Shin (ש, pronounced *SHEEN*) is on the path from Hod to Malkuth.

22. The letter Tau (ת, pronounced *TAHV*) is on the path from Yesod to Malkuth.

The transliterations of the Hebrew letter names I give here are by no means the most accurate way these names could be transliterated into English, but I use them for consistency with historical Qabalistic texts.

As with the placement of the paths themselves, there is some historical variation in the correspondence of the paths to Hebrew letters. Different Kabbalistic and Cabalistic texts assign the letters to different paths on the tree, radically changing its structure. These differences provide the subject of fruitful study, should you choose to pursue them, but for our purposes here, we will stick with this arrangement. It is the order used by the Hermetic Order of the Golden Dawn and all of its various descendants, and it is more or less the gold standard of modern-day occult Qabalah.

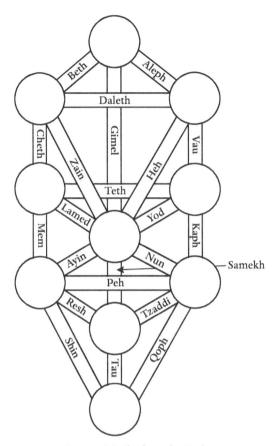

Letters Marked on the Paths

The connection of the paths to the letters of the Hebrew alphabet opens up a whole universe of other magical correspondences. As in the previous chapter, we will focus on only a few key ones, which can be used to establish a basic magical foundation from which other correspondences can be discovered. These correspondences all depend on a threefold division of the twenty-two letter alphabet. In the *Sepher Yetzirah*, three different groups of letters are identified based on their linguistic properties:

- Aleph, Mem, and Shin are the three so-called "mother" letters. They supposedly represent the most basic sounds in the Hebrew language, from which all the other letters come.

- Beth, Gimel, Daleth, Kaph, Peh, Resh, and Tau are the seven so-called "double" letters. In medieval Hebrew, each of these letters had two different pronunciations, depending on the context of the word they were situated in.
- Heh, Vau, Zain, Cheth, Teth, Yod, Lamed, Nun, Samekh, Ayin, Tzaddi, and Qoph are the twelve so-called "simple" letters.

ELEMENTAL AND ASTROLOGICAL CORRESPONDENCES

Out of this threefold division of the letters (and therefore of the paths), we derive a set of elemental and astrological correspondences:

- The mother letters correspond to three of the four elements: Aleph to air, Mem to water, and Shin to fire.
- The double letters correspond to the seven classical planets: Beth to Mercury, Gimel to the Moon, Daleth to Venus, Kaph to Jupiter, Peh to Mars, Resh to the Sun, and Tau to Saturn.
- The single letters correspond to the twelve signs of the zodiac: Heh to Aries, Vau to Taurus, Zain to Gemini, Cheth to Cancer, Teth to Leo, Yod to Virgo, Lamed to Libra, Nun to Scorpio, Samekh to Sagittarius, Ayin to Capricorn, Tzaddi to Aquarius, and Qoph to Pisces.

You'll notice that only three of the four elements are represented on the paths. We have air, water, and fire, but what of earth? The reason for this absence has to do, once again, with the *Sepher Yetzirah*, which only mentions three elements, since there are only three mother letters. In the *Sepher Yetzirah*, earth is not treated as an element in its own right, but is instead seen as a product of water.[16] To account for this imbalance, and to represent all four elements in the paths, the Golden Dawn added a second correspondence to the path of Tau, so that it corresponds both to the planet Saturn and to the element earth. If the lack of earth bothers you, feel free to use this additional correspondence.

This can be a lot of information to take in all at once. It's okay if you don't memorize all of these correspondences right away. You can always refer

---

16. Kaplan, *Sefer Yetzirah: The Book of Creation,* 274.

back to an image or a table, here or in your own notebook. The key thing for you to process now is that these correspondences are based on the division of mother letters, double letters, and single letters. If you just look at the elemental and astrological correspondences of the paths on the Tree of Life, without any context for where they came from, they seem confusing and arbitrary. If, however, you can look at them and see the structure underlying them—the reason that they are arranged the way they are—they become a lot less scary and a lot easier to manage. For ease of reference, here's a cheat sheet with the correspondences laid out in a table, and with them arranged visually on the Tree of Life:

Letter	Mother/Double/Single	Path Between	Correspondence
Aleph	Mother	Kether and Chokmah	Air
Beth	Double	Kether and Binah	Mercury
Gimel	Double	Kether and Tiphereth	The Moon
Daleth	Double	Chokmah and Binah	Venus
Heh	Single	Chokmah and Tiphereth	Aries
Vau	Single	Chokmah and Chesed	Taurus
Zain	Single	Binah and Tiphereth	Gemini
Cheth	Single	Binah and Gevurah	Cancer
Teth	Single	Chesed and Gevurah	Leo
Yod	Single	Chesed and Tiphereth	Virgo
Kaph	Double	Chesed and Netzach	Jupiter
Lamed	Single	Gevurah and Tiphereth	Libra
Mem	Mother	Gevurah and Hod	Water
Nun	Single	Tiphereth and Netzach	Scorpio
Samekh	Single	Tiphereth and Yesod	Sagittarius
Ayin	Single	Tiphereth and Hod	Capricorn

Letter	Mother/Double/ Single	Path Between	Correspondence
Peh	Double	Netzach and Hod	Mars
Tzaddi	Single	Netzach and Yesod	Aquarius
Qoph	Single	Netzach and Malkuth	Pisces
Resh	Double	Hod and Yesod	The Sun
Shin	Mother	Hod and Malkuth	Fire
Tau	Double	Yesod and Malkuth	Saturn, Earth

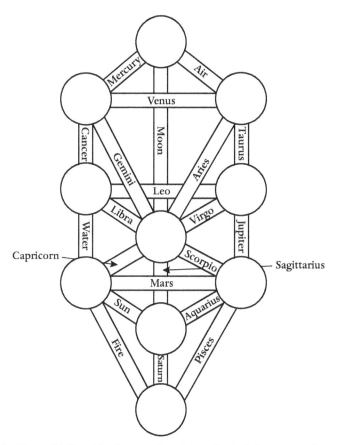

The Tree of Life with Elemental and Astrological Correspondences

Resolving Polarities

These correspondences are all very abstract, and potentially difficult to connect to. It can feel sometimes like Qabalah adds correspondences to things just for the sake of having correspondences, but that they don't actually serve any purpose. Let's take a step back and try to gain some perspective on why we have these correspondences in the first place. Despite how we might feel, the correspondences of the paths aren't just there to look pretty. They're meant to provide us with a deeper, more enriched understanding of the Sephiroth and—in the case of the twenty-two paths—of the connections between them.

In Chapter 6, we noted that although the major polarities on the Tree of Life manifest in the triads, there is a polarity of sorts formed between any two Sephiroth connected on the tree. Whenever we identify two distinct energetic centers and place them next to each other, they become opposite ends of a polar spectrum, and a tension emerges between them that is only resolved by the union of the opposite poles. Thus, there are many more polarities on the Tree of Life than those between Chokmah and Binah, Chesed and Gevurah, and Netzach and Hod. Every single path on the Tree of Life is the meeting point of two energetic poles, the product of the union between two Sephiroth whose energies have been divided and juxtaposed with each other.

There is a polarity between Malkuth and Netzach, between Hod and Gevurah, between Kether and Chokmah. Each of the twenty-two paths has a particular energy, all its own, which is born out of the division and recombination of the Sephiroth it connects. The correspondences of the paths, then, help us to understand that energy, express it, and work with it in order to deepen our knowledge of the Tree of Life, the Sephiroth, and the ways they relate to each other.

In this way, these basic twenty-two correspondences provide points of access to understanding twenty-two different polarities on the Tree of Life. We have worked our way up the tree and gained a general understanding of the

Sephiroth individually and as part of large-scale polarities; now we flesh that understanding out with a host of smaller polarities. Think about the relationship between Malkuth, the material world, and Netzach, the world of love and community. What do they share in common? How are they different from each other? What is the tension between them, and how is that tension resolved? Now look at the correspondence of the path of Qoph, which runs between them. When Malkuth and Netzach unite, the product is the astrological energy of Pisces—dreamy, intuitive, and otherworldly. What does that tell us?

Thinking about the correspondences in this way can help to make them feel useful and purposive. They're not just flourishes and decorations to crowd out the tree and make it look complicated and intimidating. They're tools to further our understanding. Learning how to use them might take time, and that's okay, but don't be discouraged. They're there to help you, not to hinder you.

Meditation on the Paths

This meditation will help you focus on the mediating energy that exists on the spectrum between any two Sephiroth, so that you can connect that energy to its corresponding path. Read through the instructions in advance so that you don't have to refer to them while you're meditating.

You Will Need
- a quiet room with no distractions, where you can meditate undisturbed

Instructions
For this exercise, choose two Sephiroth that are conjoined by one of the twenty-two paths. Sit in a comfortable position with your hands resting, palm-up, on your knees. Ground and center.

Visualize a ball of energy forming in your left hand. Fill this ball with everything you associate with the first of your two Sephiroth. Feed every concept, feeling, and keyword you associate with the Sephirah into the energy ball. See the ball starting to take shape, turning the color of the Sephirah, glowing with light. Feel its energy radiating from the palm of your left hand.

Now form another energy ball in your right hand, and fill it with the energy of the second Sephirah. Pour everything you know about this Sephirah into it, and watch it turn the appropriate color. Bring your hands close together, and feel the magnetic pull between the two energy balls. Pull your hands apart, and feel the energy flowing between them. What is the quality of that energy? How does the liminal space between your hands feel? What are the words, feelings, and images you would use to describe it?

Continue to bring your hands together and apart until you can clearly discern the energetic current flowing between them. Now think about the elemental or astrological correspondence of the path between these two Sephiroth. How does the energy of that element, planet, or zodiac sign feel? Can you feel it in the current running between your hands?

When you are satisfied with what you have felt, bring your hands all the way together and clasp them over your chest. Allow the energy balls you've formed to fuse together, and feel the release of power that comes from their union. Let that power flow through your body and release it down into the earth.

THE COLORS OF THE PATHS

As with the Sephiroth, the paths have four sets of color correspondences, belonging to the four elemental worlds, but only one color scale is widely in use today. For the Sephiroth, we used color correspondences from the Queen Scale of color, which corresponds to Briah; for the paths between the Sephiroth, however, the most commonly used color correspondences are those of the King Scale, corresponding to the world of Atziluth (see the section on color in Chapter 10). The color correspondences you are most likely to see for the paths in any depiction of the Tree of Life are the correspondences of the King Scale, and unless you get really serious about Qabalistic magic, you're unlikely to use other ones. These correspondences of the paths, like the elemental and astrological correspondences, are based on the division of the Hebrew alphabet into mother letters, double letters, and single letters:

- The mother letters correspond to the three primary colors: Aleph to yellow, Mem to blue, and Shin to red.
- The double letters correspond to the seven colors of the rainbow: Beth to yellow, Gimel to blue, Daleth to green, Kaph to purple, Peh to red, Resh to orange, and Tau to indigo.
- The single letters correspond to the twelve primary and secondary colors: Heh to red, Vau to red-orange, Zain to orange, Cheth to yellow-orange, Teth to yellow, Yod to yellow-green, Lamed to green, Nun to blue-green, Samekh to blue, Ayin to indigo, Tzaddi to purple, and Qoph to red-purple.

Why the shift from the colors of Briah to the colors of Atziluth? The simple answer is that this is just the convention. A slightly more complex answer is that the Sephiroth and the paths represent divine energy in two fundamentally different states on the tree. The Sephiroth are divine energy as it *is*, ten different ways of divine power manifesting into the world. The paths, in contrast, are divine energy in the act of *becoming*, shifting states from one Sephirah to another. The interplay of being and becoming is represented with two different color scales; the passage from one Sephirah to another is a transformation, a transmutation, and consequently we represent it with colors belonging to the fiery world of Atziluth.

These color correspondences are easily visualized with the image of the Rosy Cross Lamen, which was used by the inner order of the Golden Dawn. The lamen is a cross with elemental symbols on each of its four arms and a twenty-two petaled rose in its center. The petals are grouped into an inner ring of three petals, an intermediary ring of seven petals, and an outer ring of twelve; the petals are labeled with Hebrew letters and colored according to the correspondences of those letters.

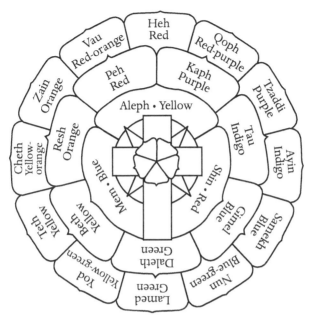

The Rosy Cross Lamen

The names of the colors in the Golden Dawn color scales were not always as straightforward as red, orange, yellow, green, blue, and purple. The Golden Dawn experimented a great deal with nineteenth-century color theory, and they designed their color scales using commercially available pigments with specific and sometimes off-putting names. Thus, tables of official color correspondences include such gems as "glowing orange scarlet," "new yellow leather," and "rich salmon."[17] These are the names of the paint colors that Golden Dawn initiates bought, but those pigments are no longer sold. For the sake of understanding the color theory and the principles behind the color correspondences on the tree, we can stick to basic kindergarten colors like red, orange, yellow, green, blue, and purple.

....

17. Regardie, 99.

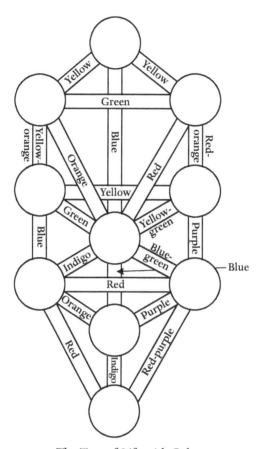

The Tree of Life with Colors

EXERCISE: CONNECTING THE
PATHS THROUGH COLOR

The correspondences of the paths don't exist in isolation; they can also provide points of reference to help you find similarities between the energies of different paths. In this exercise, you will look at paths that share a color correspondence in order to see what other qualities they may share.

You Will Need

- your journal or notebook.

Instructions

Choose two or three paths on the Tree of Life that have the same color correspondences, e.g. all three of the paths that are colored blue or both of the paths that are colored orange. Look at where they're situated relative to each other on the tree. Which Sephiroth do they bridge between? For example, if you're looking at blue paths, the path of Mem runs from Gevurah to Hod, the path of Gimel runs from Kether to Tiphereth, and the path of Samekh runs from Tiphereth to Yesod. Think about each of these polarities individually. What are they like? What kind of energy is produced on the paths between these Sephiroth?

Now think about all three paths together. What do they have in common? How is the watery energy between Gevurah and Hod similar to the lunar energy between Kether and Tiphereth, or the Sagittarian energy between Tiphereth and Yesod? What is shared between all three of these paths? What are the ways in which they are alike? Think about the energetic qualities that unite these paths, and how those qualities are expressed through the color correspondences.

If there is a Sephirah that also corresponds to this color, you may, if you choose, take this exercise one step further by looking at how that Sephirah relates to the energies of the paths. What does Chesed have in common with the paths of Mem, Gimel, and Samekh? What does Hod have in common with the paths of Resh and Zain? How do these connections help you to understand both the Sephirah and the paths in a new way?

THE MAJOR ARCANA OF THE TAROT

We will only discuss one other set of correspondences here, although—just as with the Sephiroth—there are countless more to be explored, including correspondences to magical tools, crystals, and geomantic figures. No matter how long you study Qabalistic correspondences, there will always be other ones available for you to learn. My philosophy is that the best way to start is with a few simple correspondences, familiarizing yourself with those and using them in your magic, and allowing yourself to gradually build up a wider repertoire. Don't overwhelm yourself by trying to do everything all at once.

On that note, our final set of correspondences for the paths is their relationship to the twenty-two major arcana of the tarot. Historically, there have been a number of attempts to link the Hebrew letters (and by extension, the paths on the Tree of Life) to the major arcana, but the most influential system is the one used by (surprise, surprise) the Golden Dawn. This system is the basis of the divinatory meanings assigned to the major arcana in the Golden Dawn system and its descendants, the Rider-Waite-Smith and the Thoth; consequently, its effects on occult tarot have been long-lasting and far-reaching. The cards are assigned to the paths in order, starting with the Fool on the path of Aleph and going sequentially until the World on the path of Tau.

Letter	Path Between	Tarot Card
Aleph	Kether and Chokmah	The Fool
Beth	Kether and Binah	The Magician
Gimel	Kether and Tiphereth	The High Priestess
Daleth	Chokmah and Binah	The Empress
Heh	Chokmah and Tiphereth	The Emperor
Vau	Chokmah and Chesed	The Hierophant
Zain	Binah and Tiphereth	The Lovers
Cheth	Binah and Gevurah	The Chariot
Teth	Chesed and Gevurah	Strength
Yod	Chesed and Tiphereth	The Hermit
Kaph	Chesed and Netzach	The Wheel of Fortune
Lamed	Gevurah and Tiphereth	Justice
Mem	Gevurah and Hod	The Hanged Man
Nun	Tiphereth and Netzach	Death
Samekh	Tiphereth and Yesod	Temperance
Ayin	Tiphereth and Hod	The Devil
Peh	Netzach and Hod	The Tower
Tzaddi	Netzach and Yesod	The Star

Letter	Path Between	Tarot Card
Qoph	Netzach and Malkuth	The Moon
Resh	Hod and Yesod	The Sun
Shin	Hod and Malkuth	Judgment
Tau	Yesod and Malkuth	The World

This means that the major arcana also have all the Qabalistic associations of their respective paths. The Emperor, corresponding to Heh, has a connection to the zodiac sign of Aries, and we can understand the willful, authoritative energy of this card through that lens. (Aleister Crowley maintained the tarot cards' astrological correspondences, but he swapped the path attributions of the Emperor and the Star, associating the Emperor with Tzaddi and the Star with Heh. You may sometimes see this swap replicated in Qabalistic texts.[18]) Likewise, the Empress is connected to Daleth, and thereby to loving and nurturing Venus; in the Rider-Waite Smith deck, she is even depicted with the symbol for Venus on her shield.

Some of these correspondences make perfect sense at first glance. The lion in the Strength card is Leo on the path of Teth, the scales of Justice are the scales of Libra on the path of Lamed, and the Sun in tarot corresponds to the path of Resh and the actual sun in the sky. Others, however, are initially confusing. The Chariot is attributed to Cheth and the zodiac sign Cancer. The astrological moon is paired not with the Moon card in the tarot, but with the High Priestess. It's okay if some of these correspondences don't make sense to you, or if they feel a little arbitrary at times. They function as part of a larger, interconnected system, and it can take a while to feel comfortable working in that system.

---

18. Crowley, *777 and Other Qabalistic Writings of Aleister Crowley*, 124.

The Empress

These correspondences are, however, a seminal influence on divinatory tarot. If the Qabalistic correspondences of the major arcana are uncomfortable for you, you're certainly under no obligation to use them in your tarot reading—especially if you already have an established tarot practice, and you're used to connecting to the cards in certain ways. However, if you are looking to add another layer of meaning to your tarot practice, the Qabalistic correspondences can help you to view the major arcana from a new angle. The Chariot tends to be associated with movement, journeys, and ambition, but when seen through its connection to sensitive Cancer, those concepts take on a softer, more symbolic meaning. Cancer is hard on the outside but vulnerable on the inside, and linking it to the Chariot teaches us that this card's ambition and drive can mask a deeper sensitivity and softness. Once again, remember: all of the correspondences on the Tree of Life are meant to be a help, not a hindrance. The Qabalistic associations of all the major arcana can add depth and complexity to our understanding of the cards, if we let them.

Even if you don't use Qabalah to enrich your understanding of tarot, you can go the other direction and use tarot to enrich your understanding of Qabalah. Consider the Chariot, on the path between Binah and Gevurah. Maybe the correspondence of the Chariot to Cancer doesn't make sense to you in a divinatory context, but how can the symbolism of the Chariot help you to understand the connection between these two Sephiroth? The Chariot is a card of setting your sights on the horizon and going forth to seek your fortune. In it, we find the defining power of Binah (which takes abstract ambition and forms it into a concrete goal) coupled with the discipline and drive of Gevurah. Binah without Gevurah has a goal but no way to get there; Gevurah without Binah has self-control but no direction. The Chariot brings those two energies together, providing a synthesis that moves us forward. It shows us both where we want to go and how we're going to get there.

TAROT AND PATHWORKING

One of the most important ways that tarot cards can be used to further our study of Qabalah is in pathworking the Tree of Life. The principle is fairly straightforward: tarot cards provide a visual landscape representing the energy of a particular path. Through meditation, we can mentally enter into that landscape and explore it, immersing ourselves in that path and experiencing the journey from one Sephirah to another firsthand. This is a way to take the study of Qabalah, which often feels overly intellectual and bookish, and turn it into something experiential. Rather than thinking about the paths, we walk them ourselves. By interacting with the symbols in a tarot card, seeing and hearing and touching them, we gain a first-person perspective on the path that card represents. Consequently, we can have direct experiences of the divine energy of the tree, and we can move freely between the Sephiroth in a way that's difficult, if not impossible, to accomplish merely through book study.

This pathworking technique can be used to explore the whole of the Tree of Life. You begin in your astral temple of Malkuth and follow the path of Tau (the World) to Yesod. There, you construct an astral temple of Yesod. Once it is constructed, you can move back and forth between the two temples easily, without needing to perform a complete pathworking each time. From there, you may explore new paths that take you to the temples of the other Sephiroth. The goal is, eventually, to traverse all twenty-two paths on the Tree of Life.

The World

RITUALIZING THE PATHS: A PATHWORKING OF TAU

This pathworking will help you explore the path of Tau, between Malkuth and Yesod. You can use this same general model for exploring the other paths on the Tree of Life, by writing your own pathworking with an appropriate card from the major arcana. Before proceeding with the pathworking, record yourself reading the instructions aloud, so that you can listen to them as you meditate.

You Will Need

- an image of the World card from your favorite tarot deck
- a quiet room with no distractions, where you can meditate undisturbed

Instructions

Remove the World card from your deck and study its imagery closely. If you don't have a tarot deck on hand, you can look up the card image online or use the image in this book. Examine the card until you can reproduce it perfectly in your mind's eye. Notice the expression on the central figure's face, her posture, the way the animals surrounding her frame the image. Look at the way the ribbon wraps around her.

When you can hold a consistent mental image of the card, close your eyes. Ground and center, and focus on taking deep, even breaths. As you breathe, visualize yourself in the Malkuth temple you built in the previous chapter. Take a moment to reacquaint yourself with the temple. Notice the four different colors of marble on the floor, the chandelier with ten candles hanging above your head. Walk around the temple and examine any other furnishings you have brought into this space. Keep doing so until you feel totally grounded and present in your temple of Malkuth.

Walk over to the three doors set into the wall. For now, focus your attention on the central door. Reach out and press the palm of your hand flat against it, feeling its cool surface against your skin. As you touch the door, a rich indigo color spreads out from your hand, tinting the door's surface. It spreads quickly, covering the entire door and doorframe. When the door has turned fully indigo, open it and walk through.

On the other side, you find yourself in a free fall, tumbling downward through the crystal blue sky. At first, the feeling is dizzying, terrifying. You feel like you are spinning out of control. But as you continue to breathe evenly, you realize you are not falling; you are flying. Stretch out your arms and feel the joy of the wind rushing through your hair, around your body, blowing past you in a jet stream. At any point, if you are uncomfortable with what you encounter here or if you fail any of the trials that lie ahead, you will be able to fly back to the door through which you came and return to your temple of Malkuth. Once you have gained control of your flight, look around yourself and get your bearings. There's a speck of color in the distance, a bright flash of green, red, and indigo. You fly toward it.

As you get closer, the figure of a winged man forms in front of you.

"I am the guardian of the element of air," the man says, "Who goes there?"

Give him your name. When you have told him who you are, he says:

"Those who would meet the spirit of the World must seek wisdom and truth. What is the truth you seek?"

Answer him honestly. What do you hope to learn on this journey? When you have given your answer, if the guardian is satisfied with it, he will let you pass. Continue flying toward the spot of color in the distance. As it starts to grow larger, the figure of a lion forms in the air in front of you. It says:

"I am the guardian of the element of fire. Who goes there?"

When you have told the lion your name, it replies:

"Those who would meet the spirit of the World must have passion and will. What is your will?"

Answer honestly, and if the lion is satisfied, it will let you pass. You continue to fly through the air. When you are close enough that you can start to make out the details of the figure in the distance, an eagle appears in front of you.

"I am the guardian of the element of water. Who goes there?"

When you have answered, it challenges you:

"Those who would meet with the spirit of the World must have compassion and heart. Where does your heart lie?"

When you have answered to the guardian's satisfaction, it lets you pass. You continue your journey, and now you can see that the figure in the distance is a woman, wrapped in an indigo ribbon. Floating in the air around her is an enormous, verdant wreath. Before you can quite reach her, though, the figure of a bull takes shape in the air between you and her.

"I am the guardian of the element of earth," the bull says, "Who goes there?"

You give it your name, and it replies:

"Those who would meet with the spirit of the World must be steadfast and patient. Are you willing to wait patiently for the Mysteries?"

Answer. If the guardian is satisfied, you may finally pass, and approach the World. She floats serenely in the center of the wreath, her ribbon entwining her body, shimmering like a veil that obscures your view of her.

"I am the Great Mother of all things," she says, "I am the spirit of the earth, of the stars, and of the whole of the World. It is I who give things form, I who gave birth to you and me to whom you shall return when you die. You who have come in adoration of me, you have passed the trials that brought you here. Are you ready to pass the gate into the world beyond?"

Give her your answer. She will decide whether you are telling the truth. If she determines that you are ready, she will say:

"Go, then, into the next world, blessed with truth, will, heart, and patience. Proceed with my blessings, and may the strength of the Goddess guide you on your path."

At this point, you may ask her one question or make one request. She will answer you. When she has done so, thank her, then move past her and through the wreath that encircles her. As you pass through the wreath, you find yourself in a wide, well-lit purple room. The floor is made of smooth purple stone, and the ceiling is painted with a night sky and a crescent moon. There are nine torches placed in sconces on the walls, burning with preternatural purple flames. You have found your way to the temple of Yesod.

Take some time to explore this temple, just as you did when you were forming your temple of Malkuth. There are three doors ahead of you, leading to Hod, Tiphereth, and Netzach; behind you is the door through which you came, leading back to Malkuth. Now that you have made the journey on the path of the World, you may take that door back any time, and walking through it will lead you directly to the temple of Malkuth unless you wish to explore the path a second time.

When you have explored the temple of Yesod to your satisfaction, return through that door and find yourself in the temple of Malkuth. Reacquaint yourself with your surroundings, and then allow the candles in the chandelier overhead to flicker and dim. One by one, they go out, and you are left in blackness. Open your eyes and find yourself back in the material world.

Resonance Between Paths and Sephiroth

Some paths share qualities with certain Sephiroth. We have already pointed out color-based links such as the one between Chesed and the paths of Mem, Gimel, and Samekh. Similar connections exist for astrological correspondences; for example, the path of Tau corresponds to Saturn, and therefore has something in common with the energy of Binah. It is interesting to note that Binah, the Goddess in her truest aspect as Isis Unveiled, is present in the liminal space between Malkuth and Yesod where Wiccans work our magic. Even if we cannot know the ultimate, hidden face of the Goddess, she is present with us when we walk between the worlds.

There is another way that the paths can have affinity with certain Sephiroth. We talked about the paths as the result that comes from the unity of two poles, two Sephiroth situated at opposite ends of a polar spectrum. Some of these polarities, as we have already explored in great depth, find their resolution in other Sephiroth. Thus, the path of Peh resolves the tension between Netzach and Hod—but so does the Sephirah Yesod. This path and this Sephirah share something in common; they are both products of the same polarity, although they manifest that polarity differently. Where Yesod manifests the self-other relation through intuition and dreams, Peh manifests it through the harsh, even cataclysmic energy of Mars and the Tower card from the tarot. Likewise, Tiphereth is the union of Chesed and Gevurah, but so is the path of Teth, in a slightly different way.

The paths give us a new, different insight into the Sephiroth. Remember, the Sephiroth are complicated, and we can never reduce them to just one set of ideas. The dynamics between them play out in a number of different ways, and each way we express that dynamic gives us a fuller, more robust understanding of something we will never know in its entirety.

Journal Prompts

- What's the point of studying the paths on the Tree of Life? What can they tell you about the Sephiroth that you wouldn't have been able to learn otherwise?

- What are some correspondences or connections on the paths that you find surprising or difficult to understand? Write them down and then spend some time brainstorming ways to interpret them.

- Once you've performed the pathworking with the World, try another. Write and perform a working on the path of Shin (corresponding to the Judgment card in the tarot), and construct an astral temple of Hod. Write down your experiences in your journal. How did this pathworking differ from the one you had pre-written for you?

CHAPTER 12

QABALAH FOR SPELLS

We come at last to one of the most pressing questions that face Wiccans who are trying to get into Qabalah: What good is it all? How do we actually use it? It's all well and good to study the Tree of Life and talk about the higher planes of existence, but at the end of the day, that's armchair occultism. It's all books and correspondences and charts, with the occasional meditation thrown in. What's the part where Qabalah gets practical? What can we do with it?

There are a couple of answers to this question. The first is that ritual, all ritual, can be understood in Qabalistic terms. As we've seen throughout this book, various aspects of Wiccan ritual put us in contact with the energies of the Sephiroth. A Qabalistic framework is in no way necessary to the successful practice of Wicca, and some of the most extraordinary witches I know have absolutely no knowledge of or interest in the Qabalah. But if we choose, we can use Qabalah to add dimension to the rituals we already perform, either explicitly (by adding Qabalistic symbolism to our ritual actions) or implicitly (simply by understanding that these rituals tap into the energies of the Sephiroth). The Tree of Life can add meaning and structure to Wicca without fundamentally altering Wiccan practice, because it is an interpretive lens that is compatible with any preexisting ritual format. As Wiccans, we perform Wiccan ritual; as Qabalists, we interpret that same ritual and find additional meaning in connecting it to the Tree of Life.

The second major way that Qabalah can be put to practical use in Wicca is for us to leverage Qabalistic symbolism and correspondences in our spell-work. Most of the magic that Wiccans perform is sympathetic magic; it operates on the principle that whatever is like a thing, is that thing. In our magical spaces, we create a microcosm of the universe. Sympathetic magic takes advantage of the affinity between that microcosm and the macrocosm it represents, the principle of "as above, so below." The symbolic universe we recreate within a magic circle is like the macroscopic universe around us, and therefore, by the principle of sympathy, it is the universe. What happens in the macrocosm also happens in the microcosm, and vice versa. By manipulating events in the symbolic universe, we can affect their outcome in the physical universe.

When I cast a spell, I use an object that in some way resembles or is connected to the target of my spell. I bring that object into my circle and ritually declare that this object is not only *like* my target, it *is* my target. Then, whatever I do to the object will happen to the thing or person it represents, because they are one and the same. I use the affinity between them to give myself direct causal influence over a target I wouldn't have otherwise been able to affect.

Of course, casting a spell requires more than just establishing a sympathetic link. Sympathy brings the target of a spell into my circle, but then I still have to act on it. In the non-magical world, an object at rest will only move if some impulsive force is applied to it; likewise, in magic, we must apply force in order to effect change. It's not enough just to form a sympathetic link; we also have to raise magical power and send it into the sympathetic object, so that whatever actions we perform on that object will exert a force on its counterpart in the macrocosm.

Establishing a Sympathetic Link

This is a quick and dirty explanation of the principles underlying sympathetic magic. Entire books can be (and have been!) written about what magic is, how it works, and how to cast a spell. For our purposes here, however, we'll focus on symbolism and sympathy, because that is the part of spellwork where Qabalah comes into play. Sympathetic magic requires us to represent objects and energies in the external world using symbols that are like them in some way, microcosmic versions of them that can be effectively manipulated to produce results at the macrocosmic level. Qabalah, as we have seen in the past few chapters, is replete with magical correspondences, and there are countless different connections whereby to symbolize any one of the Sephiroth or the paths. Qabalistic magic, then, is actually quite straightforward: It is magic that uses the energies and correspondences of the Tree of Life to establish a sympathetic link to a spell's target or desired outcome.

The process of writing a Qabalistic spell is much the same as writing any other spell; the only difference is that it centers Qabalistic correspondences and symbolism. You form your intention and choose the target for your spell just as you would for any other work of sympathetic magic. Then, stop and think about your spell in terms of the energy on the Tree of Life. Is there a particular Sephirah (or Sephiroth) associated with what you are trying to accomplish? Or maybe there's a particular path that expresses the energy of your spell? Find the subject matter of your spell on the Tree of Life. Then, think about how you would represent that part of the tree in magic, using colors, shapes, planetary herbs, crystals, or anything else you can think of. Use these materials, with as many layers of symbolism as feel appropriate to you, as the basis of your spell.

Qabalistic magic has a reputation for being complicated and overwrought, but in practice it can be incredibly simple. Sometimes, it's as straightforward as identifying the Sephirah with the energy most relevant to your working and pulling in one or two correspondences in order to make that Sephirah present in your magical work.

Sample Spell: For Leniency in Court

Perform this spell when you have a speeding ticket or other legal dispute that you want resolved with leniency and a forgiving eye toward yourself. The spell draws on the Qabalistic energy of Chesed, in order to incline the court toward mercy.

You Will Need

- four unlit blue candles. The number four and the color blue correspond to Chesed
- a piece of blue chalk
- the legal documents relevant to your dispute
- a wand or athame (optional)
- a space to use as an altar

Instructions

Place the candles on your altar so that they form a square (the geometric shape corresponding to Chesed), and put the legal documents in the center of the square. Ground and center; form a clear intention that these documents will attract mercy and goodwill from those who read them. Using your wand, athame, or fingers, trace the perimeter of the documents, channeling your intention into them. Say aloud:

"I consecrate these documents to the purpose of clemency. May all who read them look upon my case with kindness and favor."

Now place your hands around the first of the four blue candles. Rub it gently between your palms, charging it with your intention. Softly chant to yourself:

"Mercy, mercy, mercy, mercy."

Light the candle. Then, using the blue chalk, draw a line from that candle to the next unlit blue candle. Take this second candle between your hands, charge it, and light it in the same manner. Then draw a line to the third candle and the fourth in turn, charging and lighting each. Finally, draw a line of chalk back to the first candle, completing a square around your consecrated documents.

Sit in meditation and allow your candles to burn while you hold your intention in your mind. If your candles are small enough, stay at your altar until they have burned all the way down. Otherwise, let them burn a quarter of the way down, then extinguish them. Return to your altar for the next three days, burning down another quarter of the candles each time. This way, your spell lasts four days, reinforcing the number correspondence of Chesed once again.

Layering Qabalistic Correspondences

Other times, depending on the spell you're casting, you may want to add a couple of layers of symbolism. Some spells harmonize the energy of two or more Sephiroth, or involve a progression from one Sephirah to another. In such cases, you may want to incorporate symbols relevant to each Sephirah. There are a handful ways you could do this.

First, and most obviously, you could simply double up your symbols. Let's imagine a student who is falling behind in their studies due to a lack of focus and discipline. They decide to make a magical anointing oil, which they can wear to help them focus every time they study. Furthermore, they decide that they want to combine the energies of Hod (for study) and Gevurah (for discipline), so they make their anointing oil using eight herbs with mercurial associations and five herbs with martial associations. This is a simple way of combining the correspondences of two Sephiroth in one spell, for a magical working that unites them.

The second option is to combine the symbols of the Sephiroth in a more subtle way, taking one set of correspondences from one Sephirah and another set for the other. In our example of the struggling student, rather than using a total of thirteen herbs for their oil, they may instead choose to use only five, and have them all be herbs of Mercury. In doing so, they combine the numerical correspondence of Gevurah with the planetary herbal correspondences of Hod, bringing both Sephiroth together seamlessly into one spell.

Thirdly, if your spell involves a movement from one Sephirah to another, you can ritually enact that change by starting the spell with symbols of the first Sephirah and then replacing them with symbols of the second. Let's suppose the reason our student is having difficulty focusing is that they've overcommitted themselves to clubs, extracurricular activities, and staying out late partying. They're giving too much of their time to other people and not enough time to their own academic commitments, and they realize that their life suffers from an overabundance of Netzach and a deficiency of Hod. Rather than creating a Hod/Gevurah anointing oil, they decide to cast a spell to shift themselves from Netzach into Hod.

For a working of this sort, they could start the spell with a rolled-up photograph of themselves, tied up with a green ribbon. This would represent who they are currently, encumbered by the energy of Netzach. Then, during the ritual, they could cut and ritually discard the ribbon, unroll the photograph, and lay it face-up on their altar, placing eight pieces of agate (or another mercurial crystal) on it to hold it flat and keep it from rolling up again. In a spell like this, the harmful habits of Netzach are ritually cut away, and they are replaced with the positive qualities of Hod that the student wants to bring into their life. Of course, the goal should never be to eliminate the energy of one Sephirah completely; all of the Sephiroth are necessary to a functional, balanced life, and the goal with a spell like this is simply to slough away the excess of one Sephirah and bring it into balance by amplifying the energy of another.

Yet another way that two Sephiroth can be represented in a single spell is to use the correspondences of the path between them on the Tree of Life. In our example, the struggling student may wish to use correspondences of the path of Mem (between Gevurah and Hod) or the path of Peh (between Netzach and Hod), depending on which energy they want to target for their spell. If they were drawing on the path of Mem, for example, they could take a ritual bath, using the elemental correspondence of water to wash away their bad habits.

The energy of a Sephirah or path can also always be brought into magical space through the use of tarot cards or the elemental tools. Every card in the tarot deck connects to the Tree of Life in some way, and if you want to single out some part of the tree, a tarot card can be a perfect symbolic representation of it. Our student is looking to bring Hod into their studies—and not just Hod, but specifically the grounded, practical, earthy energy of Hod in Assiah. They may, therefore, wish to use their altar pentacle (corresponding to elemental earth) to focus their spell in the world of Assiah. Alternatively, they could use the Eight of Pentacles from their tarot deck as a representation of Hod in Assiah on their altar, grounding them and focusing their intent for the duration of their ritual. In this way, tarot cards can provide a Qabalistic focal point for any spell. The student could even just keep the Eight of Pentacles on their altar, pausing to contemplate it every morning before they went to class. This act alone is a Qabalistic spell, reminding the student of their commitment to their studies.

There are innumerable ways to apply Qabalistic correspondences in spell-work, and the only limitation is what you can think of. For any given spell, you may have as much or as little Qabalistic symbolism as you like. Qabalah is part of a tradition of ceremonial magic that has a reputation for being complex and requiring a lot of incredibly specific ingredients: a magic circle of a certain diameter, drawn on the ground with a certain color chalk, surrounded by particular geometric figures and names of angels and archangels, at a particular planetary day and hour, with an altar of a certain height and design, candles of a specific color, ceremonial robes designed for the occasion, and so on. If you want to draw on Qabalistic correspondences in any of those ways, you certainly can. One extra layer of symbolism won't hurt, and if you want to wear a special black robe just for spells relating to Binah, go for it. At the same time, though, don't feel like you have to do all that. A simple spell can be just as effective as a complicated one—sometimes, even more so. Just because you have access to all these Qabalistic correspondences doesn't mean you have to use all of them every time you cast a spell.

One of the great virtues of witchcraft is that it simplifies magic. Wiccans do magic when it needs to be done, and we use the materials available to us. From a Wiccan perspective, the point of Qabalah in our magic is not to over-complicate things and burden us with a new set of correspondences and rules that have to be followed in order for a spell to be done properly. Rather, it's to open up a new set of resources, so that when magic needs to be done, we have a whole host of new ways to form sympathetic connections, symbolize and ritualize the energies we are directing, and achieve the results we want. The Qabalah becomes one tool in our magical toolbox, to be used when it's what'll get the job done.

Don't feel like you're expected to use all Qabalah all the time, any more than you would be expected to use a screwdriver to fix every leaky faucet and busted appliance in your house. There are other tools in your toolbox, and sometimes they'll be more effective and better suited to the needs of a particular spell. You may find that some of the spells you cast are beautifully suited to Qabalah, and that you want to cram them full of symbols from the Tree of Life, while others end up having nothing Qabalistic about them whatsoever. That's okay. Being a Qabalistic magician doesn't entail shoving Qabalah into everything you do. Rather, it's about knowing enough to use Qabalah exactly when it's helpful for your magical purposes—no more and no less.

Exercise: Retooling a Spell

One of the most helpful ways to incorporate Qabalah into your extant magical practice is to look back at magical work you've already done, and to think about how you could amend it. This exercise will help you bring a Qabalistic perspective to your past spellwork.

You Will Need

- notes or a ritual script from a spell you have previously cast
- your journal or notebook

Instructions

Think about a spell you have performed in the past, which might have lent itself to Qabalistic symbolism. Which Sephirah, Sephiroth, or path would that spell connect to? If you were to perform that spell again, would you do it differently in light of what you've learned in this book? Are there any things you would add, remove, or alter in order to bring Qabalistic energy explicitly into the spell? Take a moment to rewrite that spell, noting the places where you have incorporated a sympathetic connection to the Tree of Life.

Qabalah and High Magic

As you dive into the wide world of Qabalah, you will notice that the sympathetic magic we've described so far in this chapter is only a small fraction of what could be described as Qabalistic magic. Qabalah is historically used primarily in high ceremonial magical traditions of evocation and theurgy, as opposed to the low folk magic that is common in witchcraft. What we have discussed here is an application of Qabalistic magical principles to the sort of magic that Wiccans already do, because this is a book directed at a Wiccan audience. However, there are many ways of doing magic, and not all spellcraft works on the principle of sympathy that underlies most Wiccan spells. In particular, a great deal of ceremonial magic involves the evocation of noncorporeal spirits—angels, demons, and so on—and petitioning or commanding them to accomplish a particular task. This is a technique also used in some forms of Qabalistic magic, and the Tree of Life is replete with correspondences to the names of angelic, archangelic, and demonic spirits who may be summoned to perform a magician's will.

In Chapter 9, I mentioned one such technique: performing magical work in a Sephirah by evoking the God-name of the Sephirah in Atziluth, then the archangel of the Sephirah in Briah, the choir of angels of the Sephirah in Yetzirah, and finally the planetary power of the Sephirah in Assiah. In a similar vein, S. L. MacGregor Mathers's translation of the *Goetia* instructs the magician to draw a magic circle inscribed with forty-five Hebrew names corresponding to the Sephiroth.[19] Techniques like these can be quite effective, but they're alien to the simple folk magic found in most Wiccan circles. If you're interested in learning ceremonial and theurgic magical techniques like this, I wholeheartedly encourage you in that endeavor. Qabalah is a symbolic framework that can be overlaid with any type of magic, and it can enrich the practice of spirit evocation in much the same way it enriches sympathetic magic.

A second common feature of Qabalistic magic is that much of what you'll see is personal, psychological, and directed at self-improvement. Magical lodges like the Hermetic Order of the Golden Dawn had wealthy members whose material needs were, by and large, taken care of; they pursued magic as a form of spiritual development, not a way to make sure the bills got paid. As a consequence, most of what you'll find in Qabalah books is magic geared toward enlightenment, spirituality, and personal growth. You'll see things like Aleister Crowley's infamous "knowledge and conversation of the Holy Guardian Angel"[20] (coming into contact with a tutelary spirit who guides you up the Tree of Life), but not a whole lot of Qabalah to attract a lover, Qabalah to sell a house, or Qabalah to heal an illness. These practical, worldly things simply weren't what nineteenth- and twentieth-century Qabalists were interested in using magic for.

....

19. Mathers, *The Goetia: The Lesser Key of Solomon the King*, 70.

20. Lon Milo DuQuette, *The Magick of Aleister Crowley: A Handbook of Rituals of Thelema*, 121–40.

However, that does not mean that Qabalah is incompatible with practical magic. Far from it. The key takeaway here is that Qabalah is a symbolic, magical, and theoretical lens through which any kind of magic or ritual can be viewed. Whatever sort of magic you already practice, the principles underlying the Qabalah can be applied to that practice. Being a Qabalistic magician need not be a monstrous undertaking where you unlearn everything you thought you knew about magic. You don't need to stop using sympathetic magic and start evoking angels, nor do you need to stop casting spells to meet your worldly needs. Rather, you can take your extant magical practice, view it in a Qabalistic light, and continue working the same kind of magic with added meaning and depth. Your magic doesn't have to look like something out of the Golden Dawn in order to count as legitimate Qabalah.

The point of this book is to show how Qabalistic principles fit within a Wiccan religious, magical, and ritual framework—that Qabalah and Wiccan magic are already compatible with each other. I invite you to experiment with other, more ceremonial forms of Qabalistic magic if they interest you, but you absolutely do not have to practice Golden Dawn-style magic in order to be a legitimate Qabalistic magician. If you want to practice Qabalistic magic, there are only two requirements: study Qabalah and use it in your magic. The details of how you do that are entirely up to you.

THE PLANETARY HEXAGRAMS

In Chapter 2, we discussed the magical pentagrams that were used by the Hermetic Order of the Golden Dawn to invoke and banish the energies of the four elements. In Golden Dawn Qabalistic magic, there is a sister to the system of the elemental pentagrams: a set of invoking and banishing hexagrams used to direct the energies of the planets and the Sephiroth. Any time you wish to invoke one of the planetary Sephiroth into your magical working, you may use these hexagrams to call their energy, the same way that you use the pentagrams to call the energy of the elements.

Just as each point on the pentagram is assigned to one of the elements, each point on the hexagram is assigned to a planet. The topmost point corresponds to Saturn, and proceeding clockwise around the hexagram, the other points are assigned to Jupiter, Venus, the Moon, Mercury, and Mars, respectively—with the Sun sitting in the center. This arrangement is based on the planetary correspondences of the Tree of Life: Tiphereth (the Sun) sits at the center, with Yesod (the Moon) below it. On the right-hand side, the Pillar of Mercy, we have Chesed (Jupiter) and Netzach (Venus); on the left-hand side, the Pillar of Severity, we have Gevurah (Mars) and Hod (Mercury). Finally, Binah (Saturn) is above Tiphereth on the Tree of life; thus, even though it's on the left-hand pillar, it gets assigned to the topmost point of the hexagram.

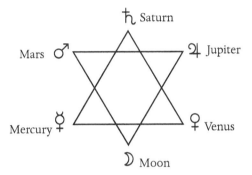

Hexagram with Planetary Points

To invoke the energy of one of the planetary Sephiroth, you draw a hexagram made up of two equilateral triangles. For the first triangle, you begin at the point of the planet you are invoking, and you draw your first stroke clockwise. Then, you draw the second triangle starting at the point opposite the planet you're invoking, once again moving in a clockwise direction. For example, to draw the invoking hexagram of Saturn: trace a clockwise triangle starting with a stroke from the point of Saturn (topmost) to the point of Venus (bottom right), then trace another clockwise triangle starting with a stroke from the point of the Moon (bottommost) to the point of Mars (top left). For the invoking hexagram of Jupiter, start with a stroke from the point of Jupiter (top right) to the point of the Moon, then draw the second triangle from the point of Mercury (bottom left) to the point of Saturn. And so on for the remaining planets. You seal the hexagram by stabbing its center, the same way you seal the elemental pentagrams.

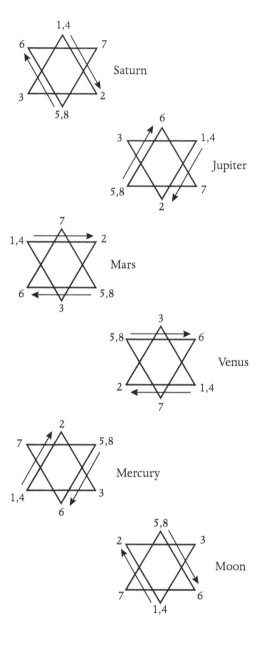

Saturn

Jupiter

Mars

Venus

Mercury

Moon

Sun = all the above in order

Invoking Hexagrams

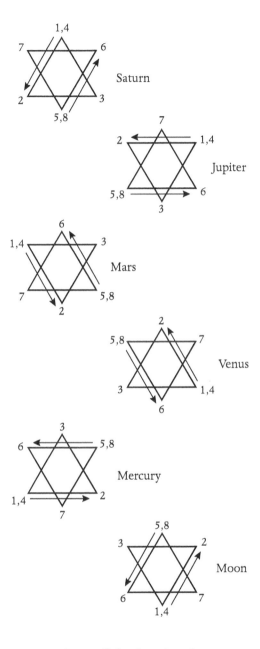

Saturn

Jupiter

Mars

Venus

Mercury

Moon

Sun = all the above in order

Banishing Hexagrams

The Sun sits at the center of the hexagram, so there is no planetary point where we can start drawing the invoking hexagram of the Sun. Instead, to invoke solar energy, you draw all six invoking hexagrams in succession, starting with the invoking hexagram of Saturn, then Jupiter, Mars, Venus, Mercury, and the Moon (following the Sephiroth in the order of emanation down the tree).

To banish planetary energies, you draw the hexagrams starting from the planetary points, but moving in a counterclockwise direction. The banishing hexagram of Saturn consists of triangles beginning with strokes from the point of Saturn to the point of Mercury, and from the point of the Moon to the point of Jupiter, respectively. For the banishing hexagram of Jupiter, you begin with a stroke from the point of Jupiter to the point of Mars, and then draw the second triangle with a stroke from the point of Mercury to the point of Venus. You get the idea. For the banishing hexagram of the Sun, you would draw all six banishing hexagrams, in order once again from Saturn to the Moon.

As with the elemental pentagrams, this can be a lot of information, and can feel overwhelming. If it's too much for you to memorize, you can always use the invoking and banishing hexagrams of Saturn as a default for directing any of the planetary energies—much the same way that you can use the invoking and banishing pentagrams of earth in place of the pentagrams of other elements. If you just want a basic invoking gesture for your work with the Sephiroth, without having to learn a different way of drawing the hexagram for each individual Sephirah, start with the hexagrams of Saturn. You can always add the other planetary hexagrams into your practice as you grow more confident, should you choose to do so.

Sample Spell: For Pleasant Dreams

This spell uses the energy of Yesod, the Sephirah of dreams and intuition, to create a talisman that will bring you good dreams. It uses the hexagram of the Moon to help direct that energy, but if you prefer, you can always use the hexagram of Saturn as a default for any planetary ritual.

You Will Need

- a purple handkerchief. Purple is the color of Yesod
- about ¼ cup of poppy seeds or dried poppy petals. Poppies are associated with sleep and dreams, and are astrologically governed by the Moon, and because of these associations, they correspond to Yesod
- a 9-inch length of twine or thin cord. The number nine corresponds to Yesod
- a wand or athame
- a teaspoon for measuring
- a space to use as an altar

Instructions

Spread out the handkerchief on your working surface. Ground and center. Using your wand or athame, draw an invoking hexagram of the Moon (or Saturn, if you prefer) over the handkerchief. As you do so, send power into it and visualize it glowing with the purple light of Yesod. Say:

"By the power of the moon above, who rules all hidden things in the night, I create this charm. May I dream sweet dreams so long as it is near."

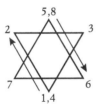

Invoking Hexagram of the Moon

Seal the hexagram in place by stabbing its center with your wand or athame. Then, place a spoonful of the poppy in the center of the handkerchief. Say:

"May my dreams bring me rest."

Add another spoonful, saying:

"May my dreams bring me peace."

Add seven more spoonfuls (nine in total), saying in succession:

"May my dreams bring me comfort. May my dreams bring me joy. May my dreams bring me renewal. May my dreams bring me tranquility. May my dreams bring me pleasure. May my dreams bring me contentment. May my dreams bring me happiness."

These are the nine qualities (nine, again, being the number of Yesod) with which you are imbuing your spell. When you have finished, fold the handkerchief up with the poppy inside; tie the bundle together with the twine. Extend your hands over the talisman and direct energy into it, chanting:

"Rest. Peace. Comfort. Joy. Renewal. Tranquility. Pleasure. Contentment. Happiness. Rest. Peace. Comfort. Joy ..."

When you have raised power to its peak, use your wand or athame to draw a second invoking hexagram of the Moon (or of Saturn) over your talisman, again visualizing the power flowing out of your tool as a brilliant purple light. Seal the hexagram with a stroke to the center, and declare:

"So mote it be!"

Keep this talisman under your mattress to ensure good dreams.

THE HEXAGRAMS AND THE FOUR WORLDS

If you choose, you can add a layer of complexity to the planetary hexagrams, using them not only to invoke the powers of the Sephiroth, but specifically to invoke the Sephiroth in one of the four worlds. A planetary hexagram is made up of two equilateral triangles; we are used to thinking of a hexagram as one upright triangle overlaid with an inverted triangle, forming a six-pointed star. However, the Golden Dawn system included four unique ways of arranging the triangles relative to each other, four ways of drawing the hexagram. Each different design is associated with one of the four elements, and thereby with one of the four elemental worlds.

If you were already feeling overwhelmed by the fourteen different invoking and banishing hexagrams, and it's sending you into a panic to learn that each of those has four different elemental variations (leaving us with a total of fifty-six different hexagrams to memorize), don't worry. You can stop right here and skip over this whole section. It's optional. You can always get by with just two hexagrams, the invoking and banishing hexagrams of Saturn that I've already introduced. I provide information about the other planetary hexagrams, and about the elemental variations thereupon, in case it's useful and interesting to you, but if you are not interested and don't intend to use them, that's fine. Take what works for you, leave the rest, and don't feel like you're expected to master all of this at once.

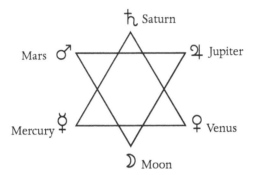

The Hexagram of Earth with Planetary Points

The hexagram we already know, and the shape we think of when some-one asks us to picture a hexagram, is the hexagram of earth and Assiah. It consists of an upright triangle (with the point of Saturn at the top) superimposed over a reversed triangle (with the point of the Moon at the bottom). When you draw a regular old invoking hexagram of Mars, then, you are actu-ally invoking Gevurah in Assiah: you are causing the power of the Sephirah to manifest in the material world. This is, after all, the purpose of most prac-tical magic, and the hexagrams of earth are the ones you'll use most often. If you want to invoke or banish a particular Sephirah in your magic, but you don't want to go into the nitty-gritty of which elemental world you're work-ing with, use the hexagrams of earth.

The hexagram of air and Yetzirah takes the two triangles and slides them apart from each other. Rather than having an upright triangle superimposed on an inverted one, the hexagram of air has an upright triangle (with the point of Saturn at the top) placed above an inverted one (with the point of the Moon at the bottom), so that the base of the upper triangle aligns with the topmost edge of the lower one. The name "hexagram" is a misnomer here; rather than a six-pointed star, this configuration is shaped like a rhombus.

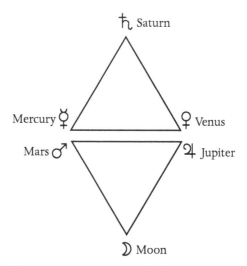

The Hexagram of Air with Planetary Points

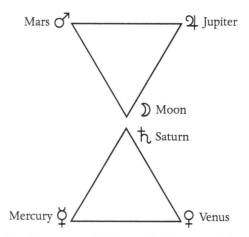

The Hexagram of Water with Planetary Points

The hexagram of water and Briah likewise pulls the two triangles apart from each other, but it moves them in the other direction. It has an upright triangle (with the point of Saturn at the top) underneath an inverted triangle (with the point of the Moon at the bottom), so that the points of Saturn and the Moon meet in the center. Thus, it looks like an hourglass.

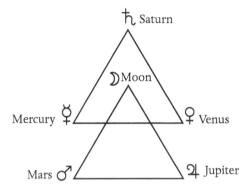

The Hexagram of Fire with Planetary Points

Finally, the hexagram of fire and Atziluth is a bit tricky. Like all the others, it has an upright triangle with the point of Saturn at the top. However, the second triangle is *not* an inverted triangle; instead, it is another upright triangle, with the point of the Moon at the top. The point of Jupiter remains on the right-hand side of this triangle, and the point of Mars remains on the left. The only difference is that the triangle has been flipped upright. The two triangles overlap so that the top of the second one (the point of the Moon) is placed at the center of the first one, producing a shape vaguely like a Christmas tree.

In all cases, the basic procedure for drawing the hexagram remains the same: first you draw one triangle, starting at the point of the planet in question, and then you draw a second triangle starting at the complementary point—moving clockwise to invoke and counterclockwise to banish. Suppose, for example, that you wanted to invoke the energy of Netzach in Briah. You would first draw an upward-pointing triangle, starting with a stroke from the bottom right to the bottom left. Then, above that, you would draw a downward-pointing triangle, starting at the top left and moving to the top right, so that the tips of the two triangles met in the middle and formed an hourglass shape. This can take a while to get used to, but with a bit of practice, you'll get the hang of it. This technique allows you to be specific and focused when bringing a particular kind of energy from a Sephirah or Sephiroth into your spellwork.

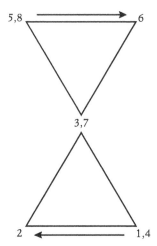

The Invoking Water Hexagram of Venus

Journal Prompts

• What kinds of symbols, images, and ingredients do you already use in your spellwork? How could these be overlaid with Qabalistic symbolism?

• Write a Qabalistic spell. Now rewrite that spell, creating a second version of it that's written for the same purpose but uses totally different Qabalistic symbolism. Do this two or three times, to habituate yourself with the creative use of Qabalah in spellwork.

• For each Sephirah, write out a list of practical goals or intentions for which you might use that Sephirah in magic. For example, you might use Netzach for love spells or Tiphereth for spells dealing with your budget.

CHAPTER 13
QABALAH AND THE GODS

Throughout this book, we have danced around the subject of how the Tree of Life relates to the Gods. The Sephiroth are emanations of divine energy, flowing forth from the source of Kether to manifest in the world. What does this say about the nature of divinity? On a Qabalistic picture, who are the Gods, and how do they relate to the tree?

In books on Qabalah, it is common to find tables of correspondences matching Pagan deities up to particular Sephiroth on the Tree of Life. Love Goddesses like Aphrodite or Freyja, for example, are attributed to Netzach, while solar deities like Apollo and dying-and-resurrecting Gods like Osiris are assigned to Tiphereth. These correspondences are based on a surface-level understanding of the Gods' mythos and the areas of the universe (and of human life) over which particular deities preside. Because of these correspondences, Qabalists are sometimes accused of having a "plug-and-play" attitude towards deities, treating the Gods merely as another set of correspondences to be used in ritual, rather than as independent spiritual entities deserving of worship and respect.

This will be a familiar charge to many Wiccans. Wicca has garnered the same reputation for plug-and-play theology, due in large part to perceptions that Wiccans "use" deities as magical tools rather than worshipping them in earnest. For some Wiccans, particularly those who view deities more as metaphors or archetypes than as literal spirits, devotional practices such as sacrifice and prayer don't form an important part of their interactions with the

Gods. This sometimes leads to accusations of frivolity or even of sacrilege, coming from people who view the Gods differently. Understandably, this allegation raises some hackles. People making the allegation feel that "those" Wiccans (and perhaps even all Wiccans) disrespect the Gods and don't take religious veneration seriously. On the other end of things, Wiccans against whom the charge is leveled often feel called out, accused of insincerity by people who don't know the intimate details of their personal practice.

Personally, I think there's nothing wrong with differing approaches to religious practice. My personal relationship with my Gods is built on regular worship, prayer, offerings, and devotion; the rest of this chapter is informed by that perspective. However, Wicca is by nature personal and experiential. I'm not in the business of telling people what they should or shouldn't believe, nor how they should or shouldn't practice. For the most part, people are drawn to Wicca (and to Paganism more broadly) because they feel a reverence for nature and a connection to Pagan Gods—even though different people have different understandings of who and what the Gods are. Wiccan practice is built on a desire to further that connection, and people do so in a variety of ways. Anyone who is earnest about their spiritual path will approach it with sincerity and respect, and in my experience, Wiccans are just as likely to be earnest as people on any other path.

WHO ARE THE GODS?

The anxiety about plug-and-play deity comes from the core issue of theology: Who or what are the Gods? Are they spirit-people walking around in the sky, watching over us? Are they psychological projections of forces in our own psyches? Are they personified forces of nature? Are they archetypes of the collective human unconscious? Do they exist independently of, and prior to, us? Or do they somehow depend upon our worship, changing as we change? Are all Gods ultimately just different names for the same divine power, or are the Gods numerically distinct beings?

I don't know the answers to these questions. The truth is, no one knows the answers, and anyone who claims to know is blinded by hubris. The answers to these questions deal with the nature of ultimate reality, as it exists independently of our perceptions, and that is something we can never know with absolute certainty. The nice thing about Wicca is that it doesn't impose theology. I have met Wiccans who believe that all Goddesses are one Goddess and all Gods are one God, that the Gods are all separate from each other, that the Gods are psychological archetypes, and even that the Gods are metaphors through which we describe the natural world. Worries about plug-and-play treatments of the Gods are usually voiced by polytheists who worry that others are not treating the Gods as "real," but all of the people I listed above have profound, intimate devotional relationships with the Gods. The Gods are very real to them; they just understand that reality differently.

No one knows what the Gods really are. Personally, I think there's some truth in all of the above stances. I believe in the Gods as literal spiritual entities with the power to act upon the world, but I also think they exist as archetypes in the unconscious mind. I believe that each deity has their own individual personality, but also that there is a sense in which the Gods all share of some common divine nature. I believe that the Gods exist prior to us and have their own agency, but I also think the Gods evolve alongside human culture. I don't know exactly how all of these things can be true at once, but somehow, I think they are.

The truth, whatever it is, is larger than us. It is messy, and mysterious, and bigger than any one person's ability to comprehend. It may even be contradictory at times; the Gods aren't limited by the rules that govern our world, and they can simultaneously exist in two totally contradictory ways. That's part of the mystery of it all. All of the various theologies found in the Pagan community, all of the ideas about who the Gods are, are attempts to categorize and explain something that is fundamentally beyond explanation. Each theological perspective can give us some insight into a larger truth, but none of them can, on its own, give us the whole truth. Any attempt to limit or define the Gods will inevitably fall short, because the Gods are greater than any concept by which we might define them.

In trying to understand the Gods, then, it helps to realize that there are multiple lenses through which we can view them, and that each of those lenses will tell us something new about them—just as we understand the Sephiroth in a variety of ways, extended through the four elemental worlds. The Gods, like the Sephiroth, are at once cosmic, psychological, personal, transpersonal, within us, larger than us, transcendent, and physically manifest. We should be careful not to limit our understanding of them by saying they are *not* any of these things. They are all of them, and more. However, what we can say is that they are *not only* any particular one of these things. Their true nature is, and will always be a mystery; we can never draw back the veil of Isis.

Exercise: Reflecting on Theology

There are a number of potential ways to bring Qabalah into your relationships with the Gods, and what works for you will largely depend on your theological point of view. Understanding how you view the Gods will, in turn, help you to understand how best to introduce Qabalah into your work with them. Remember, theology is intensely personal, and there is no official or right way to view the Gods in Wicca.

You Will Need

- No materials are necessary for this exercise, but I recommend having your journal on hand to note down your thoughts.

Instructions

What is your stance on these big theological questions? Do you see the Gods as independent spiritual entities? Personifications of the natural world? Psychological archetypes? What about the theological perspectives that don't resonate with you? Think about why some perspectives on the Gods appeal to you more than others.

Are you a hard polytheist, who believes that all the Gods are totally separate from each other? If so, how do you think about deities whose cults were historically connected through syncretism or cultural development, such as Artemis and Diana or Ishtar and Inanna? If you are a soft polytheist, who believes that all Goddesses and Gods are ultimately just different names we give to the Divine, what do you make of deities whose myths and cults are strikingly different from each other, such as Set and Thor or Venus and the Morrigan?

Whatever your answers to these questions are, they're okay. We're not here to prescribe theology or to say that one way of relating to the Gods is right and another is wrong. Keep these questions (and your answers to them) in the back of your mind as we continue our discussion of Qabalah in light of Pagan worship and our relationships with the Gods.

THE GODS PERVADE THE TREE

With that caveat about the mysterious true nature of the Gods, let us turn our attention to the relationship between the Gods and the Tree of Life. If the Tree of Life is at once a map of the universe and of the human soul, and if the Gods are at once immanent in the universe and manifest in the human soul, then the Tree of Life is also a key to understanding the Gods themselves. Everything we have said about the Sephiroth and the way their energies balance each other on the tree is also true at the level of the Gods. The Sephiroth themselves are, among other things, aspects of divine power and faces of the Gods. We can, therefore, use the Tree of Life to gain a better understanding of the Gods—or we can go in the other direction and use our understanding of the Gods to help connect us to the Tree of Life.

Crucially, all of the Gods express the energy of all ten Sephiroth, to some extent. They all contain the divine spark of Kether, which flows through all things, and if we are working in a Wiccan context and presuming a theology of immanence, they all manifest somehow in the physical world of Malkuth. They have both force and form, they are both merciful and severe, they have self-identity and relationships with others. The Gods are complex personalities, just like we are, and that complexity is only properly shown if we understand that they pervade the whole of the Tree of Life. Every single deity can be found in every single Sephirah. They might manifest in different ways—the Yesod of Arianrhod will look very different from the Yesod of Hermes—but they each express all ten Sephiroth, to greater or lesser extents.

If we can relate to a deity in all ten Sephiroth, then we can begin to appreciate the complexity of that deity's personality, and our worship will benefit accordingly. For any given God or Goddess, ask yourself:

1. What is the divine spark that unites this deity to others? What is the source of creation in their mythos, and how do they relate to that source? How are they understood as belonging to a greater whole?

2. What sort of force does this deity bring into the world? What are the ways in which they are creative, dynamic, and energetic? How are they free and unrestrained? Where do they bring growth and change into the universe?

3. What do they give form to? What do they shape, limit, and define? What do they bring into manifestation by giving it purpose and direction?

4. How are they merciful? What are the ways they show kindness, compassion, or goodwill? What kind of blessings do they bestow, and what kind of help do they offer?

5. How is this deity severe? What sort of demands do they make, and what conduct do they require? Which rules, laws, or codes of honor do they take seriously? What kind of infraction would upset them? What are the ways in which they can be unkind or even cruel?

6. In which areas of life does this deity bring harmony, success, and virtue? How do they bring balance to the world? What does a good life look like according to them?

7. Which relationships are most important to them? How do they relate to other deities? How do they relate to their worshippers? What kind of relationships do they expect their worshippers to cultivate in day-to-day life?

8. What defines this deity's individual identity? What are the characteristics that make them different from any other God or Goddess? What sets them apart?

9. What are the symbols and images associated with this deity? What are the key myths about them? How would you recognize if they were communicating to you in a dream or some other way?

10. How does this deity appear in the physical world? What are the ways you can feel their presence in your everyday life? How are they immanent, immediate, and present?

By asking all of these questions and getting a sense of how a deity exists across all ten Sephiroth, you can form a much deeper relationship with them, exploring sides of them you might not otherwise have considered. Rather than just seeing Aphrodite as a generic love Goddess, you might begin to think about how she connects to the primordial force of Eros, about the devotion she requires to pleasure and beauty, about the myth of the magic girdle she lent to Hera and her affair with Ares. You might do research into the specifics of her cult, learning about Aphrodite Ourania and Aphrodite Pandemos. And in all of this, you would be able to build a close, intimate, specific relationship with her—banishing the specter of plug-and-play polytheism once and for all.

EXERCISE: THE GODS AND THE TREE

Take this schema and apply it to your own relationship with the Gods, looking at how a particular deity's energies manifest all throughout the Tree of Life. This is also a handy way to get to know new deities with whom you're not already familiar.

You Will Need

- the list of questions provided in the previous section
- your journal or notebook

Instructions

Choose a deity with whom you already have a close devotional relationship. Using the above list, or other questions based on the ten Sephiroth, explore how that deity manifests in all ten Sephiroth on the Tree of Life. Notice which questions are easier to answer, and which ones you struggle with. Is it easy to find the presence of this deity in one Sephirah versus another?

When you have finished, repeat the exercise with a deity you have not worked with previously, but whom you would like to get to know. This may require some research on your part. Compare the two experiences. What did you learn from each? How did your prior knowledge affect the process of exploring the deity's personality through the Tree of Life?

WHERE THE GODS FEEL AT HOME

We've talked about the sense in which all of the Gods exist everywhere on the Tree of Life, and this is an important big-picture perspective to maintain. However, there is also a more localized perspective in which certain deities have more natural affinity with some of the Sephiroth than with others. Every God can be found in every Sephirah, but at the same time, it's easy to see how some Gods rule over the energy of particular Sephiroth. Thoth is a deity of writing, wisdom, and science, all of which we can find in Hod. Likewise, we find the wild fecundity of Pan in Chokmah, and the honor and courage of Tyr in Gevurah. Deities are complex personalities, just like people. And like people, different deities have different interests, histories, and qualities. Some deities will feel more comfortable with certain Sephiroth, which express the divine energies over which those deities preside—the same way that each individual person will find some Sephiroth easier to connect to than others.

When we look at tables of correspondences that place deities on certain Sephiroth, then, we should understand that these are the Sephiroth where those deities feel most at home. Pan is perfectly comfortable with the omnidirectional, expansive energy of Chokmah, but he's out of his element in restrictive Binah or intellectual Hod. Arawn, the king of the Celtic otherworld, is most at home in Yesod, but he would hardly be comfortable in social, love-oriented Netzach. Each God or Goddess is comfortable, familiar, and at ease in some Sephiroth, and maladapted, uneasy, and out of sorts in others. When we use Qabalah to aid in the worship of Pagan deities, part of what we want to do is to identify which Sephiroth a deity likes and dislikes.

These Sephiroth help us to understand what kind of offerings a deity would like and what kind of things it would be appropriate to pray to them for. If I am praying to Thoth, I'm likely to pray for things related to Hod: knowledge, introspection, eloquence in writing, and so on. Because Thoth is most at home with Hod, these are the kinds of prayers to which he will be open and receptive. On the other hand, he's unlikely to respond positively if I pray to him for wealth, social status, or a flourishing sex life. It's not that he's, in principle, opposed to these things, but they're not his area of expertise, and he's not as interested in them as other deities might be.

Importantly, there doesn't have to be an exact one-to-one correspondence of deity to Sephirah. A given deity might feel at home in more than one place. We've already discussed two classic examples of this: I've talked about the Wiccan Mother Goddess as expressing herself both in Binah and Malkuth, and her consort the Horned God being affiliated primarily with Chokmah and Tiphereth. Because the Wiccan Goddess is typically associated with the full moon, she is also associated with Yesod, although personally, I feel her connection to Binah and Malkuth much more strongly. Because the Gods are complex individuals, they have varied interests and personality traits, which sometimes express themselves across multiple Sephiroth.

Using the Sephiroth for Worship

The point of having Qabalistic correspondences for deities is not to confine the Gods to a column in a chart. The idea is not to claim that any Sephirah, or even any collection of Sephiroth, exhausts everything there is to know about a particular deity—nor, conversely, that any deity or group of deities exhaustively captures the energy of a particular Sephirah. Rather, there is a symbiotic relationship between the Sephiroth and the Gods, where each helps us to understand and engage with the other. If I worship Ares and know him well, then I can use my relationship with him in order to better understand Gevurah.

Likewise, if I am trying to cultivate a relationship with Ares, one way I can begin to engage with him is through the qualities I know of Gevurah. Although the Sephiroth and the Gods are not one and the same, we can use the similarities between them to achieve a more profound connection to each.

Furthermore, by connecting a deity to particular Sephiroth, we open the door to use the correspondences of those Sephiroth in our worship. For example, I have a personal devotional relationship with the Slavic springtime deity Jarilo. Very little information about historical Slavic Paganism survives, and little is known about this God. What we do know is that he is a seasonal dying-and-resurrecting vegetation deity, who is syncretized with the Roman God Mars, is viewed as the personification of the crops, and has a secondary function as a protector deity and a God of war. Viewing Jarilo through a Qabalistic lens, then, we can associate him with Tiphereth and Gevurah: Tiphereth for his connection to agriculture and the myth of death and resurrection, and Gevurah for his warlike qualities and his connection to Mars.

In my worship of Jarilo, I draw on these connections. I decorate his shrine with red for Gevurah and yellow for Tiphereth. I burn frankincense, because it's a solar incense, and I leave him offerings of sunflower seeds. Now, of course, Qabalah has nothing to do with the way Jarilo was historically worshipped. He's a Slavic deity; his cult is rooted in Slavic folklore and customs that have no connection to Qabalah whatsoever. These Qabalistic embellishments are additions on my part, grounded in personal gnosis rather than in any historically documented ways he was worshipped. So why is it appropriate to incorporate Qabalistic correspondences into my worship of him? Or is it appropriate at all?

Here's how I think about the matter. Jarilo is a God who comes from a particular culture, with his own mythology, personality, and traditional ritual observances. He is not a Qabalistic deity, nor is he exactly the same as any other deity. However, we can identify particular things about him that are shared with other deities. We see his connection to agriculture and the cycle of the seasons, his role as a patron and protector, his ongoing death and resurrection. These are all things that are important to him, essential features of who he is. By working with Qabalistic correspondences, then, we can show respect and attentiveness to the things he cares about most.

If you're buying a gift for a friend in the mundane world, you try to buy something that aligns with what you know about your friend's interests. Using Qabalah in worship is much the same. You start by identifying the energies, symbols, and myths that are important to the deities you're trying to honor. You can then look at Sephiroth that connect to those energies and symbols; chances are good that if a deity feels comfortable with the energy associated with a particular Sephirah, they will respond positively to symbols and offerings that are also connected to that Sephirah. Using the correspondences of Tiphereth on a shrine to Jarilo is like saying, "Hey, I noticed that death and resurrection are significant to you. Here are some colors, plants, and incense that I associate with that energy. I thought you might like them."

RITUALIZING QABALISTIC WORSHIP: CONSTRUCT AN ALTAR

Choose a deity and build a ritual space dedicated to them, adding Qabalistic symbolism that helps you connect to them. This will allow you to make practical application of Qabalistic correspondences by using Qabalah to make your altar space more welcoming and comfortable for the deity to whom it is consecrated.

You Will Need

- images or items that relate to a particular deity
- Qabalistic symbols appropriate to the Sephiroth where that deity feels most at home
- a space to use as an altar

Instructions

Start by thinking about who your chosen deity is and how you relate to them. Which myths do they appear in? Which areas of life do they govern? What symbols and offerings are traditional in their worship?

Now consider which Sephiroth are most aligned with that deity. Where on the Tree of Life would you say this Goddess or God is at ease and in their element? How would you incorporate the energy of that Sephirah into a shrine or altar? You could use an altar cloth of a particular color, colored candles, particular herbs or crystals, incense, the image of an animal associated with the Sephirah, objects in a certain number, or a given geometrical arrangement. Build your altar, using both the traditional features associated with your deity and the Qabalistic correspondences you've chosen. Then consecrate the space. Lighting any candles on your altar, pass your hand over it in a clockwise motion, saying:

"Great [deity name], I come humbly before you to dedicate this space to your worship. May it be a place of peace and love, where I can find communion with you and offer my adoration. So mote it be!"

Follow this by reciting a prayer of praise to your deity and making a small offering. How does the energy of this altar feel different from previous spaces you've used to honor your deity? What has changed by bringing in the Qabalistic imagery?

WORSHIP IS PRIMARY, QABALAH IS SECONDARY

Qabalah can provide a useful supplement to religious devotion. However, I wouldn't recommend using it as a total replacement for historically documented practices, offerings, and prayers; you should still use all of the information available to you about a particular deity, and you should worship them in the way they want to be worshipped. Hecate is a lunar Goddess, so you might decorate your altar with things associated with Yesod, or you might incorporate the numerical correspondence of Yesod by saying nine prayers to her every day. If you do this, though, you should still make your altar (and your worship) specific to Hecate insofar as you are able. Leave offerings unique to her, like eggs and garlic. Use symbols like Hecate's Wheel, Hecate's Key, or the triple crossroads. If you have a statue of Hecate, put it in the place of honor on your altar. The point is not to erect a generic Yesod altar in the place of a Hecate-specific one, but rather to use Yesod as part of a broader practice of Hecate worship, incorporating the Qabalah to enrich your devotion.

Be aware that not all deities will want Qabalistic correspondences on their altars. I've found that Jarilo responds quite positively to sunflower seeds, which I wouldn't have thought to offer him without the association with Tiphereth, but some other deities I worship show no interest in offerings that come from correspondences on the Tree of Life. Moreover, different people may have different relationships with the same deity; a Goddess may welcome Qabalistic offerings from one person and be indifferent to them from another person. My advice is to try making Qabalistic offerings if they appeal to you, and then perform divination or otherwise open yourself to communication from your deities, in order to see how those offerings are received. If your deities like what you're doing, keep going; if they don't, stop and try something else.

As you experiment with Qabalah, you may find that your worship of the Gods shifts in a Qabalistic direction. On the other hand, you may find that the religious part of your practice remains largely untouched, and that your interest in Qabalah remains primarily magical, meditative, and theoretical. Either outcome is okay. Qabalah is a tool to be applied only when it's useful. Different people will find different uses for it, and some people will want to use it only for magic, while others will form deep, intense connections to their Gods using the Tree of Life.

The ideas and techniques provided in this and the previous chapter are just suggestions to get you started. My hope is that you will use the tools provided in this book and discover your own ways of applying Qabalah to your extant religious and magical practice. Whether it provides a new interpretive lens for what you already do or a way to incorporate new symbolism into your ritual, meditation, and prayer, the Qabalah is an opportunity to enrich the Wicca you already know. You just have to find the ways of doing so that work for you.

Journal Prompts

- Write a prayer to a deity you worship, and incorporate explicitly Qabalistic language. You could use the (translated) name of a Sephirah or imagery from one or more correspondences. Use this prayer as an opportunity to experiment with framing your worship in openly Qabalistic terms.

- Find two deities who preside over similar domains and who would connect to the same Sephirah or Sephiroth. Write down the differences in how you would worship them if you used Qabalistic correspondences. How would you honor the individuality of each deity, to avoid reducing them to just a set of correspondences?

- Write down a list of all the deities you work with regularly, then take note of the Sephiroth you would associate with each of them. What patterns do you notice? Are any Sephiroth over-represented? Are any missing? Is there another deity you would consider reaching out to, who could bring the energy of the missing Sephiroth into your life and help balance out the energy of the tree?

THE MYSTERY OF IT ALL

We have reached the end of our journey together. My goal with this book was twofold: to show you what Qabalah is and to tell you why you should care. I have endeavored not only to introduce you to the basic principles of Qabalah, but also to show you why these principles matter to you as a Wiccan, and how they apply—insofar as generalizations can be made—to what Wiccans do and believe. While knowledge of Qabalah is in no way necessary for a successful Wiccan practice, Wicca is loaded with the potential for deep, rich Qabalistic symbolism. So many Pagans are discouraged from Qabalah because they think it's a totally alien magical system, but Wicca doesn't need to change in order to be compatible with Qabalah. Qabalah is already present in Wicca if you want it. You just have to know how to look for it.

My hope is that this book has shown you how to look. If your study of Qabalah ends here, I thank you for taking the time to learn Qabalah with me. Even if you do not intend to go on to become a serious Qabalist, I sincerely hope that you have found something of value for yourself in these pages. At the very least, I hope I have demystified Qabalah and made it less intimidating and more approachable, so that when you hear people talking about the Tree of Life, you have some sense of what they mean and you don't feel the urge to run screaming from the room. You may have decided that Qabalah isn't for you, and that's okay, but now you at least understand what it is, how it holds together, and why someone else might find it useful.

If, on the other hand, this is only the beginning of your journey with Qabalah, I hope that this book has demystified Qabalistic tradition and opened the door for further study. With the foundational knowledge you've gained in this book, you can go on to read and study other Qabalistic works, and you will have a frame of reference with which to orient yourself. There are always new things to learn and study, and there's a whole wide world of Qabalah still waiting for you to discover it. There are not only new correspondences, but also new magical techniques and different perspectives on the Tree of Life, all of which will offer you further, deeper insight. A potential lifetime of Qabalistic study lies ahead of you.

There's a piece of conventional wisdom sometimes touted in Qabalistic circles, that when you reach the top of the Tree of Life you find yourself right back at the bottom. When you raise your consciousness all the way up to Kether, you learn that Kether and Malkuth are actually one and the same. The final revelation of the Tree of Life is the same as the first revelation, a truth that has been with you since you began your journey in Malkuth and first set your foot upon the path of Tau. When you finally understand the greatest of mysteries in the Supernal Triad, you realize that those mysteries have been with you since the beginning.

The journey up the Tree of Life is not a line. It does not start at one point and end at another; there is no place where you stop and declare your work done. It is, rather, cyclical and never-ending. The top of the tree connects to the bottom, and energy flows constantly through it in an infinite, timeless circle. When you reach Kether and find yourself back at Malkuth, you have two options: you may turn around and redescend the tree, following the path of the Flash back down and reversing the direction in which you came. Or, if you choose, you may trace the path of the Serpent up the tree a second time, rediscovering the Sephiroth in the order of ascension all over again. Following the Serpent up the tree, you reach its head, only to find it swallowing its own tail, and you continue on your infinite quest for wisdom.

Moving in either direction on the Tree of Life, you will learn new things about the Sephiroth and come to see the tree in a way you didn't before. No matter how many times you retrace your steps, there is always something you hadn't seen, some new insight to be gained. That's part of the mystery of the Qabalah. Remember, the Tree of Life is bigger than you, me, or any person. It represents the whole of the universe, and of yourself, and of the Gods. No one knows everything there is to know about the tree, because no one knows everything about the universe—but each time you explore the tree, it will show you something new, and you will feel that you understand things just a little bit better. That is the great work of Qabalah: realizing that perfect knowledge is unattainable, but striving toward it anyway.

It is sometimes also said that each Sephirah contains a whole Tree of Life within itself: that when you peer into Malkuth, you find an entire Tree of Life, and you find another one within Yesod and yet another within Hod. Moreover, the regress is infinite. When you look at the Tree of Life within Malkuth, you find ten Sephiroth, each of which contains yet another Tree of Life. And the Sephiroth on those trees contain yet other trees, and so on to eternity. It's turtles all the way down.

It can be confusing and mind-bending to think of the Tree of Life as an infinite loop or to imagine that each Sephirah contains a tree, which is made up of Sephiroth that themselves contain trees in an infinite regress. These conceptualizations of the Tree of Life are intended to be bewildering and contradictory. They express a fundamental truth about exploring the Tree of Life: the mystery never ends. There is always a deeper truth, a new piece of wisdom to be discovered, and seeking that wisdom can sometimes be maddening and paradoxical. The Tree of Life is the key to everything, and it can help you to unlock doors you didn't even know existed, but no matter how many doors you open, there will still be more that you have not touched.

You don't have to have unlocked all the secrets of the universe in order to be a good Qabalist; you just have to see the world from a Qabalistic point of view. Try to look into the world around you and see everything as a refraction of the divine energy of the Tree of Life. See the Sephiroth in everything you do, everyone you meet, every experience you have. Let the Tree of Life become, literally and figuratively, the whole of the universe. Having finished this book, you are now equipped with the skills to do so, and Qabalah is a weapon in your arsenal that you may use whenever you choose. Don't feel like you're expected to understand every facet of the Tree of Life before you can call yourself a Qabalist. Rather, know that you don't know everything, and that you will never know everything—and realize that no one expects you to. Nobody else knows everything, either.

My final message to you, then, is this: be humble and embrace the mystery of it all. Be confident in what you do know, honest about what you don't know, and open to learning more. The path of the witch is one of mystery and magic, and so is the path of the Qabalist. Both Wicca and Qabalah bring us into contact with something divine, something greater than ourselves that we struggle to understand and express. Accept that. Celebrate it. Take joy in having communion with the Divine, in having the kinds of experiences that you will never fully understand and never quite be able to put into words. That ineffable, inexpressible, mysterious quality of the Tree of Life is what makes Qabalah special.

Take a look back at the learning goals you set for yourself when you read the introduction of this book. Have you learned what you were hoping to? Have you accomplished what you set out to do? What more would you like to learn about or experiment with? Where do you want to go from here?

The path of the mystic has no beginning and no end. I thank you for having walked this section of it with me, and I wish you wisdom and understanding as we part ways. Blessed be.

Pronunciation Guide

Qabalah: kuh-BAH-luh

Sephirah: seh-FEE-rah

Sephiroth: sfee-ROAT

Kether: KAY-tehr

Chokmah: KHOAKH-mah, where the KH sound is like the Scottish "loch"

Binah: BEE-nah

Chesed: KHEH-sed

Gevurah: guh-VOO-rah

Tiphereth: teef-AIR-et

Netzach: NET-zakh

Hod: HOAD

Yesod: yih-SOAD

Malkuth: mal-KHOOT

Daath: DAH-aht

Ain: AIN, as in "rain"

Ain Soph: AIN SOAF

Ain Soph Aur: AIN SOAF OAR

Atziluth: aht-zee-LOOT

Briah: beh-REE-yah

Yetzirah: yet-zee-RAH

Assiah: ah-SEE-ah

Aleph: AH-lef

Beth: BET

Gimel: GEE-mel, with a hard G

Daleth: DAH-let

Heh: HEY

Vau: VAHV

Zain: ZEYE-n

Cheth: KHET

Teth: TET

Yod: YOOD

Kaf: KAHF

Lamed: LAH-med

Mem: MEM

Nun: NOON

Samekh: SAH-mekh

Ayin: EYE-in

Peh: PAY

Tzaddi: TZAH-dee

Qof: KOOF

Resh: RESH

Shin: SHEEN

Tau: TAHV

God-Names, Archangels, and Angels

Sephirah	God-Name of Atziluth	Transliteration	Pronunciation	Translation
Kether	אהיה	Eheieh	eh-HEY-eh	I Am
Chokmah	יה	Yah	YAH	Lord
Binah	יהוה אלהים	YHVH Elohim	YOOD HEY VAHV HEY eh-loa-HEEM	Lord God
Chesed	אל	El	EL	God
Gevurah	אלהים גבור	Elohim Gibor	eh-loa-HEEM gi-BOOR	Almighty God
Tiphereth	יהוה אלוה ודעת	YHVH Eloah Vedaath	YOOD HEY VAHV HEY eh-LOA-ah vey-DAH-aht	God of Knowledge
Netzach	יהוה צבאות	YHVH Tzabaoth	YOOD HEY VAHV HEY tzah-vah-OAT	Lord God of Hosts
Hod	אלהים צבאות	Elohim Tzabaoth	eh-loa-HEEM tzah-vah-OAT	God of Hosts

Sephirah	God-Name of Atziluth	Transliteration	Pronunciation	Translation
Yesod	שדי אל חי	Shaddai El Chai	shah-DEYE EL KHEYE	Supreme Lord of Life
Malkuth	אדני הארץ	Adonai ha-Aretz	ah-doa-NEYE hah-ah-RETZ	Lord of the World

Sephirah	Archangel of Briah	Transliteration	Pronunciation	Translation
Kether	מטטרון	Metatron	may-tah-TROAN	Who Serves at the Throne
Chokmah	רציאל	Ratziel	raht-zee-EL	Secret of God
Binah	צפקיאל	Tzaphkiel	tzahf-kee-EL	Knowledge of God
Chesed	צדקיאל	Tzadkiel	tzahd-kee-EL	Righteous-ness of God
Gevurah	כמאל	Kamael	kah-mah-EL	Wrath of God
Tiphereth	רפאל	Raphael	rah-fah-EL	Healer of God
Netzach	האניאל	Haniel	hah-nee-EL	Grace of God
Hod	מיכאל	Michael	mee-khah-EL	Who Is Like God
Yesod	גבריאל	Gabriel	gah-vree-EL	Strength of God
Malkuth	סנדלפון	Sandalphon	sahn dahl-FOAN	Confrere

Sephirah	Angels of Assiah	Transliteration	Pronunciation	Translation
Kether	חיות הקדש	Chayoth ha-Qadesh	kha-YOAT hah-kah-DESH	Holy Living Creatures
Chokmah	אופנים	Auphanim	oa-fah-NEYE-m	Wheels
Binah	ארלים	Aralim	ah-rahl-EEM	Thrones
Chesed	חשמלים	Chashmalim	khah-shmah-LEEM	Brilliant Ones
Gevurah	שרפים	Seraphim	say-rah-FEEM	Fiery Serpents
Tiphereth	מלכים	Melekim	meh-lah-KHEEM	Kings
Netzach	אלהים	Elohim	eh-loa-HEEM	Gods
Hod	בני אלהים	Beni Elohim	BEH-nee eh-loa-HEEM	Sons of Gods
Yesod	כרובים	Kerubim	khuh-roo-VEEM	Angels of Elements
Malkuth	אשים	Ashim	ay-SHEEM	Flames

Recommended Reading

Bardon, Franz. *The Key to the True Kabbalah.* Sixth edition. Merkur Publishing, 2015.

Bardon is best known for his *Initiation Into Hermetics*, but this text is his Qabalistic tour de force. It makes explicit a number of the implicit Qabalistic principles found elsewhere in his work.

Barrabbas, Frater. *Magical Qabalah for Beginners: A Comprehensive Guide to Occult Knowledge.* Llewellyn, 2013.

This is one of the most accessible introductory Qabalah texts written in recent years. Barrabbas has a clean, no-nonsense approach to Qabalistic subject matter, and while this book is written for aspiring ceremonial magicians, there's good material in it for Qabalistically inclined witches, as well.

Cicero, Chic, and Sandra Tabatha Cicero. *Golden Dawn Magic: A Complete Guide to the High Magical Arts.* Llewellyn, 2019.

The Ciceros are largely responsible for the renaissance of Golden Dawn magic in contemporary America. This book introduces the reader to the Golden Dawn system of magic, demystifying it through the inclusion of practical exercises and ritual workings.

Crowley, Aleister. *777 and Other Qabalistic Writings of Aleister Crowley: Including Gematria and Sepher Sephiroth*. Edited by Israel Regardie, revised edition. Weiser, 1986.

This is the definitive text on Qabalistic correspondences. If you are looking to expand your understanding of the Tree of Life and its magical correspondences, this is a must-have reference book for your shelf.

DuQuette, Lon Milo. *The Chicken Qabalah of Rabbi Lamed Ben Clifford: Dilettante's Guide to What You Do and Do Not Need to Know to Become a Qabalist*. Weiser, 2001.

Possibly the most widely recommended introductory Qabalah book out there. DuQuette writes through the fictional voice of Rabbi Lamed Ben Clifford, and provides a friendly, readable introduction to Qabalistic concepts.

———. *The Magick of Aleister Crowley: A Handbook of the Rituals of Thelema*. Revised edition. Weiser, 2003.

DuQuette breaks down Aleister Crowley's religious and magical rituals in a straightforward, approachable way. This text is still rather difficult, simply because Crowley is difficult, but DuQuette makes the material much easier to understand. This is a must-read for anyone who is looking to learn more about Crowley.

Fortune, Dion. *The Mystical Qabalah*. Second edition. Weiser, 2000.

This is an incredibly dense, challenging book, but it contains some of the most profound passages I've ever encountered in a Qabalistic text. Not for the faint of heart, but if you only read one book from this list, let it be this one.

Gray, William G. *Qabalistic Concepts: Living the Tree*. Weiser, 1997.

A great read for more advanced Qabalah students. Gray was self-taught, and some of his correspondences differ from established tradition, but he shows a tremendous amount of insight into the Tree of Life, including the ways it can be used for ritual and magic.

King, Francis, and Stephen Skinner. *Techniques of High Magic: A Handbook of Divination, Alchemy, and the Evocation of Spirits*. Reissue edition. Destiny Books, 2000.

This book is the source of the wand/dagger elemental correspondence swap, and is worth reading for its historical significance alone, but it also provides an excellent grounding in the fundamental principles of ceremonial magic. Much of it is not explicitly Qabalistic, but it pairs nicely with Qabalistic study.

Knight, Gareth. *Practical Guide to Qabalistic Symbolism*. Weiser, 2002.

Knight is the most famous of Dion Fortune's students and is a master Qabalist in his own right. This book provides a straightforward, grounded guide to otherwise difficult Qabalistic concepts.

Penczak, Christopher. *The Temple of High Witchcraft: Ceremonies, Spheres and the Witches' Qabalah*. Llewellyn, 2007.

Penczak is one of the most prolific and successful Pagan authors of the twenty-first century, and his book on Qabalah shows why. Full of meditations and practical work, this book targets what Qabalah is and how it can be used in witchcraft, although it's not specific to Wiccan practice.

Reed, Ellen Cannon. *The Witches Qabala: The Pagan Path and the Tree of Life*. Revised edition. Weiser, 1997.

Reed was a high priestess of the Isian Tradition of Wicca; her book is one of the only Qabalah books available that are written for Pagans. Some of her ideas are idiosyncratic to the tradition she practiced, but this book remains one of the best Qabalah texts for Wiccan and Pagan readers.

Regardie, Israel. *A Garden of Pomegranates: Skrying on the Tree of Life*. Edited by Chic Cicero and Sandra Tabatha Cicero, revised, subsequent edition. Llewellyn, 1995.

Israel Regardie was a student and friend of Aleister Crowley, and was one of the world's foremost authorities on Qabalah. This essential book helps the reader explore the Tree of Life through scrying and pathworking.

————. *The Golden Dawn: The Original Account of the Teachings, Rites, and Ceremonies of the Hermetic Order*. Revised edition. Llewellyn, 2016.

Regardie's magnum opus is the single most authoritative text on the Hermetic Order of the Golden Dawn. It contains all the rituals and teaching materials of the original order—many of which had not previously been made available to non-initiates.

Wang, Robert. *The Qabalistic Tarot: A Textbook of Mystical Philosophy*. Marcus Aurelius Press, 2004.

This gem of a book takes an in-depth look at the tarot through a Qabalistic lens. Invaluable for tarot readers who want to further their divinatory practice with Qabalistic understanding.

BIBLIOGRAPHY

The Bible. New International Version, Ezekiel 1:10.

Agrippa, Henry Cornelius. *Three Books of Occult Philosophy.* Translated by James Freake, edited by Donald Tyson. St. Paul, MN: Llewellyn, 2004.

Aristotle. *Nicomachean Ethics.* Translated by H. Rackham. Loeb Classical Library 73. Cambridge, MA: Harvard University Press, 1926.

———. *On the Heavens.* Translated by W. K. C. Guthrie. Loeb Classical Library 338. Cambridge, MA: Harvard University Press, 1939.

Blackless, Melanie, et al. "How Sexually Dimorphic Are We? Review and Synthesis." *American Journal of Human Biology* 12, no. 2 (2000): 151–66.

Blavatsky, H. P. *Isis Unveiled: Secrets of the Ancient Wisdom Tradition, Madame Blavatsky's First Work.* Edited by Michael Gomes, abridged edition. Wheaton, IL: Quest Books, 1997.

Crowley, Aleister. *777 and Other Qabalistic Writings of Aleister Crowley: Including Gematria & Sepher Sephiroth.* Edited by Israel Regardie. Rev. ed. Newburyport, MA: Weiser, 1986.

DuQuette, Lon Milo. *The Magick of Aleister Crowley: A Handbook of Rituals of Thelema.* Newburyport, MA: Weiser, 2003.

Dweck, Yaacob. *The Scandal of Kabbalah: Leon Modena, Jewish Mysticism, Early Modern Venice.* Princeton, NJ: Princeton University Press, 2011.

Farrar, Janet, and Stewart Farrar. *A Witches' Bible: The Complete Witches' Handbook.* Bicester, UK: Phoenix Publishing, 1984.

Kaplan, Aryeh. *Sefer Yetzirah: The Book of Creation*. Rev. ed. Newburyport, MA: Weiser, 1997.

King, Francis, and Stephen Skinner. *Techniques of High Magic: A Handbook of Divination, Alchemy, and the Evocation of Spirits*. Reissue edition. Destiny Books, 2000.

Mathers, S. L. MacGregor. *Book T: The Tarot*. 1888, www.tarot.org.il/ Library/Mathers/Book-T.html.

———. *The Goetia: The Lesser Key of Solomon the King*. Edited by Aleister Crowley. Revised and corrected second printing. Newburyport, MA: Weiser, 1997.

National Library of Ireland. "The Life and Works of William Butler Yeats." nli.ie/yeats/main.html.

Plutarch. *Moralia: Volume V. Isis and Osiris. The E at Delphi. The Oracles of Delphi No Longer Given in Verse. The Obsolescence of Oracles*. Translated by Frank Cole Babbitt. Loeb Classical Library 306. Cambridge, MA: Harvard University Press, 1936.

Regardie, Israel. *The Golden Dawn: A Complete Course in Ceremonial Magic*. 6th ed. St. Paul, MN: Llewellyn, 2003.

To Write to the Author

If you wish to contact the author or would like more information about this book, please write to the author in care of Llewellyn Worldwide Ltd. and we will forward your request. Both the author and the publisher appreciate hearing from you and learning of your enjoyment of this book and how it has helped you. Llewellyn Worldwide Ltd. cannot guarantee that every letter written to the author can be answered, but all will be forwarded. Please write to:

Jack Chanek
℅ Llewellyn Worldwide
2143 Wooddale Drive
Woodbury, MN 55125-2989
Please enclose a self-addressed stamped envelope for reply,
or $1.00 to cover costs. If outside the U.S.A., enclose
an international postal reply coupon.

Many of Llewellyn's authors have websites with additional information and resources. For more information, please visit our website at http://www.llewellyn.com.